# THE STATE
## IN
## INTERNATIONAL RELATIONS

Chandler Publications in
POLITICAL SCIENCE
VICTOR JONES, *Editor*


WORLD POLITICS SERIES
PAUL SEABURY, *Editor*

# THE STATE
# IN
# INTERNATIONAL
# RELATIONS

◇◇

Compiled and Edited by

## *Richard H. Cox*

STATE UNIVERSITY OF NEW YORK, BUFFALO

CHANDLER PUBLISHING COMPANY

124 Spear Street, San Francisco, California 94105

# CONTENTS

v

# PREFACE

This collection of readings is one in a series on International Relations. It treats the general nature of the basic units of international relations; it leaves to other volumes in the series the treatment of more specific aspects of such relations.

# INTRODUCTION

## PREMISES

I have selected and edited this collection of readings on the basis of certain premises about the study of international relations. A brief account of those premises may be helpful both to the instructor who considers assigning the book, and to the student who reads it.

A glance at the table of contents reveals certain facts about the selections: they are not descriptive but interpretive; they are for the most part statements by either political theorists or political practitioners; and they were written anywhere between the fifth century B.C. and the twentieth century A.D. Thus, men as different as Aristotle, an ancient Greek philosopher, Joseph Stalin, a modern totalitarian leader, Francisco Suarez, a sixteenth-century Spanish Jesuit, and Wendell Willkie, a defeated candidate for President of the United States, speak to the reader.

This selection of materials reflects certain basic premises. The first is that relations between political societies are essentially political relations, and therefore are fundamentally the object of political science. By this statement I do not mean to deny the existence or the importance of trade, cultural or other kinds of relations. I mean only to indicate that such relations are best understood as operating within a more fundamental, political framework. Today, for example, questions of trade or cultural relations between persons or groups within the United States and the Soviet Union are settled, in the final analysis, by political leaders and with reference to political considerations. In a less

1

obvious way, the same is true for such relations between the United States and Canada, or France and Great Britain.

My second basic premise is that the object of political science is to understand the nature of political phenomena. As applied to the present subject matter, this means that the object of the study is to understand what the essential qualities of political entities are insofar as those entities are both separate from, yet somehow related to, other such entities. Furthermore, the apparent disagreement among theorists and practitioners concerning what those qualities are has been regarded as a fundamental aspect of the phenomena in question. In other words, I hope that the readings will bring forcefully to the attention of the student the way in which such disagreement constitutes one of the *problems* of international relations. My object, therefore, is to encourage thinking about the nature of international relations, not to supply information which can and should be obtained in other ways. For example, a student is assumed to bring to the study of the materials in this collection a general knowledge of modern diplomatic history and of the development and operation of basic political institutions. He is then expected to draw upon such knowledge in reading and reflecting upon the arguments and opinions contained here.

A third guiding premise is that contemporary international relations is a specific case of the coexistence and interaction of separate political entities. There are, indeed, enormous differences of form and detail between cities of ancient Greece and their relations with each other, on the one hand, and modern nation-states and their relations, on the other hand. And yet, anyone who seriously reads a work such as Thucydides' *History of the Peloponnesian War* is seized with the thought that the underlying issues are the same for him and for us. The same may be said as we read men such as Niccolo Machiavelli, Francisco Suarez, or Woodrow Wilson. The object, then, is to seek clarification of the basic issues with the help of men of any century. Political science, if it is true to its purpose, is not bound by divisions created by historians for purposes of their own.

The preceding premises, taken together, imply two complementary uses of the readings. The first use is what I will call "analysis of the fundamental problems of international relations." The second I will call "understanding of the specific form in which historical international relations occur." By the first I mean the attempt to clarify, through analysis of the problems presented, exactly what is involved when one speaks of the "relation" of a "state" to another "state." By the second, I mean the attempt to clarify exactly what kinds of conceptions, motives, and objects have been involved in specific, historical relations of political societies. Perhaps the difference in emphasis of these complementary ways of thinking may be best understood by a brief consideration of some examples from the readings.

The first example is Jean Bodin's treatment of monarchy as a form of government. Bodin, writing in the sixteenth century, argues that monarchy is the naturally best form of government. Monarchy—as distinguished from tyranny or despotism—is best because it reflects the natural order of the world; because it is the rule of wise men for the common good; and because it provides the most efficient conduct of both internal and external affairs of the state. Applied to the relations of states, this argument means that if all states were governed by monarchs, the prospect for moral and efficient conduct of such relations would be optimal.

Given this very compressed summary of Bodin's argument, we may now look at it in the two ways suggested above. If we look at it from the perspective of trying to analyze the fundamental nature of the relation of states to each other, the task is fourfold: (1) to determine what his basic premises are and to connect them to his conclusions; (2) to think of his premises and conclusions in relation to the evidence he presents—evidence, for example, concerning the existence of a "natural order" in the world; (3) to compare his general, substantive argument to the arguments of others—such as Tom Paine, who most emphatically denies that monarchy is the best form of government and who in fact traces the existence of war to the prevalence of that form; and, (4) finally, to test his arguments against historical experience. The object here, in sum, is to treat his arguments seriously with respect to their essential validity. That this will be difficult to do is easily granted: first, because the kinds of intellectual exercise I have sketched are difficult no matter what the subject matter; second, because the disappearance of monarchies in the modern age, and the moral and practical objections to them, constitute a formidable barrier to thinking in the terms and the framework indicated by Bodin.

It is at this point that the second, complementary use of the readings supplies some additional reasons for making the attempt. The reasons are these: It happens that Bodin lived and wrote at a time when the typical form of government was, indeed, monarchy. Furthermore, his conception of monarchy is based upon the notion that the world of human actions, like the natural world, is controlled by natural laws. It does not automatically follow, of course, that all monarchs of the period simply acted according to the principles laid down by Bodin. But it is possible, by reading Bodin, to learn something of the *kind* of thinking concerning the state and its relations to other states that an influential writer of the period felt impelled to offer to the learned public of his age. It is possible also to compare his principles to actual actions of monarchs of the period, and to raise the question whether the even limited acceptance of such principles as he advocates really affected international relations.

This kind of investigation has, I believe, two purposes. The first is simply to understand what specific political forms and concepts had to do with the actual international relations of the period. The second purpose is to make use of such understanding to compare one type of international relations to another, trying to determine what differences and similarities have existed in different periods and situations. The object here, in sum, is to treat Bodin's arguments as materials in an historical warehouse of experience. Given the fact that both the statesman and the political scientist must constantly fall back upon such a warehouse for comparative examples in attempting to understand contemporary problems, the value of this use of Bodin's views becomes obvious. But having arrived at this point, we realize that the historical use joins the analytical use in a never-ending interchange: the particular points to the general, and the understanding of the general requires that one constantly return to examine the particular, or concrete.

The second illustration of the complementary use of the readings is provided by the selections from Sir Winston Churchill's memoirs on the Second World War. Here, the "historical" use is the most obvious: Churchill's statements are the reflections of one of the great political practitioners of modern times; such reflections have a presumptive value as evidence of what kinds of considerations, purposes and conceptions have helped to give form to the international relations of the twentieth century. Thus when Churchill says that he has followed the four-hundred-year-old British principle of opposing the actual or potentially dominant power on the European continent, we have some concrete evidence of the specific sense in which one of the most influential of modern statesmen understood the purpose of the state. Similarly, when he says that this continuity of purpose has persisted in spite of differences of governmental forms within Britain, and in spite of different types of opposition on the continent, we have some sense of why he believes that such a purpose is so rooted in British state practice as to amount to a "law" of "public policy," as he himself refers to it. Viewed from this angle, the statements by Churchill give color and depth to the abstract notion of "modern international relations."

But it is also possible to view Churchill's statements as data for the purpose of helping to clarify the fundamental problem of international relations. His contention that the resistance to the dominant power on the continent amounts to a "law of public policy" must at first, of course, be understood as the pronouncement of a political practitioner, not that of a theorist. However, since he makes that statement based on a wealth of political experience, it is desirable to try to understand more precisely what he means, on the assumption that perhaps such experience can be analyzed and judged within a larger and more theoretical framework. The underlying issue here may then be formulated in these terms: What is the validity of making such a principle as the balancing of power part of the fundamental purpose of state policy? It is true that Churchill does not formulate the problem in such general terms. But it is also true that if we analyze his argument, and place it in the context of his general perspective on foreign relations, we discern the outlines of a thesis. That thesis is the inevitability of a contest for power among separate states, regardless of the forms of government or other historical variables. The conclusion is that balancing of power is a dictate of policy.

Churchill's thesis may then be compared to parallel theses by other men of great political experience, such as Woodrow Wilson. The difference between the views of the two men is not a simple one, but for purposes of clarification of the use of these readings, I will reduce it to a single point. Wilson's conception of the relations of states seems to be based on the thesis that the historical and contemporary contest for power among states is largely attributable to a fundamental defect in the form of governments. That thesis consists of four interrelated propositions: (1) Policies of balancing power almost inevitably end in war. (2) Such policies are due to the selfish and short-sighted operations of anachronistic monarchical and aristocratic governments in Europe and elsewhere. (3) Democratic governments, because they represent the desires of the people, do not deliberately engage in a contest for power and therefore have no need to pursue policies of balancing power. (4) Hence, a transformation of all governments into democracies will end the conditions which give rise to policies of balancing of power, and therefore will end the likelihood of aggressive war.

We are now confronted with the judgements of two men of great political experience. Given the fact that I have somewhat simplified each of their views for the purposes of illustration, it would be incorrect to say that they flatly oppose each other. But making allowance for this simplification, the fact remains that there is a wide area of disagreement between them concerning a fundamental problem. The student confronted with this disagreement will be impelled, I hope, to reflect upon what is meant by "experience"; to refine the terms of the problem; to consider more deeply than I have been able to do here the premises which are involved; and to broaden the statement of the alternatives to include, for example, the possibility that governmental *forms* are but one factor in the complex equation of the relations of states. In doing so, what begins as the attempt to understand the specific historical forms of contemporary international relations becomes, almost imperceptibly, the attempt to analyze the fundamental problems; once again, the particular points to the general, and the understanding of the general requires constant looking at the particular.

The preceding remarks concerning the two uses of the readings may now be reformulated in more technical terms. The first use is to help the student understand the theoretical side of the study of international relations; and the second use is to help him understand the practical side of that study. But from what has been said just above about the views of men such as Bodin, Paine, Churchill and Wilson, it appears that theory and practice are not antithetical but complementary in the sense that true theory grows out of the problems of practice and seems naturally to seek to guide practice. The next question is whether practice necessarily reflects theory, or is susceptible of guidance by it. The answer to this question may be given in the form of two further examples from the readings.

The student will discover, in reading the numerous selections on "sovereignty," that the interaction of theory and practice is particularly striking. Jean Bodin and Thomas Hobbes consciously strive to state what the essential property of a separate political society is, both with respect to its internal government, and with respect to its relation to other societies. Their formulations are systematically based upon certain premises concerning the nature of man, political society, law, and government. If time and space permitted, it would be possible, by the inclusion of a number of documents such as treaties, speeches of political leaders, laws, court decisions, and treatises of writers on international law, to trace in detail the great impact of these theories on practice. One example must suffice. In eighteenth-century treatises on international law, the concept of sovereignty occupies a central position. It is regarded both as a valid theory and as descriptive of actual practice. The treatises, in turn, were used to educate citizens and political leaders. They thus tended to reinforce both the theory and the practice of sovereignty.

The student may observe this complex interaction in the selection by David Jayne Hill, a former ambassador of the United States. Mr. Hill roundly castigates the concept of sovereignty, while explicitly calling attention to the way in which it has determined the practice of modern states. But there is no need to multiply cases. The student will discover, as he encounters the great variety of interpretations of sovereignty, that it is virtually impossible to say where the "theory" of sovereignty ends and the "practice" of sovereign states begins, so closely intertwined are the two. Perhaps another way of saying this would be that theory has so coalesced with practice that men's perceptions and actions are applied theory.

Whether this kind and degree of coalescence of theory and practice is the rule or the exception is another question, and it is not possible here to settle that question in general terms. It is sufficient for present purposes to consider one more example, this time one in which the "theory" contained in one of the readings seems to be—contrary to the case of "sovereignty" —at best tenuously connected to practice. I will then offer a comment on the purpose of including such a theory in the readings.

The selection from Aristotle treats the question whether the purpose of political society is to be good at making war, or to be good at producing the good life, which Aristotle defines as one of dedication to civic leadership and intellectual activity. It is important to realize that, in this case, the theory—that of the purpose of the state—is consciously in opposition to political practice. For according to Aristotle, Sparta is the model for most cities; and Sparta is dedicated to excellence in making war. Conversely, Aristotle argues that this object of political societies is so rooted in political conditions and human desires that only an elaborate program of public and private moral education, combined with the most fortunate of circumstances, would make it remotely possible for a truly well-ordered political society to exist. In this sense, Aristotle's "theory" of the purpose of the state has found little direct application in the political practice of either his time or any other.

Why then include such a "theory" in readings of this kind? The answer is that the comparison of various theories to each other, as well as to the practices of states, provides an occasion for reflection upon the fundamental problems by revealing the scope and difficulty of them. In this process of reflection, the ability to consider all the relevant alternatives is important; and it is to that end that the consideration of a seemingly "utopian" theory is recommended. For although the relation of the possible to the desirable is believed by most people to be one of tension, it is important in the study of international relations to clarify the nature and extent of that tension. Thus, if one compares Aristotle's arguments to those of John Locke, or Niccolo Machiavelli, he will discover that there are very great differences in emphasis, which reflect differences in premises and in the calculation of practical possibilities. It is in the examination of these differences that the desired clarification may take place: the clarification is at the level of theory, yet it pertains to the *limits* of practice.

## CONCLUSION

I have assumed, in the preceding remarks, that the existence of separate political societies constitutes a fundamental and continuing problem for political theory and practice. The question may be raised, of course, whether this particular political problem is not "temporary" in the sense that it is at least possible to conceive—and there are those who have advocated, and continue to advocate—a political unification of all mankind in one political society. If such a unification were to occur, what we call international relations would disappear as a practical problem. Without arguing the merits of the issue at this point, it is sufficient to observe that such a unification is nowhere in prospect. Thus the situation remains basically what it has been for centuries. This being so, the contemporary student is faced with the need to understand the problem; and since it is still doubtful whether such understanding is cumulative, progressive and additive, in the sense that, say, physics, chemistry and

geology are today generally thought to be, I have operated on
the general premise that each new generation of students
needs to think afresh about the elements of the problem by
reading, reflecting upon, and discussing original statements by
political men, both theoretical and practical.

## CONCEPTS

I should now like to call attention to certain ambiguities in
the main concepts by which these readings are ordered. My
purpose here is to help the student understand the specific
sense in which such concepts are used, and the limitations of
the present set of readings.

### THE "STATE"

As the title of the readings indicates, the basic unit of international relations is something called the "state." I have deliberately used that term, in a general way, to mean any territorial, relatively integrated, self-governing political society. It
can and does generally refer, therefore, to political entities as
different in time, place, and quality as the ancient Greek "city-
state," the early modern "dynastic state," and the contemporary
"nation-state." Now obviously, by admitting the use of the adjec-
tives "city," "dynastic," and "nation," a qualification is implied.
The question here is the relevance of such qualification.

The indicated qualification is not very important when it is
simply a question of the general problem created by the existence and interaction of separate political societies. Thus whether
the independence, as such, of separate political societies is held
to have one or another effect on the nature of the relations
between them does not seem to depend very much—in the view
of the authors included—on whether the entities in question
are city-states, dynastic states, or national states. Similarly,
whether the purpose of the political society in its relations to
others is held to be the protection of men and their properties
(Locke), the protection of the society and the development of
virtuous men (Aristotle), or the creation of a potential for expansion because of posited "necessities" of foreign relations
(Machiavelli), the argument in each case has to do only second-
arily with the different types of political societies. On the other

hand, when it is a question of understanding either the specific nature of the relations among given historical types of political society, or the connection between a given type and the theoretical or practical justification of its efficacy, then the differences are important. It is for this reason that the student should be aware of certain basic facts concerning the more technical meaning of the term "state."

The "state," as an abstract noun, is a modern concept of politics. It is derived, initially, from the Latin *status,* beginning in about the sixteenth century. At first it meant the "position" or "standing" of the person in authority—usually a monarch. Gradually, it came to mean the specifically political organization of any territorial political society. The intention of those writers who contributed to its development as a concept was to abstract from all the diverse qualities of political societies— qualities such as size and population, the form of government, the culture, the general and specific moral purposes of given institutions and laws, and the ethnic composition of a people— those attributes which are held to be the irreducible signs that a political entity exists. This process of abstracting finally settled upon four basic attributes: a people, a territory, a government, and the capacity to enter into foreign relations. In this framework, one can say that political entities as different as ancient republican Athens, Elizabethan monarchical England, the Venetian and Florentine republics of the fifteenth century, the Soviet Union, Nigeria, Panama, and India are all "states." On the other hand, when it is a question of distinguishing the specific differences among them, then it is necessary to make precise qualifications.

The earliest writings included in the collection—excerpts from Thucydides and Aristotle—refer essentially to the *polis.* Although this term is today often translated simply as "state," or "city-state," the translation is misleading because it is anachronistic: it reads back into the Greek term the connotations of what modern political theory, jurisprudence, and state practice have led us to believe is the standard way of thinking about political society. In historical fact, the ancient *polis* was fundamentally different both practically and theoretically from the modern "state." It was different in practice in that ancient polities such as Athens and Sparta included not just the attributes referred to above as belonging to a "state," but included virtually every aspect of human life: religion, culture, education and politics were but different aspects of an integrated whole. It was different in theory in that the ancient Greek poets, historians and philosophers all conceived of the *polis* as the highest form of human organization; and although the philosophers in particular criticized the specific content and purpose of given institutions, they posited the essentially integral quality of the whole as being natural to political society. Thus both the practice and the theory of the ancient *polis* posit a qualitative dimension which goes well beyond the abstractness of the notion "state."

To see this more concretely, we may consider two important points. Let us first take the matter of size and population. The modern term "state" refers, as we have seen, to any political entity, regardless of size or population: Luxembourg is as much a state as Communist China. But the *polis,* by its very definition, is a "city," a community of citizens which *can* be a community by virtue of its very limited size, small population and relatively homogeneous stock of people.

Let us take, second, the matter of form of government. The modern term "state" refers essentially only to the existence of a "government"—that is, to some organizing, ruling group which has control of the people within a territory. In this case, a change in the government in no way changes the nature of the state. But according to the theoretical analysis of the *polis,* as it is found, for example, in Aristotle, a basic change in the form of government—from oligarchy to democracy, for example—also involves a basic change in the nature of the specific *polis.* This is so because "government" is conceived of not just as having certain abstract functions, such as the maintenance of internal order and the conduct of foreign relations, but as giving substantive direction to the whole life of all its citizens: once the substance of that life changes, the *polis* is a different *polis.* Applied to the relations among different types of *polis,* this would mean that there are typical modes of inter-*polis* actions, dependent upon the given types; Aristotle's theory therefore implies a qualitative conception both of the *polis* and of its foreign relations. There would be, in principle, an optimum or best mode of inter-*polis* relations: this would consist of the relations among a number of *poleis,* all of which were governed by the best form of government. Conversely, his theory implies that among actual, different *poleis*—among oligarchies and democracies, for example—there would be qualitative differences in the mode of such relations, the modes being relative to the type of *polis.*

The conclusion to which this brief analysis points is that if we would speak very precisely, we should confine the use of the term "state" to modern political societies in Western Europe, and to those societies in other parts of the world which have taken over certain essential concepts and practices of the "state" from Western Europe. Similarly, we should confine the notion of relations among "states" to modern political societies. Thus, when the "state system" is referred to, the reference will be understood to have a precise rather than a general meaning.

Proceeding from this general delimitation of the term "state," I would now like to indicate the significance of other qualifications, in particular "dynastic state" and "nation-state." These expressions refer to different phases in the evolution of the theory and practice of the modern "state." As we have already seen, the general concept of the "state" came into being in the sixteenth century in Europe. It appears, therefore, at a period when most political societies were ruled by hereditary monarchs. This situation remained relatively the same until well into the nineteenth century, so that for about three centuries the emphasis, in theory and practice, was upon "states" which were ruled by dynasties; hence, the idea of a "dynastic" state.

An important point here is that a "dynastic" state might, and in fact very often did, include a number of "nations" under its jurisdiction. Let us take the example of what is today called Great Britain. This name came into being in 1707, when England and Scotland were joined in a single kingdom. When this happened, many ancient "nations"—using the term here in its original sense of a group of people of the same "stock," ethnically, linguistically, culturally, and so on—were combined within one "state." Thus, although they were no longer distinctly recognized as such within England, there were the remnants of ancient "nations" called Celts (Wales), Angles, Saxons and Jutes;

and in Scotland, there were similar remnants of Norse, Celts, Picts and others. Similarly, if we look at the continent, we see the development of the Austro-Hungarian Empire, which, in the nineteenth century, was a "state" including many diverse "nations."

The fact of the coexistence of different "nations" within the same "state" does not mean that there were no problems—on the contrary. However, it is one thing to speak of the conflicts among such nations within a multinational state; it is another thing to speak of the modern phenomenon of "nationalism." The latter developed upon the basis of the prior existence of distinct nations; but beginning at the end of the eighteenth century it also included a special element which was missing earlier, and that is the conscious conception that every nation has a kind of natural right also to be an independent state. It is impossible here to enter upon a substantive discussion of the complex evolution of modern nationalism. It is sufficient, for my purpose, simply to call attention to the fact that when, as happens so frequently today, the terms "nation" and "nation-state" are used to mean contemporary independent political societies, the implication is that nationalism is the basis of the society governed by a given "state." The fact remains that both in practice and theory, the fundamental relationship between such independent societies is conceived to be between the "state" mechanisms of each. Thus, when the question of "recognition" arises, the basic problem is whether a "state" exists, not whether that state is in every respect consistently based upon a true "nation." If one looks at the contemporary situation in sub-Saharan Africa, one of the basic political problems is whether the "states" there will include various ancient "nations" and then attempt to transform all of them into one "nationalistic" nation, or whether the ancient nations should be separate states. But whichever alternative is followed, the relations of the resultant political societies will continue, for the foreseeable future, to be based on the modern concepts and practices of the "state."

## INTERNATIONAL RELATIONS

The second element in the title of these readings is as ambiguous as the first. The expression "international relations" is today the standard way to refer to the relations among contemporary political societies. The expression itself, however, is a relatively new one as compared to "state." In fact, it was first coined, apparently by Jeremy Bentham, the English philosopher and jurist, around the end of the eighteenth century; but it did not really become the dominant mode of expression until the development of nationalism in the nineteenth century reinforced its usage.

Taken literally, the expression seems to mean "the relations among nations." But in spite of its popularity, and in spite of the fact that it does convey the sense that modern nationalism is a key element in the creation and maintenance of contemporary political societies, the expression is anything but precise. To be precise, one should probably speak of "inter-nation-state" relations; or simply of "interstate" relations; or if one wishes to be even more exact, of the "interaction of those persons who wield the powers of the state mechanism of the various contemporary nation-states." For it is a fact, in the final analysis, that no "nation" qua "nation," has any means by which to engage in relations with other nations. This is so because the so-called "international" arena is really peopled not by nations as such, but by public personalities called the "state."

In a sense, of course, this is a fiction, and yet a fiction which is an essential part of theory and practice. No one disputes, for example, that it is real men who carry on foreign relations. But it is important to distinguish the sense in which they carry on this activity. Obviously, they do it at one level as real human beings. But they also do it at another level as men who "personify" the entity which they direct or represent. It is in the latter capacity that such men are, in a peculiar way, conceived to *be* the "state." When, for example, the late President Kennedy ordered United States military forces, in October, 1962, to prevent further delivery of Soviet missiles to Cuba, he acted in his capacity as Commander-in-Chief of the United States armed forces. His actions, in that capacity, are understood in the practice and the theory of "international relations" to constitute ultimate actions of the "head of a state." Similarly, the actions of Premier Khrushchev in reply to those of President Kennedy, constituted actions of the "head" of the Soviet state.

It is true that, in this case, the underlying political relationship of each head-of-state to his "nation" is very different. Kennedy acted as head of a state which is democratic in its political form; Khrushchev acted as head of a state which is communist in its political form. Yet each acted toward the other in a capacity possessed by *all* heads of state, regardless of the internal ordering of the "nation" which that state represents. Furthermore, if we look into the United States Constitution, we find that the powers allocated to the President simply *assume* the existence of general powers of a head-of-state in relation to other heads-of-state; these powers are then allocated to the President. Such powers are, one might say, the only powers which are indispensable to the separate existence of the "people" or the "nation" in its external capacity; and they are the only powers which heads-of-state are bound, as such, directly to recognize in others.

The existence of such powers, possessed by the head of every state, naturally raises the further and critical question: What, if any, limitations exist on the *use* of such powers against other states? We here enter the shadowy, complex terrain of the interstate relationship itself. It is a terrain which is the object of study from many angles within the broad field of "international relations": diplomacy, including the whole range of political techniques by which states use their powers to carry on relations with other states; international law; international organization (the latter two subdivisions of study might more properly be called, given what I have said earlier in this section, "interstate law" and "interstate organization"); and military theory and practice. One purpose of this collection of readings is to reveal, in an introductory way, that these various aspects are combined in the real world of politics, however much they may be separated to facilitate study. Thus, when the student reads the first selection, which is a statement by a United States delegate to the United Nations, he will be observing the interaction of all these aspects. He will observe a diplomatic representative acting in relation to other diplomats; he will notice that the policy of the United States is formulated in the context of the United Nations Charter, traditional international law, modern state practice, and moral issues as defined by the United States government. For purposes of precise analysis, each of these elements may be abstracted from the complex whole; but for purposes of understanding what the whole "feels" like, in reality, it is necessary to confront the elements in their integrated form.

Similarly, the purpose of the readings is to make the student aware that, although it is necessary to try to understand what the "relationship" aspect of states is, such understanding must always take account of the fact that it is certain kinds of entities which are carrying on such relations; that the entities in question are in one sense, but only in one sense, "states," in the abstract; that behind "states" lie concepts and practices of political societies, in the more extended sense of groups of humans, politically organized in certain ways, for both similar and different purposes; that these purposes enter into the behavior of states; and that, therefore, in the final analysis, to understand "international relations" is to understand the *wholeness* of the internal and external aspects of political societies. Thus, when the student reads selections by men as diverse in their views of the purpose of the state as Adolph Hitler and Woodrow Wilson, he should be aware that at one level, both men accept certain premises about the power mechanism of the state: for example, both accept the fact that states have the capacity to make war. On the other hand, he should then try to understand how the use of that capacity is also understood in a very different framework by each man. It is this kind of double understanding which binds the two halves of the study together: the half which looks at the rather abstract quality called "relations of states," and the half which looks at the inner form or substance of political societies acting through the mechanisms of the "state."

RICHARD H. COX

# Part One

◇◇◇◇◇◇◇◇◇◇◇◇

# ATTRIBUTES

*The four generally recognized attributes of states are: a territory, a people, a government, and the capacity to enter foreign relations. Each attribute taken individually, and all four taken collectively, presuppose a fundamental fact: the division of the earth's surface and population into separate, "political" segments. It is the reality and the implications of this separateness which constitute the focus of attention in this first set of readings.*

*It is easy enough to speak of "the earth," meaning the physical entity or planet, independent of any human activity with respect to it. It is also easy enough to speak of "mankind," meaning the total human population, past, present, and future. But when we want to speak concretely and politically, we are compelled to recognize that neither "the earth" nor "mankind" exist in the abstract way which these terms imply. In the first place, the human use of the earth's surface is necessary to provide shelter, clothing and food, to mention only bare necessities. These goods may be obtained by wandering peoples—we still witness nomads in remote areas—but certainly not so lavishly as is possible by settling upon a given territory. And yet, it is obvious that by settling in such a way, a given portion of the earth is thereby pre-empted, usually for the exclusive use of the inhabitants, or*

*at least only on certain conditions for noninhabitants. Thus
the territoriality of political society comes into being. Secondly, and parallel to this separation of the earth's surface
into territories, is the separation of human beings into peoples. The difference between one people and another may
be very hard to discern: Canadians who reside just across
the Niagara River from Buffalo, New York, look, sound and
live practically identically the way Americans do who reside
on the other side of the river. And yet a fundamental difference exists: each is a citizen of a different state. Neither
has any right, except on certain conditions set by the government of the other state, to enter the other territory, or to
engage in any activity there. Thirdly, it is precisely by virtue
of the existence of a government that can command at least
a minimum of support from its people that separate territories and peoples are maintained. If we take the example of
physical boundaries, we find that such boundaries are ultimately a reflection of political boundaries: it is only by
political actions, past and present, that even such imposing
physical features as wide rivers or massive mountains become
the line of demarcation between different states. Similarly, it
is only by the actions of the two governments upon their
respective citizens that peoples as culturally similar as Canadians and Americans are differentiated. The fourth and final
attribute of a state, the capacity to carry on foreign relations
is, in a sense, then a final proof of its true separateness: it
is able to define, through its government, both the mode
of life within, and its mode of conduct outside its borders.
The conduct outside does presuppose the existence of the
other states, their territories, peoples and governments; but
within that presupposition, a wide range of different modes
of conduct exists: peaceful and cooperative at one end of a
continuum, all the way to warlike and hostile at the other end.*

*Many kinds of questions about the separateness of political
societies can be raised: How did it come about historically?*

*Is it justified in terms of its consequences? If it is not justified, how can it be brought to an end? All of these questions are important for a comprehensive understanding of the phenomenon in question, and various answers to them are at least implied in the readings which follow. What is most important for the student to realize, and to reflect upon, is that there is a wide area of disagreement concerning the consequences of the separate existence of political societies; that the disagreement focusses upon the question whether separate states are naturally in harmony or at enmity with other states; and that the answer to this question depends on complex premises concerning man and political institutions.*

*The readings which follow are divided into six sections: I, General Attributes of States, contains a brief, but very revealing statement of the way in which the four attributes of a state are in fact used as criteria to decide what government policy should be toward an aspirant for admission to the state-system.*

*II, Independence, then proceeds to present a continuum of points of view concerning the implications and consequences of the "independence" of political societies. Here, the emphasis is upon interpretations, by both political theorists and practitioners, of the mere fact of separateness; and the range of interpretations goes from men such as Suarez, who posits the existence of a "community" in spite of the independence of the various states; to men such as Hobbes, who posits the absence of any real "community" precisely because of that independence. In each case, the difference of interpretation turns upon questions of human inclinations; the extent to which institutions can control or direct those inclinations; and the resultant over-all consequences, for the conduct of relations among states, of the fact of separateness.*

*III, Sovereignty: Basic Theory, next provides a complementary treatment of "sovereignty," that aspect of separateness which emphasizes the exclusive governmental direction of a given people. Here again, there is a long continuum, both theoretical and historical. The first set of readings, by Bodin, Hobbes, and Treitschke, supply the student with the core of the theoretical foundations of modern sovereignty as a political concept. IV, The Case for Sovereignty in the Twentieth Century, focuses upon later interpretations of, and reactions to, that concept. Here, the range of views is as wide as the spectrum on independence. At one end of the spectrum, we find a resolute defense of sovereignty, in spite of all the transformations in political life and technology which have taken place since the time of Bodin and Hobbes, and in spite of the fact that the exercise of sovereignty has, indeed, been involved in the causality of modern wars. At the other end of the spectrum, V, The Case against Sovereignty in the Twentieth Century, we find just as resolute a criticism, even rejection of, sovereignty. In its place, the critics would have men develop international organization, or some kind of federation of smaller or larger groups of states. In the limiting case, the concept of separate sovereignties would be replaced, according to the arguments of the late United States Secretary of State, Robert Lansing, by a "world sovereignty." VI, Integration into Larger Sovereignties, presents three statements on the topic of its title.*

# I. General Attributes of States

## 1. When Does a State Exist?

*In 1948 the United States government was obliged to take a position on whether to "recognize" the existence of the new state of Israel. The idea of recognition is, technically, part of international law; but it has, in the final analysis, a political foundation, for it is only when a new state has been properly recognized by the political branches of various governments that political relations between two different states are acknowledged to exist. In the selection which follows, we find Mr. Phillip Jessup, a scholar and teacher of international law, speaking as a political representative for the United States at the United Nations. In speaking as he does, Mr. Jessup clarifies, in remarkably brief compass, the criteria by which the United States government reached its decision. The selection reveals that there is a continuing interplay between abstract concepts and political actions; that the United States government feels itself bound by the basic concepts of what a state is; and that it may expect other governments to accept the same concepts.*

### PHILLIP C. JESSUP*

Following the proclamation of the independence of Israel on May 14, 1948, the United States extended immediate and full recognition to the state of Israel and recognized the Provisional Government of Israel as a *de facto* authority of the new state. On frequent occasions since that date American officials, including the President and the Secretary of State, have affirmed that the United States looks forward to the admission of the

---

* From "Discussion of Israeli Application for Membership," *Department of State Bulletin,* December 12, 1948, pp. 723–724.

state of Israel to the United Nations. In the remarks which I had the honor to make on behalf of my Delegation in the First Committee of the General Assembly on November 19th, I invited the attention of the Committee to the statement which the Foreign Minister of the Provisional Government of Israel had made asking for the admission of Israel to the United Nations, and I then said on behalf of my Delegation:

"The United States looks forward to the admission of the state of Israel to the United Nations and to its active participation in our work. To this end we hope that the Security Council will be able, in the near future, to recommend Israel as a state duly qualified for membership."

The Charter of the United Nations in article 4 specifies that membership in the United Nations is open to—and I quote the words of the Charter—"peace-loving states which accept the obligations contained in the present Charter and, in the judgment of the Organization, are able and willing to carry out these obligations". This formulation comprises the requirements laid down by the Charter for admission of new members to the United Nations. Reduced to their essence these requirements are as follows: The political entity in question must be a state; it must be a "peace-loving" state; it must accept the obligations contained in the Charter; and it must be able and willing, in the judgment of the United Nations, to carry out these obligations. My Government considers that the state of Israel meets these Charter requirements.

The first question which may be raised in analyzing this fourth article of the Charter and its application to the membership of the state of Israel is the question whether Israel is a "state", as that term is used in article 4 of the Charter. It is common knowledge, Mr. President, that while there are traditional definitions of a state in international law, the term has been used in many different ways. We are all aware that under the traditional definition of a state in international law all of the great writers have pointed to four qualifications:

*First:* There must be a people.
*Second:* There must be a territory.

*Third:* There must be a government.

*Fourth:* There must be capacity to enter into relations with other states of the world.

So far as the question of capacity to enter into relations with other states of the world is concerned, learned academic arguments can be and have been made to the effect that we already have among the Members of the United Nations some political entities which do not possess full sovereign freedom to form their own international policy which traditionally has been considered characteristic of a state. We know, however, that neither at San Francisco nor subsequently has the United Nations considered that complete freedom to frame and manage one's own foreign policy was an essential requisite of United Nations' membership. I dwell upon this point, Mr. President, not because anyone has ever questioned that in this respect Israel is free and unhampered; in this respect I believe that there would be unanimity that Israel exercises complete independence of judgment and of will in forming and in executing its foreign policy. The reason I mention the qualifications of this aspect of the traditional definition of a state is to underline the point that the term "state" as used and applied in article 4 of the Charter of the United Nations may not be wholly identical with the term "state" as it is used and defined in classic textbooks of international law. When we look at the other classic attributes of a state we find insistence that it must also have a government. No one doubts that Israel has a government. I think the world has been particularly impressed with the way in which the people of Israel have organized their government and have established a firm system of administration and of lawmaking under the most difficult conditions. Although, pending their scheduled elections, they still modestly and appropriately call themselves the "Government of Israel", they have a legislative body which makes laws; they have a judiciary which interprets and applies these laws; and they have an executive which carries out the laws and which has at its disposal a considerable force which is responsive to its will.

According to the same classical definition, we are told that a state must have a people and territory. Nobody questions the fact that the state of Israel has a people. It is an extremely homogeneous people: a people full of loyalty and of enthusiastic devotion to the state of Israel.

The argument seems chiefly to arise in connection with territory. One does not find in the general classic treatment of this subject any insistence that the territory of a state must be exactly fixed by definite frontiers. We all know that historically many states have begun their existence with their frontiers unsettled. Let me take as one example my own country—the United States. Like the state of Israel it had at its origin certain territory along the seacoast. It had various indeterminate claims to an extended territory westward, but in the case of the United States, that land had not even been explored and no one knew just where the American claims ended and where French and British and Spanish claims began. To the north, the exact delimitation of the frontier with the territories of Great Britain was not settled until many years later. And yet I maintain, Mr. President, that in the light of history and in the light of a practice and acceptance by other states, the existence of the United States of America was not in question before its final boundaries were determined.

Although the formulas in the classic treatises vary somewhat one from the other, both reason and history demonstrate that the concept of territory does not necessarily include precise delimitation of the boundaries of that territory. The reason for the rule that one of the necessary attributes of a state is that it shall possess territory, is that one can not contemplate a state as a kind of disembodied spirit. Historically the concept is one of insisting that there must be some portion of the earth's surface which its people inhabit and over which its government exercises authority. No one can deny that the state of Israel responds to this requirement.

# II. Independence

## 2. A Community of Independent States

*The modern state-system really came into being when the sep-
arate states established, and could enforce, their claim to be
independent of each other. But independent in what sense?
That is the problem which Francisco Suarez treats in the follow-
selection. Suarez (1548–1617), a Spanish Jesuit, wrote at a
critical time in the development of the modern system. He
points, on the one hand, to the growing reality of independent
states; but he argues, on the other hand, that their independence must be understood in relation to a still more fundamental
principle. That principle is the common humanity of all men.
By this he means, generally, that man is naturally a rational
and moral being, who is subject to certain universal principles
of right and justice. These principles are known either in their
abstract form (natural law), or in their applied form (law
of nations—which later comes to be called "international law").
In either case, independent states are joined in a unity which
can be transgressed by unjust actions, but can never be denied
in principle.*

### FRANCISCO SUAREZ*

The rational basis [of the law of nations] consists in the fact
that the human race, into howsoever many different peoples
and kingdoms it may be divided, always preserves a certain
unity, not only as a species, but also a moral and political

---

* From Francisco Suarez, *De Legibus, Ac Deo Legislatore,* 1612.
Selections are from the "Classics of International Law" translation
of parts of three of Suarez's works: Book I, Ch. 19, sec. 9 (pp.
348–349); Book III, Ch. 2, secs. 4–6 (pp. 375–377). Reprinted by
permission of the Carnegie Endowment for International Peace.

unity (as it were) enjoined by the natural precept of mutual love and mercy; a precept which applies to all, even to strangers of every nation.

Therefore, although a given sovereign state, commonwealth, or kingdom may constitute a perfect community in itself, consisting of its own members, nevertheless, each one of these states is also, in a certain sense, and viewed in relation to the human race, a member of that universal society; for these states when standing alone are never so self-sufficient that they do not require some mutual assistance, association, and intercourse, at times for their own greater welfare and advantage, but at other times because also of some moral necessity or need. This fact is made manifest by actual usage.

Consequently, such communities have need of some system of law whereby they may be directed and properly ordered with regard to this kind of intercourse and association; and although that guidance is in large measure provided by natural reason, it is not provided in sufficient measure and in a direct manner with respect to all matters; therefore, it was possible for certain special rules of law to be introduced through the practice of these same nations. For just as in one state or province law is introduced by custom, so among the human race as a whole it was possible for laws to be introduced by the habitual conduct of nations. This was the more feasible because the matters comprised within the law in question are few, very closely related to natural law and most easily deduced therefrom in a manner so advantageous and so in harmony with nature itself that, while this derivation [of the law of nations from the natural law] may not be self-evident—that is, not essentially and absolutely required for moral rectitude—it is nevertheless quite in accord with nature, and universally acceptable for its own sake.

[Having established that all states are subject to natural law and the law of nations, Suarez raises a further question concerning the power of governments to make laws for their citizens: Does this power reside in the whole body of mankind collectively? His answer to this question supplies a basis for the proposition that mankind is properly separated into independent political societies.]

. . . The multitude of mankind is regarded in two different ways.

First, it may be regarded simply as a kind of aggregation, without any order, or any physical or moral union. So viewed, [men] do not constitute a unified whole, whether physical or moral, so that they are not strictly speaking one political body, and therefore do not need one prince, or head. Consequently, if one regards them from this standpoint, one does not as yet conceive of the power in question as existing properly and formally; on the contrary, it is understood to dwell in them at most as a fundamental potentiality, so to speak.

The multitude of mankind should, then, be viewed from another standpoint, that is, with regard to the special volition, or common consent, by which they are gathered together into one political body through one bond of fellowship and for the purpose of aiding one another in the attainment of a single political end. Thus viewed, they form a single mystical body which, morally speaking, may be termed essentially a unit; and that body accordingly needs a single head. Therefore, in a community of this kind, viewed as such, there exists in the very nature of things the power of which we are speaking, so that men may not, when forming such a group, set up obstacles to that power; and consequently, if we conceive of men as desiring both alternatives—that is to say, as desirous of so congregating, but on the condition (as it were) that they shall not be subject to the said power—the situation would be self-contradictory, and such men would accordingly fail to achieve any [valid end]. For it is impossible to conceive of a unified political body without political government or disposition thereto; since, in the first place, this unity arises, in a large measure, from subjection to one and the same rule and to some common superior power; while furthermore, if there were no such government, this body could not be directed towards one [common] end and the general welfare. It is, then, repugnant to natural reason to assume the existence of a group of human beings

united in the form of a single political body, without postulating
the existence of some common power which the individual members of the community are bound to obey; and therefore, if this
power does not reside in any specific individual, it must necessarily exist in the community as a whole.

To what has been said above, we should add the statement
that the power in question does not reside in the multitude of
mankind by the very nature of things in such wise that it is
necessarily one sole power with respect to the entire species,
or entire aggregate, of men existing throughout the whole world;
inasmuch as it is not necessary to the preservation or welfare
of nature, that all men should thus congregate in a single political community. On the contrary, that would hardly be possible,
and much less would it be expedient. For Aristotle (*Politics,*
Bk. VII, chap. iv [, § 7]) has rightly said that it is difficult
to govern aright a city whose inhabitants are too numerous;
accordingly, this difficulty would be still greater in the case of a
kingdom excessively large, and therefore, it would be greater
by far (we are referring to civil government) if the whole world
were concerned.

Consequently, it seems to me probable that the power of
which we speak never existed in this fashion in the whole assem-
blage of mankind, or that it so existed for an exceedingly brief
period; and that, on the contrary, soon after the creation of the
world, mankind began to be divided into various states in each
one of which this power existed in a distinct form. . . .

Finally, it may be concluded from the foregoing that this
power to make human laws of an individual and special nature,
laws which we call civil, as if to indicate that they are ordained
for one perfect community—it may be concluded, I say—that
this power never existed in one and the same form throughout
the whole world of men, being rather divided among various
communities, according to the establishment and division of
these communities themselves. Thus we also conclude that . . .
this civil power did not reside in any one specific man with
respect to the whole world. For at no time did all men agree
to confer that power upon a particular ruler of the entire world,
neither have we any knowledge of its bestowal upon some particular individual by God. . . .

◇◇◇◇◇◇◇◇◇◇◇◇◇◇◇◇◇◇◇◇◇◇◇◇◇◇◇◇◇◇◇◇◇◇◇◇◇◇◇◇◇◇◇◇◇◇◇◇◇◇◇◇◇

# 3. Independence and Liberty

*The question whether all mankind ought to constitute a single political society raises the further question of the political effect—for example, the effect on the prospects for human freedom—of a world-state. The most concrete relevant historical information we have at our disposal is to be obtained from the conditions of men under extensive, or "world" empires. In the selection which follows, Edward Gibbon (1737–1794), the great English historian of Rome, compares the modern European state-system to the conditions which prevailed under the Roman Empire.*

## EDWARD GIBBON*

The division of Europe into a number of independent states, connected, however, with each other by the general resemblance of religion, language, and manners, is productive of the most beneficial consequences to the liberty of mankind. A modern tyrant, who should find no resistance either in his own breast, or in his people, would soon experience a gentle restraint from the example of his equals, the dread of present censure, the advice of his allies, and the apprehension of his enemies. The object of his displeasure, escaping from the narrow limits of his dominions, would easily obtain, in a happier climate, a secure refuge, a new fortune adequate to his merit, the freedom of complaint, and perhaps the means of revenge. But the empire of the Romans filled the world, and when that empire fell into the hands of a single person, the world became a safe and dreary prison for his enemies. The slave of Imperial despotism, whether he was condemned to drag his gilded chain in Rome and the senate, or to wear out a life of exile on the barren rock

---

* From Edward Gibbon, *The History of the Decline and Fall of the Roman Empire* (Boston: Phillips, Samson and Co., 1851). Vol. I, pp. 99–100.

of Seriphus, or the frozen banks of the Danube, expected his
fate in silent despair. To resist was fatal, and it was impossible
to fly. On every side he was encompassed with a vast extent of
sea and land, which he could never hope to traverse without
being discovered, seized, and restored to his irritated master.
Beyond the frontiers, his anxious view could discover nothing,
except the ocean, inhospitable deserts, hostile tribes of barbar-
ians, of fierce manners and unknown language, or dependent
kings, who would gladly purchase the emperor's protection by
the sacrifice of an obnoxious fugitive. "Wherever you are," said
Cicero to the exiled Marcellus, "remember that you are equally
within the power of the conqueror."

---

◇◇◇◇◇◇◇◇◇◇◇◇◇◇◇◇◇◇◇◇◇◇◇◇◇◇◇◇◇◇◇◇◇◇◇◇◇◇◇◇◇◇◇◇◇◇◇◇◇

# 4. Independence and Conflict: Political
# Experience

*In 1787, the debate among American citizens over whether to
ratify and put into operation the newly drafted "federal" constitution produced a political classic: the series of essays now
known as* The Federalist. *These essays, written by three of the
greatest American statesmen, Alexander Hamilton, James Madison, and John Jay, range over the whole field of the problem
of governing men. In one of the essays, Hamilton treats the
problem of what will happen to the states if they remain only
loosely joined; and in order to get to the bottom of that question, he states his understanding of what political experience
has shown results from the coexistence of independent states.
His conclusion, that conflict is inevitable, reflects a view of human nature in politics which may not be easy to accept. But it
is a view which has been held by many men in all ages, and is
itself part of the problem of the existence of separate political
societies.*

## ALEXANDER HAMILTON*

If these states should either be wholly disunited, or only united in partial confederacies, a man must be far gone in Utopian speculations, who can seriously doubt that the subdivisions into which they might be thrown would have frequent and violent contests with each other. To presume a want of motives for such contests, as an argument against their existence, would be to forget that men are ambitious, vindictive and rapacious. To look for a continuation of harmony between a number of independent, unconnected sovereignties, situated in the same neighborhood, would be to disregard the uniform course of human events, and to set at defiance the accumulated experience of ages.

The causes of hostility among nations are innumerable. There are some which have a general and almost constant operation upon the collective bodies of society. Of this description are the love of power, or the desire of preëminence and dominion— the jealousy of power, or the desire of equality and safety. There are others which have a more circumscribed, though an equally operative influence within their spheres; such are the rivalships and competitions of commerce between commercial nations. And there are others, not less numerous than either of the former, which take their origin entirely in private passions; in the attachments, enmities, interests, hopes, and fears of leading individuals in the communities of which they are members. Men of this class, whether the favorites of a king or of a people, have in too many instances abused the confidence they possessed; and assuming the pretext of some public motive, have not scrupled to sacrifice the national tranquillity to personal advantage, or personal gratification.

The celebrated Pericles, in compliance with the resentment of a prostitute,[1] at the expense of much of the blood and treasure of his countrymen, attacked, vanquished, and destroyed

---

* From *The Federalist* (Hallowell: Masters, Smith and Co., 1857), No. 6. Footnotes as in source, renumbered.

[1] ASPASIA, vide PLUTARCH's life of Pericles.

the city of the *Samnians*. The same man, stimulated by private pique against the *Magarensians,* another nation of Greece, or to avoid a prosecution with which he was threatened as an accomplice in a supposed theft of the statuary *Phidias,* or to get rid of the accusations prepared to be brought against him for dissipating the funds of the state in the purchase of popularity, or from a combination of all these causes, was the primitive author of that famous and fatal war, distinguished in the Grecian annals by the name of the *Peloponnesian* war; which after various vicissitudes, intermissions and renewals, terminated in the ruin of the Athenian commonwealth.

The ambitious cardinal, who was prime minister to Henry VIIIth, permitting his vanity to aspire to the triple crown, entertained hopes of succeeding in the acquisition of that splendid prize by the influence of the emperor Charles Vth. To secure the favor and interest of his enterprising and powerful monarch, he precipitated England into a war with France, contrary to the plainest dictates of policy, and at the hazard of the safety and independence, as well of the kingdom over which he presided by his counsels, as of Europe in general. For if there ever was a sovereign who bid fair to realize the project of universal monarchy, it was the emperor Charles Vth, of whose intrigues Wolsey was at once the instrument and the dupe.

The influence which the bigotry of one female,[2] the petulance of another,[3] and the cabals of a third,[4] had in the cotemporary policy, ferments and pacifications, of a considerable part of Europe, are topics that have been too often descanted upon not to be generally known.

To multiply examples of the agency of personal considerations in the production of great national events, either foreign or domestic, according to their direction, would be an unnecessary waste of time. Those who have but a superficial acquaintance with the sources from which they are to be drawn, will themselves recollect a variety of instances; and those who have a tolerable knowledge of human nature, will not stand in need

---

[2] Madame de Maintenon.
[3] Dutchess of Marlborough.
[4] Madame de Pompadoure.

of such lights, to form their opinion either of the reality or extent of that agency. Perhaps, however, a reference, tending to illustrate the general principle, may with propriety be made to a case which has lately happened among ourselves. If Shays had not been a *desperate debtor,* it is much to be doubted whether Massachusetts would have been plunged into a civil war.

But notwithstanding the concurring testimony of experience, in this particular, there are still to be found visionary or designing men, who stand ready to advocate the paradox of perpetual peace between the states, though dismembered and alienated from each other. . . .

So far is the general sense of mankind from corresponding with the tenets of those, who endeavor to lull asleep our apprehensions of discord and hostility between the states, in the event of disunion, that it has from long observation of the progress of society become a sort of axiom in politics, that vicinity or nearness of situation, constitutes nations natural enemies. An intelligent writer expresses himself on this subject to this effect: "Neighboring nations (says he) are naturally enemies of "each other, unless their common weakness forces them to league "in a confederative republic, and their constitution pre- "vents the differences that neighborhood occasions, extinguish- "ing that secret jealousy, which disposes all states to aggrandize "themselves at the expense of their neighbors." [5] This passage, at the same time, points out the evil, and suggests the remedy.

---

◇◇◇◇◇◇◇◇◇◇◇◇◇◇◇◇◇◇◇◇◇◇◇◇◇◇◇◇◇◇◇◇◇◇◇◇◇◇◇◇◇◇◇◇◇◇◇◇◇◇

# 5. Independence and Conflict:
## A Theoretical View

*In 1651, the English philosopher Thomas Hobbes (1588–1679) published his* Leviathan. *This book is generally considered to*

---

[5] Vide: "Principes des négotiations," par L'Abbé de Mably.

*be one of the greatest works ever written on political philos-
ophy. The basic conception which is of interest to us here is
that of independent states as existing in what Hobbes calls a
"state of nature." Such a state is, in Hobbes' view, but a continuation of the original, warlike condition of men who have no
common government. Hence, even though Hobbes also refers, as
Suarez had done, to a "natural law," we find that his conception of that law is rooted in radically different premises concerning man's fundamental nature: man's basic desire, and his
fundamental right, is to be safe. This view goes far beyond
that of Hamilton, for in Hobbes' case, it is a question not
simply of historical experience, but of a new, and tradition-
shattering analysis of the basis of political life. That new analysis
came to play a crucial part in the development of modern
political conceptions. For example, within a short time of the
publication of Hobbes' works, other writers were referring to the
condition between separate political societies as one of a "state
of nature," a conception which has persisted into the twentieth century.*

## THOMAS HOBBES*

. . . In the nature of man, we find three principal causes of
quarrel. First, competition; secondly, diffidence; thirdly, glory.

The first, maketh men invade for gain; the second, for safety;
and the third, for reputation. The first use violence, to make
themselves masters of other men's persons, wives, children, and
cattle; the second, to defend them; the third, for trifles, as a
word, a smile, a different opinion, and any other sign of under-
value, either direct in their persons, or by reflection in their
kindred, their friends, their nation, their profession, or their
name.

Hereby it is manifest, that during the time men live without
a common power to keep them all in awe, they are in that
condition which is called war; and such a war, as is of every
man, against every man. For WAR, consisteth not in battle only,
or the act of fighting; but in a tract of time, wherein the will

---

* From Thomas Hobbes, *Leviathan,* Ch. 13. (In *The English Works
of Thomas Hobbes of Malmesbury,* ed. Sir W. Molesworth. London:
John Bohn, 1841, Vol. 3.)

to contend by battle is sufficiently known: and therefore the notion of *time,* is to be considered in the nature of war; as it is in the nature of weather. For as the nature of foul weather, lieth not in a shower or two of rain; but in an inclination thereto of many days together: so the nature of war, consisteth not in actual fighting; but in the known disposition thereto, during all the time there is no assurance to the contrary. All other time is PEACE.

Whatsoever therefore is consequent to a time of war, where every man is enemy to every man; the same is consequent to the time, wherein men live without other security, than what their own strength, and their own invention shall furnish them withal. In such condition, there is no place for industry; because the fruit thereof is uncertain: and consequently no culture of the earth; no navigation, nor use of the commodities that may be imported by sea; no commodious building; no instruments of moving, and removing, such things as require much force; no knowledge of the face of the earth; no account of time; no arts; no letters; no society; and which is worst of all, continual fear, and danger of violent death; and the life of man, solitary, poor, nasty, brutish, and short.

It may seem strange to some man, that has not well weighed these things; that nature should thus dissociate, and render men apt to invade, and destroy one another: and he may therefore, not trusting to this inference, made from the passions, desire perhaps to have the same confirmed by experience. Let him therefore consider with himself, when taking a journey, he arms himself, and seeks to go well accompanied; when going to sleep, he locks his doors; when even in his house he locks his chests; and this when he knows there be laws, and public officers, armed, to revenge all injuries shall be done him; what opinion he has of his fellow-subjects, when he rides armed; of his fellow citizens, when he locks his doors; and of his children, and servants, when he locks his chests. Does he not there as much accuse mankind by his actions, as I do by my words? But neither of us accuse man's nature in it. The desires, and other passions of man, are in themselves no sin. No more are the actions, that proceed from those passions, till they know a law that forbids them: which till laws be made they cannot know: nor can any law be made, till they have agreed upon the person that shall make it.

It may peradventure be thought, there was never such a time, nor condition of war as this; and I believe it was never generally so, over all the world: but there are many places, where they live so now. For the savage people in many places of America, except the government of small families, the concord whereof dependeth on natural lust, have no government at all; and live at this day in that brutish manner, as I said before. Howsoever, it may be perceived what manner of life there would be, where there were no common power to fear, by the manner of life, which men that have formerly lived under a peaceful government, use to degenerate into, in a civil war.

But though there had never been any time, wherein particular men were in a condition of war one against another; yet in all times, kings, and persons of sovereign authority, because of their independency, are in continual jealousies, and in the state and posture of gladiators; having their weapons pointing, and their eyes fixed on one another; that is, their forts, garrisons, and guns upon the frontiers of their kingdoms; and continual spies upon their neighbours; which is a posture of war. But because they uphold thereby, the industry of their subjects; there does not follow from it, that misery, which accompanies the liberty of particular men.

# 6. Independence and State-Personality

*Modern states are the "public persons" of the state-system. But the abstractness of such a concept seems, at times, to have provoked a reaction. In the following selection, we find the*

*abstract idea of the state combined with the idea that indi-*
*vidual states also have special qualities. In this case, independ-*
*ence is construed as the basic condition ensuring that each*
*state may, in fact, develop its "special" qualities. Heinrich von*
*Treitschke (1834–1896) was a famous and influential German*
*historian and political theorist.*

## HEINRICH VON TREITSCHKE *

. . . [Johann] Fichte has finely said, "Individual man sees
in his country the realisation of his earthly immortality."
    This involves that the State has a personality, primarily in the
juridical, and secondly in the politico-moral sense. Every man
who is able to exercise his will in law has a legal personality.
Now it is quite clear that the State possesses this deliberate will;
nay more, that it has the juridical personality in the most complete sense. In State treaties it is the will of the State which is
expressed, not the personal desires of the individuals who conclude them, and the treaty is binding as long as the contracting
State exists. When a State is incapable of enforcing its will, or
of maintaining law and order at home and prestige abroad, it
becomes an anomaly and falls a prey either to anarchy or a
foreign enemy. The State therefore must have the most em-
phatic will that can be imagined. . . .
    Treat the State as a person, and the necessary and rational
multiplicity of States follows. Just as in individual life the ego
implies the existence of the non-ego, so it does in the State.
The State is power, precisely in order to assert itself as against
other equally independent powers. War and the administration
of justice are the chief tasks of even the most barbaric States.
But these tasks are only conceivable where a plurality of States
are found existing side by side. Thus the idea of one universal
empire is odious—the ideal of a State co-extensive with humanity is no ideal at all. In a single State the whole range of culture
could never be fully spanned; no single people could unite the
virtues of aristocracy and democracy. All nations, like all indi-

---

* From Heinrich von Treitschke, *Politics*, trans. B. Dugdale and
T. De Bille (London: Constable and Co., Ltd., 1916), I, 15–16. Reprinted by permission of Constable and Co.

viduals, have their limitations, but it is exactly in the abundance of these limited qualities that the genius of humanity is exhibited. The rays of the Divine light are manifested, broken by countless facets among the separate peoples, each one exhibiting another picture and another idea of the whole. Every people has a right to believe that certain attributes of the Divine reason are exhibited in it to their fullest perfection. No people ever attains to national consciousness without overrating itself. . . .

◇◇◇◇◇◇◇◇◇◇◇◇◇◇◇◇◇◇◇◇◇◇◇◇◇◇◇◇◇◇◇◇◇◇◇◇◇◇◇◇◇◇◇◇◇◇◇◇◇◇◇

# 7. Independence and International Harmony

*Treitschke, writing in the nineteenth century, had emphasized the powerful assertion of the independent state's "personality." Nicholas Murray Butler (1862–1947), eminent American scholar, educator and public-spirited citizen, writing in the twentieth century after the carnage of World War I, shifted the emphasis. To him, the independence of nation-states permitted each to contribute not just to its own development, but to the creation of an international "society," under a universal law.*

## NICHOLAS MURRAY BUTLER*

It would be difficult to find any problem, either intellectual or practical, that presents itself more persistently or in more varied forms than that of the relation between the One and the Many. The ancient Greek philosophers saw its significance, and

* From Nicholas Murray Butler, "The Development of the International Mind," *International Conciliation,* No. 192, November, 1923, pp. 777–781, 783–785. Reprinted by permission of the Carnegie Endowment for International Peace.

with that naïve directness so characteristic of them, attacked it as a fundamental question that must be answered if the world was to be grasped by human intelligence. The problem of the One and the Many lies at the bottom of all logic, of all ethics, of all economics, and of all politics; it lies at the bottom of the problem of nationalism and internationalism. How can the One be enriched and perfected not only without harm to the Many, but so as to enrich and perfect the Many itself? How can the One be distinguished from the Many and given a form and a personality all its own? How can the One so guide and direct its own appetites and so shape its own conduct as to build up rather than to tear down the advantage and the welfare of the Many? Truly the relation between the One and the Many, if the oldest of intellectual problems, is also one of the most many-sided and most difficult. . . .

It may assist to propose a satisfactory answer to these difficult and perplexing questions, if we look upon a nation as endowed with personality like an individual. In that case, we gain some new comprehension of what is meant by national opinion other than the opinions of individuals, of what is meant by national feeling other than the feeling of individuals, and of what is meant by national ambition and purpose other than the ambition and purpose of individuals. . . . If a nation be a person—and I think it is—then those tested principles of ethics which have application to the conduct of individual persons, would also have application to the conduct of national persons. The same fundamental precepts, the same ruling points of view, that we call moral in the case of an individual, are also moral in the case of a nation. . . .

So soon as nations, both great and small, accept the doctrine that they are moral persons, and as such are bound to conform their conduct to moral laws, the basis is laid for the recognition of the like personality of other nations, and a true society of nations begins to appear. Just as individuals are no longer granted either moral excellence or political rights by reason of their intellectual competence or their material possessions, so nations, when judged as moral persons, are not to be given weight as large or small, rich or poor. One test of membership in a true society of nations must be like the test of membership in a society of individuals, namely, willingness and capacity to observe loyally the principles and to follow earnestly the ideals which are characteristic of civilized states. . . .

A real difficulty is found, in the life of nations as One and the Many. If a nation, representative of the One, is so reckless of moral control as to seek only its selfish aggrandizement at whatever cost to the Many, it becomes and must become the enemy of the world's peace and order, precisely as an individual acting in similar fashion becomes the enemy of the peace and order of the community in which he lives. It is essential that the gospel of service should be hearkened to by nations as well as by individuals. It is the teaching of this gospel that a nation exists not for self-aggrandizement but for the promotion of the general good, and that it may grow great and strong and rich without danger to mankind if its greatness, its strength, its wealth, and its riches be used in a spirit of friendship, not hostility, of service, not selfishness. To put it differently, it is essential that the civilized nations should develop, each for itself, what I ventured long since to describe as the international mind.

The international mind is that fixed habit of thought and action which looks upon the several nations of the civilized world as cooperating equals in promoting the progress of civilization, in developing commerce and industry, and in diffusing science and education throughout the world.

The international mind, so defined, is in sharp antagonism to that internationalism which would break down the boundaries of nations and merge all mankind, regardless of differences in tradition, in law, in language, in religion, and in government, into a single and common unit. Such internationalism, instead of being progressive, would be reactionary. It would obliterate those differences which the march of progress has developed, and it would seek to destroy those landmarks of civilization which have been set up at great cost of life and labor over twenty centuries. Such internationalism would foment discord by creating false relationships, which, having no body of facts to correspond to them, could only give rise to friction, to conflict, and to international war. The international mind, on the other hand, makes much of the spirit, the temper, and the tradition of nationality. It builds upon history and upon achievement, and it appeals to the pride, the glory, and the spirit of service of the nations, both great and small. It sees in the various civilized nations so many different facets of a single crystal, each reflecting the light of civilization in its own way, and each being a necessary part of the complete and perfect stone. . . .

. . . Just as in the philosophy of the Greeks the One and the Many had to be explained, if at all, with reference to each other, so in our modern political philosophy the individual nation and an association of nations must be looked upon, not as antagonistic but as complementary, as parts of one complete organic whole. The method of achieving this end is the method of law. The pathway to that law is provided by morals. The support both of morals and of law is to be found in public opinion. That public opinion must be taught to know the international mind, to accept it, and to guide national action and policy in accordance with it.

# III. Sovereignty: Basic Theory

# 8. The Original Conception of Sovereignty

*Jean Bodin's magisterial work,* Six Books of the Commonwealth
*(1576), contains the first detailed, explicit treatment of "sovereignty." Because that concept has come, in later times, to
be taken almost as synonomous with modern ideas, it is important to notice the precise nature of Bodin's treatment, and
to reflect on the context within which it occurs. Even though
Bodin begins by speaking of sovereignty as "absolute," we
soon find him seriously qualifying that term by references to
the limits set on the actions of princes by divine and natural
law. In this sense, Bodin stands much closer to Francisco
Suarez than to Thomas Hobbes, whose views are presented in
the next selection. Furthermore, Bodin's purpose in treating
sovereignty is not to elevate that particular conception to the
dominant place in referring to political authority, but to clarify
what he feels has been left unclear in earlier treatments. In
this sense, he stands in sharp contrast to Hobbes, whose view
of sovereignty is really the core of his treatment.*

## JEAN BODIN*

Sovereignty is that absolute and perpetual power vested in a
commonwealth which in Latin is termed *majestas* . . . The
term needs careful definition, because although it is the distinguishing mark of a commonwealth, and an understanding of
its nature fundamental to any treatment of politics, no jurist
or political philosopher has in fact attempted to define it. . . .
I have described it as *perpetual* because one can give abso-

---

*From Jean Bodin, *Six Books of the Commonwealth,* trans. M. J.
Tooley (Oxford: Basil Blackwell), Book I, Chs. 8–10, pp. 25, 27–29,
36, 43–44. Reprinted by permission of Basil Blackwell.

lute power to a person or group of persons for a period of time, but that time expired they become subjects once more. Therefore even while they enjoy power, they cannot properly be regarded as sovereign rulers, but only as the lieutenants and agents of the sovereign ruler, till the moment comes when it pleases the prince or the people to revoke the gift. The true sovereign remains always seized of his power. . . .

Let us now turn to the other term of our definition and consider the force of the word *absolute*. The people or the magnates of a commonwealth can bestow simply and unconditionally upon someone of their choice a sovereign and perpetual power to dispose of their property and persons, to govern the state as he thinks fit, and to order the succession, in the same way that any proprietor, out of his liberality, can freely and unconditionally make a gift of his property to another. Such a form of gift, not being qualified in any way, is the only true gift, being at once unconditional and irrevocable. Gifts burdened with obligations and hedged with conditions are not true gifts. Similarly sovereign power given to a prince charged with conditions is neither properly sovereign, nor absolute, unless the conditions of appointment are only such as are inherent in the laws of God and of nature. . . .

If we insist however that absolute power means exemption from all law whatsoever, there is no prince in the world who can be regarded as sovereign, since all the princes of the earth are subject to the laws of God and of nature, and even to certain human laws common to all nations. On the other hand, it is possible for a subject who is neither a prince nor a ruler, to be exempted from all the laws, ordinances, and customs of the commonwealth. . . . But notwithstanding such exemptions from the operations of the law, the subject remains under the authority of him who exercises sovereign power, and owes him obedience.

On the other hand it is the distinguishing mark of the sovereign that he cannot in any way be subject to the commands of another, for it is he who makes law for the subject, abrogates law already made, and amends obsolete law. No one who is subject either to the law or to some other person can do this. . . .

It is far otherwise with divine and natural laws. All the princes
of the earth are subject to them, and cannot contravene them
without treason and rebellion against God. His yoke is upon them,
and they must bow their heads in fear and reverence before
His divine majesty. The absolute power of princes and sovereign
lords does not extend to the laws of God and of nature. He
who best understood the meaning of absolute power, and made
kings and emperors submit to his will, defined his sovereignty
as a power to override positive law; he did not claim power to
set aside divine and natural law. . . .

If justice is the end of the law, the law the work of the
prince, and the prince the image of God, it follows of necessity
that the law of the prince should be modelled on the law of
God. . . .

Before going any further, one must consider what is meant
by *law*. The word law signifies the right command of that person, or those persons, who have absolute authority over all the
rest without exception, saving only the law-giver himself,
whether the command touches all subjects in general or only
some in particular. To put it another way, the law is the right-
ful command of the sovereign touching all his subjects in general,
or matters of general application . . . As to the commands of
the magistrate, they are not properly speaking laws but only
edicts. 'An edict', says Varro, 'is an order issued by a magistrate.' Such orders are only binding on those subject to his
jurisdiction, and are only in force for his term of office.

The first attribute of the sovereign prince therefore is the
power to make law binding on all his subjects in general and
on each in particular. But to avoid any ambiguity one must
add that he does so without the consent of any superior, equal,
or inferior being necessary. If the prince can only make law
with the consent of a superior he is a subject; if of an equal he
shares his sovereignty; if of an inferior, whether it be a council
of magnates or the people, it is not he who is sovereign. . . .

All the other attributes and rights of sovereignty are included
in this power of making and unmaking law, so that strictly
speaking this is the unique attribute of sovereign power. It in-
cludes all other rights of sovereignty, that is to say of making

peace and war, of hearing appeals from the sentences of all courts whatsoever, of appointing and dismissing the great officers of state; of taxing, or granting privileges of exemption to all subjects, of appreciating or depreciating the value and weight of the coinage, of receiving oaths of fidelity from subjects and liege-vassals alike, without exception of any other to whom faith is due. . . .

But because *law* is an unprecise and general term, it is as well to specify the other attributes of sovereignty comprised in it, such as the making of war and peace. This is one of the most important rights of sovereignty, since it brings in its train either the ruin or the salvation of the state. This was a right of sovereignty not only among the ancient Romans, but has always been so among all other peoples . . . Sovereign princes are therefore accustomed to keep themselves informed of the smallest accidents and undertakings connected with warfare. Whatever latitude they may give to their representatives to negotiate peace or an alliance, they never grant the authority to conclude without their own express consent.

# 9. The Hobbesian Leviathan

*Hobbes' treatment of sovereignty is, in certain critical respects, much more determinative of modern views than is that of Bodin. To understand Hobbes' view correctly, it should be considered in relation to his basic premise that man is by nature in a warlike "state of nature." (The student will find it helpful, at this point, to review the selection from Hobbes in the materials on Independence.) Similarly, to understand the relation of the sovereigns to each other, Hobbes' definition of "natural law" should be considered in relation to the ideas of Suarez and Bodin. For the latter two men, the natural law is essentially a set of fundamental* duties *binding individual men and sovereigns; for Hobbes, the natural law is essentially a set of fundamental* rights *of men and sovereigns. The difference, in application, is very great: Hobbes' sovereign is, in the final analysis, sole judge of what actions to take to preserve or increase the power of the Leviathan-state vis-à-vis all other states.*

## THOMAS HOBBES*

. . . Because the condition of man, . . . is a condition of war of every one against every one; in which case every one is governed by his own reason; and there is nothing he can make use of, that may not be a help unto him, in preserving his life against his enemies; it followeth, that in such a condition, every man has a right to every thing; even to one another's body. And therefore, as long as this natural right of every man to every thing endureth, there can be no security to any man, how strong or wise soever he be, of living out the time, which nature ordinarily alloweth men to live. And consequently it is a precept, or general rule of reason, *that every man, ought to endeavour peace, as far as he has hope of obtaining it; and when he cannot obtain it, that he may seek, and use, all helps, and advantages of war.* The first branch of which rule, containeth the first, and fundamental law of nature; which is, *to seek peace, and follow it.* The second, the sum of the right of nature; which is, *by all means we can, to defend ourselves.*

. . . covenants, without the sword, are but words, and of no strength to secure a man at all. Therefore notwithstanding the laws of nature, which every one hath then kept, when he has the will to keep them, when he can do it safely, if there be no power erected, or not great enough for our security; every man will, and may lawfully rely on his own strength and art, for caution against all other men. And in all places, where men have lived by small families, to rob and spoil one another, has been a trade, and so far from being reputed against the law

---

* From Thomas Hobbes, *Leviathan,* Chs. 14, 17, 18, pp. 117, 154–155, 157–158, 163–164, 166 of the Molesworth edition of the *English Works.*

of nature, that the greater spoils they gained, the greater was their honour; and men observed no other laws therein, but the laws of honour; that is, to abstain from cruelty, leaving to men their lives, and instruments of husbandry. And as small families did then; so now do cities and kingdoms which are but greater families, for their own security, enlarge their dominions, upon all pretences of danger, and fear of invasion, or assistance that may be given to invaders, and endeavour as much as they can, to subdue, or weaken their neighbours, by open force, and secret arts, for want of other caution, justly; and are remembered for it in after ages with honour.

Nor is it the joining together of a small number of men, that gives them this security; because in small numbers, small additions on the one side or the other, make the advantage of strength so great, as is sufficient to carry the victory; and therefore gives encouragement to an invasion. The multitude sufficient to confide in for our security, is not determined by any certain number, but by comparison with the enemy we fear; and is then sufficient, when the odds of the enemy is not of so visible and conspicuous moment, to determine the event of war, as to move him to attempt.

And be there never so great a multitude; yet if their actions be directed according to their particular judgments, and particular appetites, they can expect thereby no defence, nor protection, neither against a common enemy, nor against the injuries of one another. For being distracted in opinions concerning the best use and application of their strength, they do not help but hinder one another; and reduce their strength by mutual opposition to nothing: whereby they are easily, not only subdued by a very few that agree together; but also when there is no common enemy, they make war upon each other, for their particular interests. For if we could suppose a great multitude of men to consent in the observation of justice, and other laws of nature, without a common power to keep them all in awe; we might as well suppose all mankind to do the same; and then there neither would be, nor need to be any civil government, or commonwealth at all; because there would be peace without subjection.

Nor is it enough for the security, which men desire should last all the time of their life, that they be governed, and directed by one judgment, for a limited time; as in one battle, or one war. For though they obtain a victory by their unanimous endeavour against a foreign enemy; yet afterwards, when either they have no common enemy, or he that by one part is held for an enemy, is by another part held for a friend, they must needs by the difference of their interests dissolve, and fall again into a war amongst themselves. . . .

The only way to erect such a common power, as may be able to defend them from the invasion of foreigners, and the injuries of one another, and thereby to secure them in such sort, as that by their own industry, and by the fruits of the earth, they may nourish themselves and live contentedly; is, to confer all their power and strength upon one man, or upon one assembly of men, that may reduce all their wills, by plurality of voices, unto one will: which is as much as to say, to appoint one man, or assembly of men, to bear their person; and every one to own, and acknowledge himself to be author of whatsoever he that so beareth their person, shall act, or cause to be acted, in those things which concern the common peace and safety; and therein to submit their wills, every one to his will, and their judgments, to his judgment. This is more than consent, or concord; it is a real unity of them all, in one and the same person, made by covenant of every man with every man, in such manner, as if every man should say to every man, *I authorise and give up my right of governing myself, to this man, or to this assembly of men, on this condition, that thou give up thy right to him, and authorize all his actions in like manner.* This done, the multitude so united in one person, is called a COMMONWEALTH, in Latin CIVITAS. This is the generation of that great LEVIATHAN, or rather, to speak more reverently, of that *mortal god,* to which we owe under the *immortal God,* our peace and defence. For by this authority, given him by every particular man in the commonwealth, he hath the use of so much power and strength conferred on him, that by terror thereof, he is enabled to perform the wills of them all, to peace at home, and mutual aid against their enemies abroad. And in him consisteth the essence of the commonwealth; which, to define it, is *one person, of whose acts a great multitude, by mutual covenants one with another, have made themselves every one the author, to the end he may use the strength and means of them all, as he shall think expedient, for their peace and common defence.*

And he that carrieth this person, is called SOVEREIGN, and said to have *sovereign power;* and every one besides, his SUBJECT.

. . . because the end of this institution, is the peace and defence of them all; and whosoever has right to the end, has right to the means; it belongeth of right, to whatsoever man, or assembly that hath the sovereignty, to be judge both of the means of peace and defence, and also of the hindrances, and disturbances of the same; and to do whatsoever he shall think necessary to be done, both beforehand, for the preserving of peace and security, by prevention of discord at home, and hostility from abroad; and, when peace and security are lost, for the recovery of the same. . . .

[Therefore] annexed to the sovereignty [is] the right of making war and peace with other nations, and commonwealths; that is to say, of judging when it is for the public good, and how great forces are to be assembled, armed, and paid for that end; and to levy money upon the subjects, to defray the expenses thereof. For the power by which the people are to be defended, consisteth in their armies; and the strength of an army, in the union of their strength under one command; which command the sovereign instituted, therefore hath; because the command of the *militia,* without other institution, maketh him that hath it sovereign. And therefore whosoever is made general of an army, he that hath the sovereign power is always generalissimo. . . .

Concerning the offices of one sovereign to another, which are comprehended in that law, which is commonly called the *law of nations,* I need not say anything in this place; because the law of nations, and the law of nature, is the same thing. And every sovereign hath the same right, in procuring the safety of his people, that any particular man can have, in pro-

curing the safety of his own body. And the same law, that
dictateth to men that have no civil government, what they
ought to do, and what to avoid in regard of one another, dictateth the same to commonwealths, that is, to the consciences
of sovereign princes and sovereign assemblies; there being no
court of natural justice, but in the conscience only . . .

◇◇◇◇◇◇◇◇◇◇◇◇◇◇◇◇◇◇◇◇◇◇◇◇◇◇◇◇◇◇◇◇◇◇◇◇◇◇◇◇◇◇◇◇◇◇◇

# 10. Sovereignty in the Nineteenth Century

*When Treitschke formulated his views on sovereignty, in the
middle of the nineteenth century, he drew upon two sources:
first, the European intellectual tradition which developed the
concept; and second, the accumulated practice of modern, sovereign states. But it is interesting and worthwhile to note that
in at least one important particular he extends the conception
beyond even what Hobbes had maintained by singling out the
"right of arms" as the very core of sovereign, political authority. It is also interesting to notice the link which he makes
between independence, size and sovereignty per se.*

## HEINRICH VON TREITSCHKE*

. . . Jean Bodin formulated the dictum, "The State is a plurality of families *avec puissance souveraine.*" He was the first to
use the expression in the sense in which it is now indispensable
to us. Now it is the right and the duty of learning to express
certain notions of universal validity in the terms of that nation's language in which they were first generated. Therefore the word "sovereign" is, and will remain, characteristic of

* From Heinrich von Treitschke, *Politics,* trans. B. Dugdale and
T. De Bille (London: Constable and Co., Ltd., 1916), I, 27–32. Reprinted by permission of Constable and Co.

the nature of the State, since the temporal power cannot tolerate a coordinated, and still less a higher authority in its own sphere.

Human communities do exist which in their own fashion pursue aims no less lofty than those of the State, but which must be legally subject to it in their outward relations with the world. It is obvious that contradictions must arise, and that two such authorities, morally but not legally equal, must sometimes collide with each other. Nor is it to be wished that the conflicts between Church and State should wholly cease, for if they did one party or the other would be soulless and dead, like the Russian Church for example. Sovereignty, however, which is the peculiar attribute of the State, is of necessity supreme, and it is a ridiculous inconsistency to speak of a superior and inferior authority within it. The truth remains that the essence of the State consists in its incompatibility with any power over it. How proudly and truly statesmanlike is Gustavus Adolphus' exclamation, "I recognize no power over me but God and the conqueror's sword." This is so unconditionally true that we see at once that it cannot be the destiny of mankind to form a single State, but that the ideal towards which we strive is a harmonious comity of nations, who, concluding treaties of their own free will, admit restrictions upon their sovereignty without abrogating it.

For the notion of sovereignty must not be rigid, but flexible and relative, like all political conceptions. Every State, in treaty making, will limit its power in certain directions for its own sake. . . .

However flexible the conception of Sovereignty may be we are not to infer from that any self-contradiction, but rather a necessity to establish in what its pith and kernel consists. Legally it lies in the competence to define the limits of its own authority, and politically in the appeal to arms. An unarmed State, incapable of drawing the sword when it sees fit, is subject to one which wields the power of declaring war. To speak of a military suzerainty in time of peace obviously implies a *contradictio in adjecto*. A defenceless State may still be termed a

Kingdom for conventional or courtly reasons, but science, whose first duty is accuracy, must boldly declare that in point of fact such a country no longer takes rank as a State.

This, then, is the only real criterion. The right of arms distinguishes the State from all other forms of corporate life, and those who cannot take up arms for themselves may not be regarded as States, but only as members of a federated constellation of States. The difference between the Prussian Monarchy and the other German States is here apparent, namely, that the King of Prussia himself wields the supreme command, and therefore Prussia, unlike the others, has not lost its sovereignty.

The other test of sovereignty is the right to determine independently the limits of its power, and herein lies the difference between a federation of States and a Federal State. In the latter the central power is sovereign and can extend its competence according to its judgment, whereas in the former, every individual State is sovereign. . . .

Over and above these two essential factors of the State's sovereignty there belongs to the nature of its independence what Aristotle called "αὐτάρκεια," i.e. the capacity to be self-sufficing. This involves firstly that it should consist of a large enough number of families to secure the continuance of the race, and secondly, a certain geographical area. A ship an inch long, as Aristotle truly observes, is not a ship at all, because it is impossible to row it. Again, the State must possess such material resources as put it in a position to vindicate its theoretic independence by force of arms. Here everything depends upon the form of the community to which the State in question belongs. One cannot reckon its quality by its mileage, it must be judged by its proportionate strength compared with other States. The City State of Athens was not a petty State, but stood in the first rank in the hierarchy of nations of antiquity; the same is true of Sparta, and of Florence and Milan in the Middle Ages. But any political community not in a position to assert its native strength as against any given group of neighbours will always be on the verge of losing its characteristics as a State. This has always been the case. Great changes in the art of war have destroyed numberless States. It is because an army of 20,000 men can only be reckoned to-day as a weak army corps that the small States of Central Europe cannot maintain themselves in the long run.

# IV. The Case for Sovereignty in the Twentieth Century

## 11. Sovereignty in National Socialism

*The excesses committed in the name of sovereignty of the state are readily, and perhaps particularly, associated in the twentieth century with the "totalitarian" states. Hence, even though Nazi Germany no longer exists, it is important, for the study of the phenomenon, to consider the terms in which sovereignty was understood in Hitler's Third Reich. The following selection is taken from a translation, made by United States State Department experts, of a book by an influential German jurist, Ernst R. Huber. The defense of the extreme form of sovereignty which Huber gives reflects the general concentration of power, at that period, in the hands of the Nazi Party. The Party, in turn, completely controlled the state mechanism, and was therefore able to enforce its conception of sovereignty as lodged in Hitler.*

### ERNST R. HUBER *

The new constitution of the German Reich . . . is not a constitution in the formal sense such as was typical of the nineteenth century. The new Reich has no written constitutional declaration, but its constitution exists in the unwritten basic political order of the Reich. One recognizes it in the spiritual powers which fill our people, in the real authority in which our political life is grounded, and in the basic laws regarding the

---

* From E. R. Huber, *Constitutional Law of the Greater German Reich,* 1939. The excerpts printed here are taken from *National Socialism,* United States Department of State, 1943, Appendix, pp. 156, 160–161, 163.

structure of the state which have been proclaimed so far. The advantage of such an unwritten constitution over the formal constitution is that the basic principles do not become rigid but remain in a constant, living movement. Not dead institutions but living principles determine the nature of the new constitutional order. . . .

The Führer Reich of the [German] people is founded on the recognition that the true will of the people cannot be disclosed through parliamentary votes and plebiscites but that the will of the people in its pure and uncorrupted form can only be expressed through the Führer. Thus a distinction must be drawn between the supposed will of the people in a parliamentary democracy, which merely reflects the conflict of the various social interests, and the true will of the people in the Führer-state, in which the collective will of the real political unit is manifested . . .

The Führer is the bearer of the people's will; he is independent of all groups, associations, and interests, but he is bound by laws which are inherent in the nature of his people. In this twofold condition: independence of all factional interests but unconditional dependence on the people, is reflected the true nature of the Führer principle. Thus the Führer has nothing in common with the functionary, the agent, or the exponent who exercises a mandate delegated to him and who is bound to the will of those who appoint him. The Führer is no 'representative' of a particular group whose wishes he must carry out. He is no 'organ' of the state in the sense of a mere executive agent. He is rather himself the bearer of the collective will of the people. In his will the will of the people is realized. He transforms the mere feelings of the people into a conscious will . . . Thus it is possible for him, in the name of the true will of the people which he serves, to go against the subjective opinions and convictions of single individuals within the people if these are not in accord with the objective destiny of the people . . . He shapes the collective will of the people within himself and he embodies the political unity and entirety of the people in opposition to individual interests . . .

But the Führer, even as the bearer of the people's will, is not arbitrary and free of all responsibility. His will is not the subjective, individual will of a single man, but the collective national will is embodied within him in all its objective, historical greatness . . . Such a collective will is not a fiction, as is the collective will of the democracies, but it is a political reality which finds its expression in the Führer. The people's collective will has its foundation in the political idea which is given to a people. It is present in the people, but the Führer raises it to consciousness and discloses it . . .

In the Führer are manifested also the natural laws inherent in the people: It is he who makes them into a code governing all national activity. In disclosing these natural laws he sets up the great ends which are to be attained and draws up the plans for the utilization of all national powers in the achievement of the common goals. Through his planning and directing he gives the national life its true purpose and value. This directing and planning activity is especially manifested in the lawgiving power which lies in the Führer's hand. The great change in significance which the law has undergone is characterized therein that it no longer sets up the limits of social life, as in liberalistic times, but that it drafts the plans and the aims of the nation's actions . . .

The Führer principle rests upon unlimited authority but not upon mere outward force. It has often been said, but it must constantly be repeated, that the Führer principle has nothing in common with arbitrary bureaucracy and represents no system of brutal force, but that it can only be maintained by mutual loyalty which must find its expression in a free relation. The Führer-order depends upon the responsibility of the following, just as it counts on the responsibility and loyalty of the Führer to his mission and to his following . . . There is no greater responsibility than that upon which the Führer principle is grounded.

The Führer unites in himself all the sovereign authority of the Reich; all public authority in the state as well as in the movement is derived from the authority of the Führer. We must speak not of the state's authority but of the Führer's authority if we wish to designate the character of the political authority within the Reich correctly. The state does not hold political authority as an impersonal unit but receives it from the Führer as the executor of the national will. The authority of the Führer is complete and all-embracing; it unites in itself all the means of political direction; it extends into all fields of national life; it embraces the entire people, which is bound to the Führer in loyalty and obedience. The authority of the Führer is not limited by checks and controls, by special autonomous bodies or individual rights, but it is free and independent, all-inclusive and unlimited. It is not, however, self-seeking or arbitrary and its ties are within itself. It is derived from the people; that is, it is entrusted to the Führer by the people. It exists for the people and has its justification in the people; it is free of all outward ties because it is in its innermost nature firmly bound up with the fate, the welfare, the mission, and the honor of the people.

◇◇◇◇◇◇◇◇◇◇◇◇◇◇◇◇◇◇◇◇◇◇◇◇◇◇◇◇◇◇◇◇◇◇◇◇◇◇◇◇◇◇◇◇◇◇◇◇◇◇

# 12. Sovereignty in Soviet Communism

*Marxism-Leninism is the "official" doctrine of the Soviet State. What this means, basically, is that the interpretation of all political, and other phenomena of a social character, must be made within the framework of that doctrine. This may be readily seen in the selection which follows: the phenomenon of sovereignty is interpreted as having two fundamentally different senses, depending on whether it is the sovereignty of a Communist state, or that of a Capitalist state. In the first case, sovereignty is the instrument of the communist revolution; in the second, it is the instrument of capitalist oppression. The*

*selection is taken from a translation of a recent, standard text-
book on international law, used in universities in the Soviet
Union.*

## V. V. YEVGENYEV\*

Soviet scientific thought has made a particularly important
contribution to the development of the conception of state
sovereignty. Soviet theory consistently champions the principle
of sovereignty as national self-determination internally and
externally and as the principle of freedom for the peoples in
all its forms (political, economic and cultural). Respect for this
principle flows from the very foundations of the Soviet state
system, which is a voluntary union of free peoples founded
on the principle of the sovereign equality of its member nations.

An important characteristic of the Soviet conception of sovereignty lies in that it does not confine itself to the recognition
that a State has certain formal rights (equality, non-intervention). It is designed to secure the implementation of these
rights in practice, and also to uncover every attempt to infringe
state sovereignty, whatever its form (economic and military
"aid", the "open door", "equal opportunities", the theory of
the "vacuum", etc.).

Thus, in Soviet theory and practice sovereignty is raised to
a new historical level, and has acquired a new social and
political content. . . .

The definitive importance of the principle of sovereignty in
relations between States is not the same thing as the conception of "absolute" sovereignty. A sovereign State must not in
its international relations behave in an arbitrary fashion, without taking account of the generally recognised principles of
International Law and the international undertakings which it
has voluntarily assumed. To do so would mean to violate the
principle of the sovereign equality of all the members of the

---

\* From *International Law* (Moscow: Foreign Languages Publishing
House, n.d.), pp. 83, 96–98.

international community. It would undermine the international community and lead to the unlimited rule of force and violence.

The question of entry into an international organisation or of the conclusion of a treaty is decided by each State at its own discretion. In such matters each State is sovereign, and no external pressure is permissible. But in addition to rights, entry into an international organisation or the conclusion of a treaty also involves certain obligations which are to a certain extent a restriction on its sovereignty.

However, in the interests of international co-operation, States voluntarily and reciprocally restrict their sovereignty. The violation or arbitrary unilateral repudiation of freely assumed undertakings cannot be justified by reference to sovereignty.

The forcible restriction of the sovereignty of States which are members of the international community is impermissible, except following aggression. The subjection of small States to the will of large States, or the subordination of the former by the latter, is also impermissible. This is often cloaked by hypocritical reference to the weak States' "voluntary restriction of sovereignty". The utter untenability of such references is particularly manifest in the relations between the colonial Powers and the so-called non-self-governing territories—relations which are tantamount to annexation.

## THE NEED TO OBSERVE THE PRINCIPLE OF SOVEREIGNTY

The unswerving observation of the principle of sovereignty not only does not obstruct co-operation between States, as the enemies of peace frequently assert, but makes this co-operation more fruitful and successful. It enables States freely to make use of their rights, voluntarily to assume obligations under International Law and to guarantee their fulfilment. Sovereignty is a reliable means of defending the small States from the major imperialist Powers' attempts to subjugate them to their diktat.

The creation of aggressive blocs, the building of military bases abroad, intervention in the internal affairs of other countries and the suppression of the national-liberation movement

are all aggressive actions which are incompatible with the
sovereignty of States and peoples.

Many bourgeois scholars and politicians try to give some
"theoretical" justification for their views regarding the "unnecessary" and "harmful" nature of sovereignty under present-
day conditions. This point of view was most frankly expressed
by the American Adler [1] who described anarchy as the sole
cause of war. Anarchy, he said, appears everywhere where
people or nations try to live together without renouncing sovereignty. The sovereignty of nations and anarchy are insepara-
ble, he declared, and the price of sovereignty is war.

As one of the basic tenets of present-day International Law,
the principle of sovereignty is closely linked with other principles of International Law.

Its realisation is inconceivable without the strict observance
of other generally recognised principles, such as mutual respect for territorial integrity, non-aggression, non-intervention
in each other's internal affairs, equality and mutual advantage
and peaceful coexistence.

Today the struggle for sovereignty is more than ever before
linked with the struggle for peace and against imperialist aggression. In this struggle the Soviet Union has the support of
People's China and the other socialist countries, and also of the
friends of peace throughout the world.

## THE RELATIONSHIP BETWEEN STATE
## AND NATIONAL SOVEREIGNTY

The question of the relationship between state and national
sovereignty is of great theoretical importance. By national sovereignty we understand the right of each nation to self-determination and independent development. Each nation has this
right, regardless of whether or not it has its own statehood.
National sovereignty merges with state sovereignty if the nation has achieved independence and formed its own State.
When the nation has not yet been able to form its own inde-

---

[1] Mortimer J. Adler, *How To Think About War and Peace* (New
York: Simon and Schuster, 1944).

pendent State, its sovereign right to self-determination constitutes the basis for its just struggle to establish such a State.

Having established its own State, a nation can unite with
other nations on the basis of full equality.

◇◇◇◇◇◇◇◇◇◇◇◇◇◇◇◇◇◇◇◇◇◇◇◇◇◇◇◇◇◇◇◇◇◇◇◇◇◇◇◇◇◇◇◇◇◇◇◇◇◇◇◇◇◇◇◇◇

# 13. Sovereignty in Constitutional Democracy

*Given the fact that the two preceding selections reflect the
official view of sovereignty within two of the three leading
types of political systems in the twentieth century, it is fitting to add, at this point, a statement by a spokesman for the
view within constitutional, western democracy. I have chosen,
for this task, Wendell Willkie, the Republican candidate for
President of the United States in 1944, and an ardent supporter
of what is sometimes called "internationalism." Willkie's views
appeared in the midst of World War II, itself a sobering testimony to the excesses committed in the name of sovereignty,
among other principles. He looks back to the prewar situation,
but also forward to what should follow; and he concludes that
however much sovereignty may be abused, there is no reasonable alternative basis for the organization of political societies in the twentieth century.*

## WENDELL WILLKIE*

Since the turn of the century we have lost the power of directing our own national destiny. We must regain it. To show
how much we have lost control over our destiny I need only

---

* From Wendell Willkie, "The Uses of Sovereignty," *Foreign Affairs,*
XXII (April, 1944), pp. 347, 351–355, 358–359. Reprinted by permission of the Council on Foreign Relations, Inc., New York.

point to our unwilling participation in two world wars and to the instability of the American economy during the period between them. We have sought to escape war and to maintain our economy as a separate entity in the world by jealously guarding our sovereign rights. I am forced to the conclusion that something is wrong with what we have meant by the term "national sovereignty." . . .

I believe that if we are to avoid the same disastrous cycle when the present war in Europe and Asia has been won we shall have to give up the idea that sovereignty is something simply to be conserved, like the talent which was laid away in the earth in the biblical parable, and accept the idea that it is an active force to be used. That is the thesis of what I have to say here.

I want to see our Government and people use the sovereign power of the United States in partnership with the sovereign power of other peace-loving nations to create and operate an international organization which will give better protection to the rights of all nations, on a wider political, economic and social basis, than has ever yet been attempted in history. To my mind, mutuality of responsibility and service represents more real freedom, in the sense of freedom from wars and economic disaster, than can be gained through adherence to all the sterile formulas of exclusive national sovereignty written into all the books of international law ever published. . . .

Congress and the press have been discussing the steps which should be taken to bring the peacetime foreign policy of the United States into harmony with twentieth century realities. Much of the talk has centered about the term sovereignty.

In the whole literature of political theory no word has occasioned more disputes. Students of politics hold generally, I think, that few countries have contributed more significantly to the development of political institutions than the United States. But since the days when Madison, Hamilton and Jay wrote for *The Federalist* we have made few notable contributions in the realm of theory. Perhaps we should be grateful that Americans are traditionally interested in finding out, not the fine shadings in a word's meaning, so much as the essence of the thing it represents. Even so, we cannot dismiss the conflict in opinion over the term sovereignty as mere juggling with words.

The word sovereignty does represent a most important idea. And it is of additional practical importance for us now because some of our deepest emotions and loyalties, our pride in our country's past and our concern for her future, are associated with it. But we had best be aware also that it often gets into the forefront of our thoughts for other and less legitimate reasons. Often it is deliberately invoked to create confusion. And often, as with other words which receive a lot of attention, it becomes a catchword, a slogan. Many people now feel the necessity of putting the word "sovereign" into any sentence describing our relationship to other nations in the postwar world as automatically as they put on a necktie when they dress in the morning. I believe it is much too important a word to be used as a mere convention of speech. . . .

Some ardent theorists have endeavored to separate sovereignty from reality altogether in their search for a completely logical system built up out of words. Sometimes the search for a mystical point called the ultimate source of sovereignty has turned into a game for special devotees, as in the studies which find the ultimate pinpoint of sovereignty in the subsection of the Constitution which provides for the amending of the Constitution. I have no quarrel with those who enjoy such academic pleasures. But there need be no confusion regarding the central fact of the matter. Sovereignty within the United States resides in the people of the United States. The people of the United States exercise the supreme power of the state. They are sovereign.

What, then, is the difficulty? It comes from the effort to extend the sovereignty concept beyond the purpose for which it was developed and apply it in the field of relations among nations.

Does the sovereignty of the American people extend throughout the world? The question has only to be put to be answered: obviously not. Two states, at the moment, pretend that they have a right and duty to enforce their will throughout the world. They have dressed their claim up in fancy and most

offensive theories based on blood, race and mythology. It is
now in the course of being put down. The idea of the absolute
sovereignty of any nation in international relationships is as
impractical in operation as the idea of the absolute separateness of any nation.

To the extent that the term sovereignty is taken to mean
that we have the right to do exactly as we please in dealings
with other nations, and that what we choose to do is not properly of concern to any other nation, it is out of date. During
roughly 125 years of our national existence we assumed that
this conception of sovereignty was valid. We even got into the
habit of believing that it was an essential part of national freedom. Its invalidity was brought home to us only with the development of modern communications. To try to defend it against
the facts of modern life would be unrealistic and dangerous.
Nor would we thereby be preserving freedom. . . .

. . . The highways of the world now are crowded. From
Hong Kong to Narvik, and from the North Pole to the South,
there are no empty seas, no air spaces which are not tra-
versed, no land where rights and interests of many peoples
do not meet and may not conflict. The United States or any
other nation cannot make the rules of the road all by itself.

In this matter I think we must prepare to revise our ideas
even further. Nations cannot as a matter of principle refuse to
arbitrate international disputes which arise from domestic policies. Speaking on this question, one of the most distinguished
statesmen of our day, Secretary of State Charles Evans
Hughes, later Chief Justice of the Supreme Court of the United
States, said in 1923 in a speech before the Canadian Bar
Association: "In these days of intimate relations, of economic
stress and of intense desire to protect national interests and
advance national opportunity, the treatment of questions which,
from a legal standpoint, are domestic, often seriously affects
international relations. The principle, each nation for itself to
the full extent of its powers, is the principle of war, not of
peace."

Understand, I am not suggesting the abolition of sovereignty.
I am merely following out logically what seems to me an ob-

vious line of reasoning. Senator Austin of Vermont recently expressed it when he said: "In order to save sovereignty we must use sovereignty in joining other nations for security."

Sometimes the suggestion that sovereignty be used causes unnecessary alarm lest thereby sovereignty be lost. I think these fears are based on nothing more serious than a misunderstanding of method. "As I speak of sovereignty," said Senator Wiley of Wisconsin in a recent debate in Congress, "I speak of something which is precious. I speak of that which my grandfather obtained when he came to this country. Although he still could not understand the English language, he could obtain 160 acres of land, and he never forgot that that was his soil. . . . After he came to this country he became inspired with something called American sovereignty, and he was a part of the national sovereignty. I say that I do not think we, as trustees, can barter that thing away—the sovereignty of the State or the people."

Each of us shares the feeling for the American soil expressed so movingly by Senator Wiley. Each of us values the backbone which the feeling of self-reliance he extols has given the American people. Each of us, with him, gets angry at the suggestion we might "barter away" something which we hold so precious. But this, it seems to me, is another example of the way in which shades of meaning can obscure the essence of what a word stands for. The actual proceeding of give and take described by the word barter has nothing unworthy about it. Indeed, the phrase "enter into a contract to do such-and-such on such-and-such terms," which might properly be substituted in this connection, carries only honorable and businesslike implications.

I think that if we wish to establish relations between nations based on law instead of force the method which must be followed is the one employed when men enter into a contract of partnership. This has been developed over the years as a practical device for advancing the interests of civilized persons. A proper partnership involves clear rights and equivalent duties for all the partners, proportionate to their respective stakes in the common enterprise. The rights do not exist apart from the duties. This means that anyone who wants to enjoy the advantages of a partnership must give up some of his individual freedom of action. This voluntary limitation on his own future action constitutes the advantage which his partners gain in return for giving up some of their freedom of action in his favor.

. . . For most of us who look at the problem of sovereignty without personal or party bias the question that arises is simply: What specific actions are necessary and wise for the extension of the use of our sovereignty?

In the League of Nations debate of 1919 and 1920 the sharpest differences of opinion within this country arose over the question whether the United States should commit itself to the use of force in upholding international agreements. Friends and foes alike of the proposed international organization saw that this would be the test of its usefulness. Persons who wished to prevent the United States from joining any world organization at all inflamed emotions and awakened prejudice by proclaiming that such a commitment would be "treason." Those who wanted to make the organization the instrument for preventing a second world war saw that it would succeed or fail according to the willingness of member states to pledge themselves to the use of force to maintain the rule of law, by an agreed procedure and in agreed circumstances.

Today this is still the core of the decision which we must take. Are we willing only to talk when any situation arises which plainly threatens war? Or are we willing, in agreed circumstances, to act?

. . . What is important today is that unless the American isolationism which we are now putting out the door is to fly back through the window, we must preface any discussion of details of the international organization which we expect to help create by a clear statement that we are prepared in principle to join with other members of that organization in using force to sustain its decisions.

Would the creation of a joint instrument of force threaten our sovereignty? Or would it, on the contrary, represent a useful extension of our sovereign powers in an effort to protect our vital interests?

First of all let us consider the immediate and concrete post-war situation which will make an international armed force necessary. Obviously, it is the requirement that Germany and Japan be policed to make sure that they do not again acquire the military power to wage wars of aggression. The idea of "policing" parts of the world outside the boundaries of the United States is not a new one for us. Acting unilaterally—that is to say one-sidedly and by ourselves—we have used our armed forces for police work in other parts of the world more than 50 times in our history. (In this connection, incidentally, we might remind ourselves that certain of our one-sided expeditions into Latin America were part of a policy which we now believe to have been unwise and which by agreement with the Latin American countries has now been renounced in favor of cooperative action in cases where police work in this hemisphere may be necessary.)

Besides these instances of unilateral action, we have on 25 or more occasions taken police action in cooperation with other nations. . . . They represented a constructive use of sovereignty, mutually advantageous to all three parties.

This established principle of cooperative international policing gives us the foundation on which to build for the future. No dramatically long step is required. I can see the practical difficulties in attempting to create a closely integrated internationalized police force. But I do not have any difficulty in conceiving of an agreement between the peace-loving nations to the effect that each will maintain certain land, sea or air forces and that each will use them collaboratively, in agreed situations and within agreed limits, to prevent aggression.

This seems to me the minimum requirement to ensure that international disputes which are clearly covered by international law shall be submitted to courts and judges, and that those which are not shall be settled by conciliation and compromise. For such a procedure to work successfully, the members of the international organization must say plainly, in advance, that if peaceful methods fail the aggressor state will encounter sufficient armed forces to ensure his eventual defeat.

In planning how this force would be operated as a practical

matter we have a model in the combined chiefs of staff with which this war has made us familiar. Such a staff would make the necessary technical preparations for effective collaborative action in the event that should ever become necessary. I would hope that the mere preparation for action would forestall the need of ever taking it. But if the time should come when collective action had to be taken, it certainly is in the interest of the United States and of all other peace-loving states that it be taken promptly and decisively.

To repeat once more: I think that our use of our sovereignty to create an effective instrument of peace is the best way of protecting our sovereignty. If this is called "bartering," I would say that it is a profitable transaction, and I would rather see the United States enter into it than pursue its own aloof way into a third world war.

◇◇◇◇◇◇◇◇◇◇◇◇◇◇◇◇◇◇◇◇◇◇◇◇◇◇◇◇◇◇◇◇◇◇◇◇◇◇◇◇◇◇◇◇◇◇◇◇

# 14. Sovereignty and International Organization: A United States Senator's View

*When the United Nations Charter was submitted to the United States Senate for ratification, the stormy debate and subsequent refusal of the Senate, twenty years earlier, to ratify participation in the League of Nations, seemed an ominous precedent. In the event, however, the Senate ratified the document by a vote of 89–2. Lest this be taken to mean a complete reversal of earlier attitudes, it is necessary to realize the terms on which ratification was agreed to by many of the Senators. The following selection is taken from the debate in the Senate; we hear Senator Raymond Eugene Willis, a Republican Senator from Indiana, rendering his interpretation of what participation means, so far as the sovereignty of the United States is concerned.*

## RAYMOND E. WILLIS*

In my humble judgment, Mr. President, the average man in my home State—the average man everywhere in America—wants us to adopt and support this charter, implementing it in every reasonable way, but at the same time safeguarding the interests of our own Nation.

I have given countless hours to the study of this problem. I am convinced that in accepting this charter we have safeguarded those things which the common man wants to have made certain:

First. We have protected the sovereignty of the United States of America. This charter does not merge our interests as a Nation in a common body with the other nations of the world. It does not set up a superstate. The sovereign right of the United States of America is protected. We have not merged our ideals with the baser ideals of the world. We have, for the purpose of cooperation, selected only those on which we can agree. The dignity and courage of America are magnified.

Second. The power to determine to what extent the American soldiers may be used in other parts of the world is retained in the Congress of the United States. And if, in the judgment of the Congress of the United States, the acts of the Security Council are not in accord with the high purposes of the preamble of this charter, the right of the United States representative to veto the use of force is reserved. Whatever may be the thoughts of the legalistic minds, that is the thought of the common people of America.

Third. The so-called common man, filled with wishes, hopes that while we protect the United States we can help build a new spirit of cooperation, and usher in a long and prosperous peace in the world.

The average American, Mr. President, is a peace-loving,

---

\* From U. S. Senate, *Congressional Record*, Vol. 91, July 28, 1945, p. 8323.

kind and charitable person. I believe that Charles Lindbergh in a recent interview expressed his thoughts when he said:

I have always believed that America's destiny should be kept independent of the endless wars between European nations. But to make ourselves independent of Europe's welfare is impossible. The civilization which is falling to pieces in Europe is our civilization. We are bound to our civilization as a man is bound to his own family. Whether or not he takes part in the quarrels of his parents no man worthy of the name turns back on them in trouble.

Besides, as far as the present situation is concerned—

He continued—

the question of retirement is past. We have taken a leading part in this war and we are responsible for its outcome. We cannot retire now and leave Europe to the destructive forces which it has let loose. Honor, self-respect, and our own national interests prevent doing that.

The common man, Mr. President, realizes that in the end we took on a great portion of the job of reducing Germany to a shambles. The common man believes that it is our humane duty to help bind up the wounds caused by that destruction in the lands over-run by this war. In that belief, I supported the Bretton Woods legislation for economic rehabilitation of these lands.

Yes, the common man today, more than ever, believes in safe-guarding the interests of America. It is a virtue, not a crime in his eyes, to think of America first before we attempt to carry the burden of the whole world. For the weak cannot support the weak, nor the blind lead the blind.

Mr. President, America today is drifting into a new isolationism, not by any means a matter of our choice. She has become the last great Nation of the world which puts her complete faith in the philosophy of free enterprise. It was that philosophy that made America strong enough to win this war. No matter to what extent she may be restricted in this new isolationism, the common man will fight to the end for the preservation of the ideals of America. Therefore we must keep our country strong militarily, economically, morally and spiritually. The safety of America lies in our reliance on our own security and reliance on our own strength and virtue rather than in charters and compacts and treaties. "The best political systems, leagues or conferences would not be enough unless based on a dynamic strength of character and the power of Christian ethics."

◇◇◇◇◇◇◇◇◇◇◇◇◇◇◇◇◇◇◇◇◇◇◇◇◇◇◇◇◇◇◇◇◇◇◇◇◇◇◇◇◇◇◇◇◇◇◇◇◇◇◇◇◇

# 15. Sovereignty in Diplomacy

*A diplomat, especially one at the highest level of policymaking and policy-execution, must treat the existence of sovereignty less as a concept than as a hard fact of political existence. This does not mean that diplomats, as such, are necessarily committed to the persistence of sovereignty in the form it has taken over several centuries. The two, somewhat different, perspectives are represented in the following two selections. In the first, Mr. Christian Herter, former Secretary of State of the United States, is speaking to a Conference of Foreign Ministers, in Geneva, Switzerland, in 1959. His subject is the continuous, vexing postwar problem of the division of Germany into two parts at the end of World War II. His remarks reflect the intransigence of the Soviet Union in support of East Germany, and the United States position concerning the problem. In the second selection, one of the most distinguished of modern American diplomats—and scholars, for he is also a distinguished historian —Mr. George Kennan, reflects upon his own experience of the facts of sovereignty. In the final analysis, the agreement between Mr. Herter and Mr. Kennan is significantly larger than the disagreement: each points to the stubborn reality of the modern state.*

## CHRISTIAN HERTER*

In considering the feasibility of a "peace treaty" with Germany we must keep in mind certain fundamental considera-

---

*From United States Department of State, *Bulletin*, June 8, 1959, p. 819.

tions which must underlie any formulation of specific treaty terms. The United States on December 11, 1941, declared war on Nazi Germany and thereafter engaged in a major conflict with that state. Nazi Germany capitulated unconditionally in 1945.

At all times, prior to the capitulation, the Nazi government of Germany was the government of all of Germany.

It is the position of the United States that under international law the international entity known as Germany remains in existence, notwithstanding what has happened since 1945 as an incident of Four Power occupation. The Government of the United States does not consider, and will not admit, that Germany as an international entity is permanently divided into new and separate states, as was the case of Austria after World War I.

It is undeniable that a peace treaty necessarily connotes a final settlement of the problems engendered by war, such as frontiers, treaty obligations, claims and debts, and the like. It was the international entity known as Germany with which the United States was at war and with which it has outstanding problems. Accordingly, any "final settlement," so far as our Governments are concerned, must await the establishment of a government which can act for and bind Germany as a whole.

Conversely, since the United States was never at war with the Federal Republic of Germany nor with the so-called "German Democratic Republic," any "peace treaty" or definitive settlement with such portions of Germany, whether individually or collectively, could not be a final peace treaty with Germany. . . .

Quite aside from the question of recognition of the so-called German Democratic Republic—and the United States wishes to reiterate that it has no intention of recognizing the so-called German Democratic Republic as representative of any part of the German people—it is only by closing one's eyes to reality that one is able to regard the "Germany" of the Soviet proposal as anything of substance.

For example, the widely divergent views of the German Federal Republic and the so-called German Democratic Republic are matters of common knowledge. Yet article 3 of the Soviet draft "treaty" provides:

The Allied and Associated States recognize the full sovereignty of the German people over Germany, including the territorial waters and airspace.

In international relations the sovereignty of a state is one and indivisible. The concept of "two existing German states" representing the indivisible sovereignty of the German people is unacceptable, both in legal and in political theory, and would be wholly unworkable in practice. Who, it may be asked, will represent a sovereign "Germany" or "the German people" in other capitals or in the United Nations? To whom will the other signatories of the treaty look for fulfillment of the obligations of "Germany" under the Soviet proposal?

## GEORGE KENNAN*

While our subject is the very broad one of "History and Diplomacy," I thought I would narrow it somewhat and attempt merely to describe something of the aspect in which diplomatic history presents itself to a diplomatist who has turned late in life to the study and writing of history.

I must first offer the usual disclaimer about generalizations—in this instance, of course, with regard to that race of being which goes by the name of diplomatist. There are all shapes and sizes of people, today, within the increasingly generous and hazy delimitations of this profession. I naturally cannot pretend to speak for all of them. But I believe that what I am about to say would meet with understanding on the part of most of those who have had their noses rubbed for long in the classic and central diplomatic function, which is the wearisome duty of negotiating and mediating between governments with conflicting interests—and that this would be true not only of those who are our contemporaries but also of a long succession of diplomatic representatives stretching back into history at least as far as the Venetians. Prior to that,

* From George Kennan, "Diplomacy and History," *The Review of Politics*, XVIII (April, 1956), pp. 170–177. Reprinted by permission of the editor of *The Review of Politics*.

I gather, very few people were ever saddled with the necessity of practicing this thankless, disillusioning, and physically exhausting profession as a permanent and regular livelihood.

Diplomatic history is, of course, only one phase of political history generally. It is a part of the study of man in his behavior as a political animal; and it concerns itself with what occurs at that particular point of friction where the activity of one sovereign political authority rubs and grates on that of another. It is, of course, the element of *sovereignty* on both sides that gives to the contact at this point that peculiar delicacy, that charged, explosive quality, that final unpredictability by which it is distinguished. All other human contacts, it seems, take place within the limits of some recognized framework of obligation, supported by some sort of physical sanction. There is always, at least in theory, some rule or some higher authority to which appeal may be taken. But the sovereign national state, this child of the modern age, notwithstanding the mantle of nebulous moral obligation in which it likes to wrap itself, still recognizes in the crucial moments of its own destiny no law but that of its own egoism—no higher focus of obligation, no overriding ethical code. I am often accused of approving this state of affairs because I insist on the recognition of its reality. Actually, I think, no one could be more sadly conscious than is the professional diplomatist of the primitiveness, the anarchism, the intrinsic absurdity of the modern concept of sovereignty. Could anything be more absurd than a world divided into several dozens of large secular societies, each devoted to the cultivation of the myth of its own overriding importance and virtue, of the sacro-sanctity of its own unlimited independence? A thousand times right are the enthusiasts of world government in their protest against the philosophic childishness of this concept, however many times wrong they may be in their ideas as to how it might be corrected. But the diplomatist, as people frequently forget, is the servant of this system of national states; it is precisely to the working of this imperfect mechanism that his efforts are dedicated. He is professionally condemned to tinker with its ill-designed parts like a mechanic with a badly built and decrepit car, aware that his function is not to question the design or to grumble over the decrepitude, but to keep the confounded contraption running, some way or other.

When, therefore, the diplomatist thinks about diplomatic history, his thoughts turn in the first instance to the nature and personality of the sovereign state. He knows this in part, of course, from the example of those governments with which he has been obliged to deal as a foreign representative. But he knows it better still from his intimacy with his own government. The personality of his own government presses itself upon him over the course of the years with a great vividness, with a sort of inexorable and commanding finality. It is the primary, overriding, inalterable reality of his professional world. And he is often moved to reflect on the extraordinary nature of this governmental personality: on its imperious authoritarianism toward its servants; its indomitable self-righteousness; its smugness and self-centeredness; its infuriating air of optimism and unconcern; its preposterous claim to infallibility; its frequent impoliteness; its stubborn and impudent silences; its insistence on the right not to answer letters; its bland assumption that because *it* has not made up its mind, reality should be expected to stand still until it does. And when the diplomatist, saturated as he is with the consciousness of this personality, then chances to pick up a book about diplomatic history, or to thumb through old dispatches in some dusty Foreign Office archives, he soon observes, not without a touch of exquisite intellectual pleasure, that it is not only his own government and not only governments in his own age that are this way; but that governments have been this way for a long time in the past, throughout, in fact, the entire range of history of the national state.

Realizing this, the diplomatist is moved, first, to marvel that a number of institutional personalities so difficult, so impossible by every normal criterion of social behavior, so outrageous in all respects, should have been able to live side by side in the same world and to deal with each other as long as they have, without even a larger number of conflicts and catastrophes. But secondly, he would have to be very uncurious indeed if he failed to inquire what it is, in the experience of being sovereign, that makes governments behave the way they do. And in this way he soon finds himself led unerringly to the classical problems of political science: to the inquiry as to how men tend to behave in the exercise of governmental power, and why they behave just this way.

Now I cannot attempt to generalize about the political philosophy of the devotees of my former profession. There is probably not much more agreement among them than there is among the rest of us on these questions that have divided the contemplative portion of mankind since the days of Plato and Aristotle.

But the diplomatic representative is made aware at every point of one curious feature of the sovereign government: and that is the duality of its motivation as between national interest and party interest. I have often found in my friends among the enthusiasts for universal international organization what seems to be a somewhat naive view of the nature of the governmental voice in world affairs. These people assume that when a government speaks its word or casts its vote in an international forum, what one hears is the genuine expression of the aspirations of the people for whom it speaks. Now that may conceivably be the case and sometimes is; but it is not necessarily so; and it is rarely entirely so—for the following reason. It is clear that every government represents only the momentary product of the never-ending competition for political power within the respective national framework. In the most direct sense, therefore, it speaks only for a portion of the nation: for one political faction or coalition of factions. There is always another portion of the nation that is in opposition to it and either challenges its right to speak for the nation as a whole or accepts it only grudgingly and unhappily. This is true, in one version or another, whether the country's political life operates on the principle of parliamentary representation or whether it is based on some form of authoritarianism.

Yet it would be wrong to jump to the other extreme and to assume that the voices of governments, as heard on the international forums, reflect exclusively domestic-partisan interests.

The interests of every political régime will be found to be bound up with, and in a certain area identical with, the interests and fortunes of the nation as a whole.

What emerges, therefore, from the hopper of the political process in each country and proceeds to speak for the country in international affairs is always to some degree a corrupted voice—in part the expression of national interests or aspirations, as seen by those momentarily entrusted with their definition and manifestation, but also partly the expression of the desire of one group of men to retain the power they already enjoy and to defend their position against their competitors within the national framework. And the diplomatist sees that there is very often a conflict between these two elements of motivation, and that the men who write his instructions and define the governmental position he must represent are torn, in conscience and interest, between the one and the other. He sees that in the great dramatic moments of history—especially when danger presents itself in the purely physical and external form, as when war threatens or already exists—the domestic political competition is, by common consent, thrust somewhat into the background, and statesmen even find it possible to think almost exclusively, for a time, in terms of the interests of the nation as a whole.

# V. The Case against Sovereignty in the Twentieth Century

## 16. The Evils of Sovereignty

*Although the preponderant view, as represented in the preceding section, is that sovereignty is both necessary and desirable, or at least necessary, there is a vocal minority which denies this. The disillusionment with sovereignty has taken a variety of forms in the twentieth century, but at bottom all criticisms point away from sovereign states to some different form of political organization. The pace at which this development is expected to take place, and the forms which are expected to replace it vary considerably, depending on who is advancing the criticism. It seems worthwhile, then, to examine the views of some men who have themselves been responsible for the conduct of political affairs in the twentieth century, and who cannot therefore be accused of being mere visionaries, unfamiliar with the difficulties of political practice. The first selection was written toward the latter part of World War I by David Jayne Hill, educator, scholar, and diplomat. Mr. Hill had at one time been United States Ambassador to Germany, and he spoke for many men of his generation in inveighing against the evils of sovereignty; but what is more, he spoke out of a solid grounding in modern political theory and modern diplomatic practice, as is evident from his skillful marshalling of arguments. His refusal to limit the evil to "autocratic" states is especially instructive in view of the great tendency of all modern states, democratic and autocratic alike, to mobilize the total energies of a nation in the pursuit of vital objectives. The second selection is by a former Prime Minister of Great Britain, Lord Attlee. His remarks, which were delivered some forty years after those of Mr. Hill, reflect an awareness both of the evils of sovereignty and of the immense difficulties of overcoming them.*

## DAVID JAYNE HILL*

The great tragedy of history has been the conflict between the universal humanism that Rome endeavored to establish, first by law and afterward by faith, and the tribalism of the primitive European races. In the fifteenth century tribalism triumphed. In the twentieth, universal humanism may reclaim its own, and reassert the substantial unity of the human races.

In both instances there has been disillusionment. In the fifteenth century Christendom assumed the existence of a unity of belief that had not in reality been attained. Both the empire and the papacy, in which great minds had placed implicit faith, proved unable, in the face of racial conflicts, either to rule the world or to preserve the coherence of Christendom. All that had given grandeur to Rome seemed to have ended in failure when the Greek Empire, the last bulwark of Roman imperialism, already long and bitterly alienated from the Roman Curia, paid the penalty of separatism, and fell before the Ottoman assault. With it the splendid postulates of the Roman imperial idea—the essential unity of mankind, the supremacy of law based upon reason and divine command, the moral solidarity of all who accepted the formulas of faith, and the effective organization of peace as a condition of human happiness—seemed to have suffered a fatal catastrophe. In place of the *Pax Romana, Faustrecht,* the right of the mailed fist, widely prevailed within the confines of Christendom. Slowly dying during a thousand years, the traditions of the ancient world, which the Greek Empire had endeavored to preserve long after they had been undermined by tribalism in the West, were now definitively abandoned. The future was seen to belong to the separate nations, which alone possessed a strong sense of unity. The disparity of races, the spirit of local

* From David J. Hill, "Europe's Heritage of Evil," *The Century,* Vol. 94 (May, 1917), pp. 7–15.

independence, the conflict between the spiritual and the temporal forms of obedience, combined to render possible the development of powerful national monarchies, and dynastic ambition was eager to make use of them for its own designs.

It was Machiavelli who expounded the new theory of the state and the methods of securing its advancement; and in this he was inventing no system of his own, but merely stating in definite terms the principles which successful monarchs were already putting into practice. " 'The Prince,' " declares Villari, "had a more direct action on real life than any other book in the world, and a larger share in emancipating Europe from the Middle Ages"; but it would be more exact to say that Machiavelli's work, written in 1513 and published in 1532, was the perfect expression of an emancipation from moral restraints already far advanced. The Christian idealism of the Middle Ages had already largely disappeared. The old grounds of obligation had been swept away. Men looked for their safety to the state rather than to the church; and the state, as Machiavelli's gospel proclaimed it, consisted in absolute and irresponsible control exercised by one man who should embody its unity, strength, and authority. Thus began the modern world.

With the dissolution of the feudal organization through the predominance of the national monarchies disappeared the sense of mutual obligation which under the feudal régime had constituted an ethical bond between the different orders of society. What remained was the bare conception of irresponsible "sovereignty" considered as a divinely implanted, absolute, unlimited, and indivisible prerogative of personal rule, the charter right of each dynasty to seek its own aggrandizement, preponderance, and glory regardless of all considerations of race, reason, or religion.

With such a conception of the nature of the state, the whole system of international relations was necessarily based upon military force. Until Grotius appealed to the ethical motive, and the treaties of Westphalia recognized the *de jure* rights of territorial sovereignty, there was among the nations of Europe no semblance of public law which jurisprudence could recognize. But even after the Peace of Westphalia, the so-called

"law of nations" was little more than a theoretical acceptance
of the equal rights of autonomous sovereigns, each of whom
could work his will without interference within his own domains, leaving to each ruler the unquestioned prerogative of
dictating the religion of his own subjects, of taxing them, of
arming them, and of making war with their united forces for
his own advantage. In effect, the Peace of Westphalia, by
rendering even petty princes absolute, permitted more than
three hundred independent rulers to carry on the sanguinary
game of war for plunder or conquest without restraint; and
all, left free to destroy one another, were thus entitled by public
law, through war and diplomacy, to seek their fortunes with
complete autonomy. Sovereignty, defined as "supreme power,"
regardless of any principle of right, was conceived to be the
very essence of the state. It remained simply to discover by a
trial of strength which power was entitled to be esteemed supreme.

When in its moral awakening the Europe of the latter part
of the eighteenth and early part of the nineteenth century
began to think for itself,—or at least to follow the thinking of
Locke, Montesquieu, Rousseau, Kant, and others who sought
to find the true foundations of the state in the conception of
law based upon the nature and necessities of men rather than
upon dynastic power,—Europe found itself under the incubus
of this sinister inheritance.

Without a convulsion that would shake the whole of Europe
to its foundations it was powerless to throw it off. Rousseau
had in "Le contrat social" merely transferred the idea of sovereignty from the monarch to the people, but he had not
essentially altered its character. It was still "supreme power,"
still the "absolute, indivisible, and perpetual" thing which
Bodin, seeking to give royalty a philosophical pedestal to stand
upon, had said it was. Inherent in the people, it was still the
personification of all the public powers; and the *volonté
générale,* the general will, regardless of its moral qualities,
was the unlimited, irresponsible source of law, the possessor of
all, the dictator of all, and the ultimate authority in all things,
which the individual man must respect and obey.

When the French Revolution judged and condemned the king, it was done as a sovereign act, and was, therefore, not permitted to be questioned by the monarchs of Europe. Was not sovereignty territorial? Then it belonged to France. Was it not indivisible? Then it belonged to the French people. Was it not perpetual? Who, then, could ever take it away or in any way dispute it? And thus the *volonté générale* of one nation, having swept away the monarchy, soon rose to the height of a war on all kings; and in the person of the residuary legatee of the Revolution, Napoleon Bonaparte, made emperor by the assent of the *volonté générale* of France, assumed to act as sovereign over the whole of Europe. . . .

And thus the malign inheritance of Europe, in so far as it was affected by the Revolution, is essentially unchanged. Monarchy and democracy alike, without distinction, have regarded sovereignty merely as "supreme power," "absolute, indivisible, and perpetual." Thus it stands in all the text-books of the law of nations. So many sovereignties, so many absolute autocrats. Being the sole sources of law, how can they be subject to law? And there being no law which they may not set aside, since it is but their creature, sovereign nations are irresponsible, and have no more to do with moral right or wrong than so many untamed animals seeking to satisfy their appetites. The right to make war at will and to be answerable to no one, that was, and is, the accepted doctrine of the old Europe, which merely asserted itself anew in 1914.

This does not signify that it has never been contested. More than three hundred years ago a now almost-forgotten German jurist, though recognizing sovereignty as the foundation of the state, defined it as an attribute not of the people as an unorganized mass, but of a "body politic" organized for the promotion of justice, deriving its authority as a moral entity from the rights of its constituent members, whom it is organized to protect against wrong, and therefore from its very nature charged with mutual rights and obligations. The only authority it can claim is authority to defend the rights and interests thus committed to its guardianship. As a moral entity—for this is what Althusius taught that a state founded on rights necessarily is—it should be ready to apply the principles of justice and equity in its dealings with other states.

Were this conception of sovereignty generally accepted, justice and equity would not halt at the frontiers of a nation. The right of war would exist, but it would not be, as the old Europe has generally recognized it to be, a virtually unlimited right. There could be, under this conception, no permanently subject peoples. There could be no world dominion. There could be no legal schemes of conquest. War would mean the punishment of offenders against the law of nations, the suppression of anarchy and brigandage, resistance to the ambitions of the conqueror.

But the old Europe has never been disposed to give to sovereignty that meaning. It could not do so while it was identified with royal legitimacy. That principle triumphed a hundred years ago in the Congress of Vienna, which strove to neutralize the effects of the French Revolution by ending forever the sovereignty of the people. Then followed the effort to establish Europe firmly upon the principles of absolutism by crushing out all constitutional aspirations. To accomplish this the unlimited right of war was necessary, for without armed intervention by the allied sovereigns the task was hopeless. Legitimacy was to be everywhere sustained by the Holy Alliance. Wherever a state adopted a constitution, the powers bound themselves at the Congress of Troppau, "if need be by arms, to bring back the guilty state into the bosom of the Alliance."

The unlimited right of a sovereign state to make war for any reason it considered sufficient, or for no reason at all, thus seemed to be written into the public law of Europe. That was the unhallowed inheritance which modern democracies have received from absolutism. Being entitled to all the prerogatives of sovereignty as historically understood, they have not repudiated the heritage. And thus they have tacitly accepted the evil principle of the despotisms against whose iniquities they have rebelled, and whose pernicious influence they were struggling to throw off. . . .

Before attempting to find a basis for a revision of international relations it is necessary to consider how intimately national interests have become associated with war. For a long time all the interests of the state were regarded as personal to the sovereign. All its territory was his territory. All the property of the nation was his property, of which the people enjoyed only the usufruct. Even their persons and their lives were at his disposal, for they were in all respects his subjects.

To-day the identity of the sovereign is changed, but not the conception of sovereignty. The people, standing in the place of the sovereign, claim the right of succession to all the royal prerogatives. The national interests have become their interests. The appeal to their patriotism rests upon this ground. The power, gain, and glory of the state are represented to be theirs. Even where it has not entirely superseded the monarch, the nation believes itself to have entered into partnership with him, and the people consider themselves shareholders in the vast enterprise of expanding dominion. . . .

Whatever, from an internal and social point of view, the merits or defects of the extension of state functions may be, they are bristling with possibilities of war, and when modern nations engage in it, it is no longer a dynastic adventure, but a people's war. Commanding the strength and resources of a whole people, and acting for its alleged interests, these great economic corporations are fitted for aggression as well as for defense. If they were subject to the usual laws of business that prevail in the regulation of private enterprises within their own borders, in accordance with the principles they apply at home, these mailed and armed knights of trade might not be dangerous to the world's peace; but they are not subject to these or to any such regulations. They recognize no law which they feel themselves obliged to obey. Inheriting by tradition from the past alleged rights of absolute sovereignty, and equipped with military forces on land and sea, they are engaged in a struggle for supremacy which they would not for a moment permit within their own legal jurisdiction. Were a similar organization formed within their own borders, adopting as its principles of action the privileges usually claimed by sovereign states, it would be promptly and ruthlessly suppressed as a dangerous bandit. . . .

And this condition of the world is the logical outcome of the inherited theory of the state. This fact is now beginning to be recognized, and recently there has been much said regarding imperialism and democracy, often assuming that the mere internal *form* of government is responsible for the international situation in Europe. But it is not the form, it is the spirit, and above all the postulates, of government that are at fault. If democracies may act according to their "good pleasure," if the mere power of majorities is to rule without restraint, if there are no sacred and controlling principles of action, in what respect is a multiple sovereign superior to a single autocrat? If the private greed of a people is sustained by the pretensions of absolutism in international affairs, democracy itself becomes imperial, without accepting the principles of equity which give dignity to the imperial idea. In truth, the most dangerous conceivable enemy to peace and justice would be a group of competitive democracies delirious with unsatisfied desires.

If there is to be a new Europe, it will be far less the result of new forms of organization than of a new spirit of action. Europe must renounce altogether its evil heritage. It must reconstruct its theory of the state as an absolutely autonomous entity. If the state continues to be a business corporation, as it probably in some sense will, then it must abandon the conception of sovereignty as an unlimited right to act in any way it pleases under the cover of national interests and necessity. It must consent to be governed by business rules. It must not demand something for nothing, it must not make its power the measure of its action, it must not put its interests above its obligations. It may plead them, it may argue them, and it may use its business advantages to enforce them; but it may not threaten the life or appropriate the property of its neighbors or insist upon controlling them on its own terms. It may display its wares, proclaim their excellence, fix its own prices, buy and sell where it finds its advantage; but it must not bring to bear a machine-gun as a means of persuasion upon its rival across the street. . . .

States, like individual men, must henceforth admit their responsibilities to one another, accept the obligation to obey just and equal laws, and take their respective places in the society

of states in a spirit of loyalty to civilization as a human and
not an exclusively national ideal.

## LORD ATTLEE*

The root of the trouble in today's world is that we believe in
anarchy. We believe in the complete, or almost complete, right
of every nation to do what it chooses. One still has the feeling
that anything like a surrender of sovereignty is contrary to our
human nature. Although every day individuals surrender their
sovereignty inside a country for the sake of a larger freedom,
we still talk as if we were detached individuals when it comes
to international affairs.

What is needed in the world today is the rule of enforceable
law enforced. You will find some people who say that all this
is high-flying idealistic nonsense. So long as human nature remains human nature this idea of world government will remain
nothing but a comfortable dream. I wonder how many people
have said that in their time with regard to every possible
innovation. But you cannot afford to take that view today.
Unless mankind meets the challenge of the present day it will
not survive.

The United Nations doesn't yet fill the bill. The U.N. has
not yet meant the surrender of sovereignty; it is not an authoritative force—it has no instrument. I am not denying that it is
a very powerful forum of public opinion, nor am I denying
that it does all kinds of good things, but it doesn't do the
*essential* things. But there are some hopeful signs. Leaders in
our own country and others no longer shrink from world government. It has been proclaimed by our Government that we
must work towards world government—that is a great step
forward from the old days when collective security was
called midsummer madness. They also declare for absolute

---

* From Lord Attlee, "The Perils of Absolute Sovereignty," *The Saturday Review,* August 23, 1958, pp. 22–3. *The Saturday Review* obtained permission to reprint this version of a lecture by Lord Attlee
from The David Davies Memorial Institute of International Studies,
London, England. Reprinted by permission of *The Saturday Review*
and the David Davies Institute.

disarmament. Thirty or forty years ago anyone who preached that would have been answered, "Human nature never changes —people always fight." Today we have plans for disarmament.

But why do all these admirable plans break down? The late Arthur Henderson worked with great devotion between the wars on disarmament proposals. Other experts are working constantly. Yet why don't we get disarmament? I think the answer is that we always found that between the wars you cannot get disarmament without some security—it always broke down on that. How can you get security? You cannot get security internationally today. You may get a partial security in arrangements of one kind and another—such as NATO and SEATO. But I don't believe we will get real disarmament without an approach to an international force. I say it for this reason: at the present time we are held in uneasy equilibrium by the possession of two groups in the world of nuclear weapons. We hope this means that nuclear warfare will never come to the world. We hope that, but it may be that the mere fact that either side would hesitate to use these nuclear weapons may make them take a chance with what are called "conventional weapons." A good definition of an unconventional weapon was given by Sir Winston Churchill the other day: "Those the other side have got and you have not got." I don't much believe in this distinction. I don't believe that when you arm your forces with nuclear weapons you can then talk of them as conventional weapons. I think the distinction has to do with their mass destructiveness, as contrasted to comparatively light weapons for police purposes.

I think the time has come when, if we are realists, we should say that no major war would be won with nuclear weapons, and therefore if any minor trouble develops we don't want forces which would lead inevitably to the use of nuclear weapons. We want something much smaller and lighter—a form of armed police force. If we had that you could, I believe, have enough to stop incidents where there was danger developing, but we would also be saved all the immense business of these huge land armies that I believe will never fight at all.

How are you going to get such a force? People say that

there is not today the necessary unity in the world; power politics are played all the way. I don't see any reason why, apart from power politics, some of these problems that oppress us in various parts of the world should not be settled peaceably, but there are people who have an interest in stirring it up.

Can we get away from this? Let's be realists. If it is really true that the Soviet Union is inspired by a complete desire to enslave the whole world, as a combination of the old-fashioned Russian imperialism and the new Communist ideological imperialism, then the outlook is pretty bad; but I always think we are rather inclined to overestimate the solidarity and strength of the people with whom we can necessarily have only a limited contact. Looking back at the war and reading the memoirs, it is most illuminating to see what they were thinking on the "other side." At the time we were all impressed by the fact of this great military force of Germany, absolutely on top, and yet you find that the inside was quite doubtful. And the idea of an absolutely strong, monolithic power in Russia may be wrong.

I believe that despite the possession of nuclear weapons, the dominating feeling in Russia today is fear. I believe the trouble in America is fear. If we could lift off that fear we might get much further. I don't believe that the holding of the satellite states is essentially due to an imperialist desire to spread Communism. I think it is a desire to have an expendable bursting layer between East and West. I don't think that any of us, any country, even in the most extremist circles in America, imagines that one could conquer Communism by an attack on Russia. I hope Russia also realizes that they will not conquer the world by force, because the forces will be too strong for them—the spiritual forces. They are already finding difficulties in the satellite countries. That is why, I think, that if you could lift off this fear of Russia today an approach might be made which would reconcile things. And even if the nuclear weapons are held by the two rival groups instead of by a world authority it might be possible that the Russians, like everybody else, do not want to have localized little wars because they may not remain localized.

One of our difficulties in all these matters is that it is not as if the world was a very peaceful place. There are an awful lot of sore places. Any suggestion you have to stabilize the world as it is would cause a great outcry from the people under a rule they don't like. Again I don't believe, with all our sympathy for the Hungarians, Poles, Rumanians, and the rest, that one would contemplate embarking on a nuclear war to rescue them, nor do I think they would contemplate it either, because after the rescue there might be very little left of the rescued or the rescuer.

We need to make a start on the idea of an international force. That force would not be European solely, or American or Australian, but should cover Africa and Asia as well. One of the dangers I see today in the world is that out-of-date ideas still hang on. There are still out-of-date ideas about the primacy of Europe. I don't think we have shown an awful lot of commonsense in nearly committing suicide in two world wars, so we might be a bit humble on that.

I think that a world force might make the best approach to world government. I know all the difficulties of world government. You can say, "Where are you going to draw the line between what nations can do and what they cannot do?" But our aim would be to begin with the minimum, just as we did in our own domestic affairs. Our early force was really just to keep law and order, the King's peace, the Police Force gradually coming about, and it has taken very many years before we met society's other needs.

I would like to continue on the widest possible scale the work that is being done to try and raise the standards in the undeveloped countries of the world. I am all for that, but I think one cannot continue without any surrender of sovereignty. Surrender of sovereignty is what you want if you look only at this one aspect of war and peace. Could we make a start on that? I would like to see it pressed further, rather more vigorously than at present. So many of the smaller issues are pressed, but the big major one is not. I don't want it to be done by acrimonious disputes in the U. N.—there are far too many acrimonious debates. I would like it seriously discussed every-

where what the reality is—the reality that faces us, simply, is
our civilization going to continue? This question was always
at the back of my mind when I was in office. There was always
this looming danger. Yet nationalism persists. I refer to the
hope that nations may grow upon the question of sovereignty.
Sixty years ago, who would have thought of the surrender of
sovereignty in the British Commonwealth? Now today in India,
Pakistan, Ceylon, Ghana, Malaya and elsewhere we have seen
a surrender of sovereignty.

But to whom should sovereignty be surrendered? I believe
we must have a wide authority and that that wide authority
must cease to be based just on power. All the arguments (we
had them all at San Francisco) as to why the power must
be placed in the hands of a few big states—are true only if we
are going to depend on action of individual states to support
the law. If you get away from that there is no reason why we
need have this predominance of the bigger states. The interests
of the smaller ones are just as great as our own. I am not
going to argue on the subject of world government in its
detail. I have never felt that technical details were so important. If people want to get these things, they will. I would
like a movement in this country and every country in favor of
world government, not on the grounds of commonsense. It is
commonsense that we who live in a city like London should
have all kinds of things controlled—motorists must not pass a
red light; drains must be looked after and all that. It is time
we realized that the world is also a close-locked community
today. We just cannot afford to have the exercise of individual
sovereignty.

To whom are you going to hand it over? I am democratic;
I am prepared to submit to the will of a properly constituted
body representing the world. I am not prepared to submit to
a kind of junta of three or four of the strongest powers. I
have been accustomed for many years to accept the will of the
majority, and I am prepared to do it again. I would like Britain
and America and Russia also to be prepared to do it, because
I believe that unless we can get this we shall not get peace.

◇◇◇◇◇◇◇◇◇◇◇◇◇◇◇◇◇◇◇◇◇◇◇◇◇◇◇◇◇◇◇◇◇◇◇◇◇◇◇◇◇◇◇◇◇◇◇◇◇◇◇◇

# 17. World Sovereignty

*Early in this century, even before the furies of World War I had caused many thinking men to question the validity of the sovereign state, Robert Lansing, who became Secretary of State under Woodrow Wilson, completed a series of three lengthy articles for the* American Journal of International Law. *The first two articles were published in 1907, in the first volume of that journal, and treated the question of "Sovereignty in a State." The third article, which treated "World Sovereignty" was not published until after World War I, in 1921. In a prefatory note Mr. Lansing explains that his third article was not published with the others "because the logical application of the theory to the world as a whole seemed too speculative and to lack the practical value" of the first two. He then concludes that, in 1921, with World War I a still bitter memory, "the discussion seems less academic and more pertinent to present day philosophic thought concerning the political relationship between nations than it did fourteen years ago." Today, nearly a half century later, the prospects for a true "world sovereignty" are no greater than they were when Mr. Lansing finally saw fit to offer his analysis of the problem to the public. In spite of the logic of his critique of the phenomenon of separate "sovereign" states, the political reality which he hoped to be contributing to has not come into being. Nevertheless, his arguments are worthy of consideration, for they lay bare what still another political practitioner saw as the nature of the problem.*

## ROBERT LANSING*

The conception of the type of sovereignty which is manifested in the external and internal relations of a state, is necessarily limited by the point from which it is viewed. Thus far in the

* From Robert Lansing, "Notes on World Sovereignty," *The American Journal of International Law,* XV (January, 1921), pp. 13–21. Reprinted by permission of the editor of *The American Journal of International Law.* Footnotes renumbered.

discussion that viewpoint has been the state as the highest form of a political organism in that it has attained complete development. In dealing with sovereignty in a state in its external sphere of activity, that is, in the relations between the sovereigns of different states, it was necessary to rest upon the assumption that these sovereigns were equal and equally independent. An assumption, however rational it may be, is never satisfactory and never conclusive; but from the standpoint of the state, the correctness of this assumption could neither be established nor disproved. Still the truth of an assumption relating to man as a political being and not as a moral being must be capable of demonstration by historical facts. If the point of view is insufficient, it must be widened or a new one taken which will be comprehensive enough to embrace all that has been assumed, so that it may be tested by positive evidence. . . .

This more comprehensive point of view is . . . that which sees in the world but a single social organism all-inclusive and universal, which minimize the sovereignties in states, affects their realities, and raises the question whether such sovereignties are real or artificial. Confessedly, if there exists a sovereignty that is superior to the sovereignty in a state, it has not yet developed into the positive type which is manifest in a political state and which history and experience recognize. It is still unformed and necessarily a theoretical conception. Nevertheless, it will be seen, as the nature of sovereignty is viewed from the broader standpoint, that powerful political and moral influences are at work in the world to change the theory into practice. Among these influences, the most potent is the increasing realization by civilized peoples of the interdependence and mutual responsibility of states in their political and economic relations.

This realization compels the conviction that the entire human race ought to be considered, and in fact is, a single community, which awaits the further development of modern civilization to complete its organization and make of all mankind a great, universal political state. There is, therefore, sufficient ground for an examination of sovereignty from this standpoint;

and it will be found that, though there has been no formal recognition of the existence of such sovereignty, the great states of the civilized world have recognized, perhaps unconsciously, its existence in the applied law of nations, just as they have recognized it in the sphere of morals by giving binding effect to the principles of humanity.

## THE IDEA OF A WORLD COMMUNITY AND WORLD SOVEREIGNTY

Since it is possible to conceive of the human race as one body composed of a large number of political groups including millions of individuals, or as one body with these individuals as units, and, in either case, as a community, it follows from the very nature of things that in this unorganized mass of humanity there *must* be a certain body of individuals possessing a physical might sufficient to compel obedience by every member of the human race throughout the world. Such superior physical might constitutes sovereignty, and, since its only limit is the earth, it may properly be termed *World Sovereignty.*

The objection may be made that this physical force has never been subjected to organization and has never been exerted, and that having remained without definite manifestation it is purely hypothetical and its existence theoretical rather than actual. But the existence of such supreme force is self-proving. Since each human being possesses a measure of bodily strength, the union of the physical strength of all the human beings in the world must represent the collective might of mankind. Divide that collective might unequally and a preponderance rests with a certain body of individuals and a lesser portion of such physical power with the remainder of the race. The possessors of the preponderant amount of power, including as a factor intelligent cooperation, are humanly supreme in that they can enforce their collective will throughout the earth. That dominant body of individuals possesses the *World Sovereignty* and is itself the *World Sovereign.*

If the opinions of those writers, who maintain that the state possesses the sovereignty or that the state is preëxistent to sovereignty, are accepted as correct, any discussion of World

Sovereignty prior to the actual organization of the entire human race into a universal political state would be illogical; but, [if we assume, conversely] . . . that there is a sovereign before there is a state, that the organization of a state is an act of sovereignty, and that the existence of a community is conclusive evidence of the existence therein of superior physical force, *i.e.,* of sovereignty, the very conception of a *World Community* compels the recognition of a World Sovereign and of World Sovereignty.

## THE IDEA OF A WORLD STATE

The first positive and direct expression of World Sovereignty must of necessity be the organization of a *World State,* which presumably will be of a federal character for two reasons, first, because the world is already divided into organized groups of individuals forming political states, and, second, because the federal state is the most highly developed political organism of modern civilization. The idea of a World State is not new; in fact prior to Grotius the idea was general; but under the artificial sovereignty of the Middle Ages it was substantially an impossibility. Today, however, based upon a higher conception of sovereign authority and a more enlightened code of political ethics, the idea is gathering new force.

Bluntschli says:

It will take many centuries to realize the Universal State. But the longing for such an organized community of all nations has already revealed itself from time to time in the previous history of the world. Civilized Europe has already fixed her eye more firmly on this high aim. . . . Meanwhile unconquerable time itself works on unceasingly bringing the nations nearer to one another, and awaking the universal consciousness of the community of mankind; and this is the natural preparation for a common organization of the world. . . . Only in the universal empire will the true human state be revealed, and in it international law will attain a higher form and an assured existence. To the universal empire the particular states are related, as the nations to humanity.[1]

---

[1] Bluntschli, Theory of the State, 3d Edition, pp. 26, 31, 32.

In the last sentence quoted the idea of the writer that the "universal empire" will have a federal organization is brought out, but, since he gives the state precedence of sovereignty, he could not logically consider World Sovereignty as existing until the World State is *in esse*. Accepting the conclusions reached in the previous Notes that sovereignty is coëxistent with the community, and that the state is one of the manifestations of sovereignty, it is impossible to recognize the Community of Mankind without acknowledging the existence of World Sovereignty.

## INDEPENDENCE OF STATES

This sovereignty, which as yet lacks positive and direct expression, may be seen by a survey, from the broader point of view, which has been assumed of the external sovereignty of a state. Independence is the outward manifestation of such sovereignty: . . . real sovereignty in a state must possess that attribute. This assertion needs no further proof of its correctness than the statement. When sovereignty is viewed from within the State, it is easy to understand and evident in the various phenomena of society; but, when two or more states, each with an independent sovereign, come into opposition so that the wills of their sovereigns do not harmonize, and each sovereign attempts to be independent and to exercise exclusive sovereignty, the state of affairs resulting is paradoxical, for manifestly two supreme authorities cannot exist within the same sphere.

Take, for example, the specific instance of two states territorially contiguous, one of which is physically stronger than the other and could, if it so willed and was not prevented by other states, destroy the sovereignty of its weaker neighbor by depriving it of independence.[2] In the instance given, is not the weaker state *dependent* upon the volition of the more powerful for its independence? Or, if the more powerful is re-

---

[2] In this and in subsequent places where the sovereignty and independence of a state are spoken of, the phrases are used for the sake of brevity. On all such cases it should be understood that the sovereignty and independence of the sovereign of the state are intended.

strained from aggression by the fear that other states might
intervene, is not the weaker state *dependent* upon the combined physical force of these other states for its independence? Can there be such a thing as *dependent* independence?
Under such conditions, what becomes of the *reality* of the
independence of the sovereign of the weaker state, and what
becomes of the *reality* of its sovereignty?

The answers to these questions are obvious. The idea is thus
stated by Bluntschli: "If a state is compelled to recognize the
political superiority of another it loses its sovereignty and becomes subjected to the sovereignty of the latter" (Bluntschli,
p. 506). . . . The conclusion is that, no matter how *real*
sovereignty in a state may be when viewed from the standpoint
of the state itself, *it is not real in fact but artificial* unless the
sovereign of that particular state possesses the physical force
which, if exercised, can compel obedience from all mankind
throughout the world. Doubtless the sovereign of the Persian,
the Macedonian, or the Roman Empire, as each in its turn
attained the zenith of its glory and might, may have reasonably
claimed real sovereignty even in the broader sense and maintained the claim against the united strength of all other peoples; but in later centuries the Saracens, Charlemagne, and Bonaparte attempted and failed to establish an empire and obtain
universal sovereignty. In the past one hundred years no state
has become so powerful as to hope, much less has had the
temerity to assert, that it could hold its sovereignty supreme
and independent against a coalition embracing the other states
of the world.

## ARTIFICIAL CHARACTER OF SOVEREIGNTY
## IN A STATE

It is evident from the foregoing that the sovereignty in every
modern state lacks the essential of real sovereignty, namely
independence. Sovereignty, as it exists in a state, stands in
much the same relation to the supreme might of the world
that civil liberty stands in relation to the sovereign power in
a state. From the broader point of view, therefore, the sovereignty in a state is dependent upon the collective physical force

of mankind, or rather upon the collective will of those, whether considered as political groups or as individuals, who possess the preponderance of such force, and who are because of such possession actually independent. In the case of this dominant body all the essential qualities and attributes of real sovereignty are present, but it is unorganized, undetermined, and necessarily variable, composed of a multitude of individuals who are members of numerous states and offset against one another by race, national allegiance, and other differences. But *what* individuals and *what* states enter into the composition of this sovereign body are equally uncertain from the fact that this World Sovereignty has never been directly exercised by the possessors or by an agent directly authorized by them to carry out their sovereign will.

The artificial character of the sovereignty in a state when compared with the reality of World Sovereignty, while demonstrable by abstract reasoning, may be also proved by reference to concrete facts.

History furnishes numerous instances of the loss and restoration of sovereignty in a state—lost through the exercise of physical force external to the state and superior to that within the state, and against the will of the sovereign of the state; and restored by the voluntary act of the possessor of the superior external force or under the coercive influence of other external forces, and not by the physical might within the state itself. Such evidence is conclusive of the fact that the sovereignty in a state is artificial and that the independence of its sovereign, though asserted by it and acknowledged by other states, is not real and self-maintained.

To illustrate the force of this evidence, a few examples will suffice.

An event in recent history belonging to this particular class of proof was the result of the Franco-German War in 1871. After French sovereignty and independence had been swept away by the victorious armies of Germany, the sovereignty and independence were restored by the conquerors in exchange for the undertaking of the French Government to pay a large war indemnity and the cession of Alsace-Lorraine. This restoration was the voluntary act of the possessor of a physical force proven by actual demonstration to be superior to any such force within the French state. Clearly the sovereignty and independence of the latter rested for their continuance upon the will of the victor, or possibly upon the fear of Germany that continued possession would arouse the hostility of other European Powers. In either case, French sovereignty and independence lacked reality and were manifestly artificial.

A similar example of conquest and restoration was presented in the war between the United States and Mexico. The military forces of the United States overthrew the Mexican Government and acquired the sovereignty of the republic, but it was voluntarily restored upon Mexico agreeing to certain conditions. Mexico could not have secured such restoration by its own power. Mexican sovereignty was, therefore, dependent upon the will of the conquerors; and, since it was dependent and not independent, it was artificial. . . .

From these illustrations it is apparent how artificial are the sovereignty and independence which are assigned by international usage to a state, feeble and powerless though it be to repel the hostile act of any one of the great national states of the world.

As has been said, no single state, however vast its resources and population, could under existing conditions successfully withstand the combined and organized opposition of the rest of the states in the world, any more than one individual member of a modern state could maintain his absolute liberty against the collective will of his fellow members. In each case superior physical strength is lacking to the individual state or person, and without superior physical strength the result cannot be accomplished.

It may be said then that every state, whether strong or weak, whether great or small, whether rich or poor, whether civilized or barbarous, is in a sense a protectorate, a ward of the other states of the world, holding its political powers of them and responsible to them for its international conduct. In a word, every state is a member of the *Community of Nations,* wherein resides World Sovereignty, and which in the fullness of time will become, through the positive expression of that sovereignty, an organized political union, a *Federal World State*.

## EQUALITY OF NATIONS

Having reached this point in the discussion, and having seen that a bond of interdependence makes of the states of the world something more than a mere collection of separate and independent units, each moving irresponsibly in its own distinct sphere; having seen that they in fact form an embryonic political state, analogy to the fully developed type of the state previously considered offers a reason for the hypothesis so universally adopted by publicists and governments, that *every nation is the equal of every other nation in the world*. From the consideration given to the character of independence and sovereignty in a state, it is evident that this cannot be an *actual* equality, a fact which has been forced upon some writers who have attempted to explain it by limiting the subject of equality, but the result has been destructive of the value of the assertion. . . .

In discussing sovereignty from the point of view of the state, it was shown that in times of domestic peace individuals having certain qualifications attained through development are presumed to possess an equal share of the sovereignty of a single state, and that the same is true of states which as units composing a federal state are presumed to share equally in the federal sovereignty. The fiction of this assumption is proven when tested by the exercise of physical force, the ultimate appeal of the real sovereign. Since a war between two, three or four nations is no more destructive of the general peace of the world community than a conflict between a few individuals in a state is destructive of its domestic peace, the persistent international condition is that of peace, as no conflict of modern times has been of sufficient magnitude to constitute a World War, thereby imposing upon the Community of Nations a general condition of belligerency. As a result the assumption of equality in the possession of sovereign power during times of peace in the world, when a state possesses certain qualifications, such as a recognized sovereign and an organized and operative government, is never withheld from such a state in international intercourse.

It should always be borne in mind, nevertheless, that the equality of individuals in a state, the equality of states in a federal union, and the equality of nations in the Community of Nations are all artificial and based upon assumed qualities which can only be tested by the actual exercise of physical force. It is true that a war between two states may demonstrate the relative amount of real power possessed by each, but, since the *world* is at peace, they remain to neutral states presumptively equal until the sovereignty of one is actually absorbed by the other. It matters not how great is the contest or how decisively victorious one of the belligerents may be, to the rest of the world the assumption of equality continues unaffected, for general peace prevails.

Thus, although the Community of Nations lacks the organization essential to make of it a political state, the individual nations, by general though independent consent and not by direct command of a World Sovereign, employ that fiction of equality which in a state relates to the possession by individuals of the sovereignty. In the Community of Nations this is applicable to the equality of nations in the possession of the World Sovereignty. This assumption, so firmly imbedded in the Law of Nations, is a conscious or unconscious recognition of the unity of the states of the world in the possession of a universal sovereignty; and it is, furthermore, a manifestation of the tendency of modern thought towards an organized World Community.

## SUMMARY

To summarize the conclusions reached:

*First:* There is possessed by a body of individuals in the world the physical might to compel absolute obedience from all other individuals in the world considered collectively, and from all individuals in the world considered separately.

*Second:* This all-powerful body of individuals possesses therefore the real sovereignty of the world, the world being considered as a unit or a single and universal community.

*Third:* The sovereignty in every state as now organized politically is artificial when viewed from the standpoint of the world as a single community; and such sovereignty depends for its sphere of operation and exercise upon the will of the body of individuals possessing the World Sovereignty.

*Fourth:* Since only the sovereignty existing in a state has been directly exercised, World Sovereignty has not up to the present time been positively expressed. It remains passive through lack of harmony of purpose and unity of action by its possessors, and through the absence of proper channels of expression.

*Fifth:* The nature of World Sovereignty in its present state of development is similar to that of the lesser sovereignty, which, viewed from the standpoint of the community or state, is real. The condition existing is analogous to that in a community, wherein the real sovereignty has never been exercised although its existence is certain. Such a community is unorganized, for organization is a positive exercise of real sovereignty.

# VI. Integration into Larger Sovereignties: A Half-way House

*The seemingly insuperable difficulties of transforming the separate sovereign states of the world into a single, world-state have led all but a small minority of critics to advance other alternatives. One alternative, suggested at least in outline already by some of the preceding readings, is that of a general international organization. But as we have also seen, the terms in which the present international organization is framed retain the sense of the sovereignty of separate states; and the practice of states within the United Nations has amply confirmed the expectation of most of the founders—that the basic unit is still the state. A second alternative is to form present sovereign states into larger political entities. Each of these would, of course, remain sovereign with respect to other similar entities. But the implication is, at least so far as proponents of such a development are concerned, that by a gradual process of integration—for example, in Western Europe—the old rivalries and the old effects of sovereignty may be abated on an increasing scale, and that this process would become cumulative. In the collection of readings which follow, various perspectives on, including reasons for attempting to produce, such an integration are presented.*

◇◇◇◇◇◇◇◇◇◇◇◇◇◇◇◇◇◇◇◇◇◇◇◇◇◇◇◇◇◇◇◇◇◇◇◇◇◇◇◇◇◇◇◇◇◇◇◇

# 18. The Schuman Plan: Integration by Economic Means

*On May 9, 1950, the French cabinet, under the leadership, for this purpose, of the Foreign Minister, Mr. Robert Schuman, agreed to an historic arrangement: to coordinate, under a single authority, the coal and steel production of France and Germany. This action, coming only five years after the end of World War II, and given the generations of enmity between these two proud states, was regarded at the time as a great and bold experiment. The connection between this economic action and the anticipated political consequences is made quite clear by Mr. Schuman: it is a move in the direction of a "united" Europe.*

## ROBERT SCHUMAN*

It is no longer a question of vain words but of an act, a bold act, a constructive act. France has acted, and the consequences of her action may be immense. We hope that they will be.

France has acted essentially for peace. If peace is to have a chance, there must first of all be a Europe. Five years almost to the day after the unconditional surrender of Germany, France is taking the first decisive act in the construction of Europe and is associating Germany with it. This act must necessarily transform European conditions. This transformation will make it possible to take other common actions that have been impossible until now.

Out of all this will emerge a sound, united and strongly constructed Europe, a Europe whose standard of living will rise, thanks to the pooling of production and the extension of markets which will bring about a drop in prices. In this Europe, the Ruhr, the Saar and the French basins will work together, and their peaceful labor, followed by United Nations observers, will benefit all Europeans, Eastern as well as Western, and all lands, especially Africa, that look to the old Continent for their development and prosperity.

Such is France's decision, and these are the considerations that inspired it: World peace cannot be safeguarded without creative efforts proportionate to the dangers that threaten it. The contribution that an organized and vital Europe can make to civilization is indispensable to the maintenance of peaceful

---

* From Robert Schuman, "Franco-German Steel and Coal Pool," *Vital Speeches of the Day,* XVI (June 1, 1950), pp. 482–483. Reprinted by permission of the editor of *Vital Speeches.*

relations. As the champion of a united Europe for more than twenty years, France has always had one main objective: to serve the cause of peace. Europe has not been organized. We have had war.

Europe will not be built at one stroke or by means of one over-all structure. It will be built, first, by means of concrete steps that create real solidarity. The unification of the European nations demands that the age-old enmity of France and Germany be eliminated; the action undertaken must apply primarily to France and Germany. To this end, the French Government proposes immediately to take action on a limited but decisive point: it proposes to place all French and German steel and coal production under a common high authority in an organization open to the other European countries.

The pooling of coal and steel production will insure the immediate establishment of common bases of economic development, the first stage in European federation, and will change the destiny of these regions which have long been devoted to the manufacture of weapons of war of which they themselves have been the most constant victims.

The solidarity of production thus established will prove that any war between France and Germany has become not only *unthinkable,* but materially impossible. The creation of this powerful production pool, open to all countries that wish to participate in it, and making available to all its members on the same conditions the basic necessities for industrial production, will lay the real foundations for the economic unification of these countries. The output of this pool will be offered to the whole world without discrimination or exclusion, as a contribution to the improvement of living standards and the advancement of peaceful enterprises. Europe will have increased means with which to promote the realization of one of her essential tasks: the development of the African continent.

The fusion of interests, indispensable to the establishment of a broader and deeper community between countries that have long been kept apart by bloody conflicts, will thus be realized simply and rapidly. By pooling their basic industries and establishing a new high authority whose decisions will be binding for France, Germany and the other participating countries, this proposal will lay the first concrete foundations of a European federation that is essential for the safeguarding of peace.

In order to work toward the realization of the objectives defined above, the French Government is ready to open negotiations on the following basis: the common high authority will be charged with insuring in the shortest possible time the modernization of production and the improvement of its quality; the supplying of coal and steel on the same terms to the markets of France, Germany and other member countries; the increase of joint exports; the improvement and equalization of the living conditions of the industrial workers in the participating countries.

Since production conditions are very different in the member countries, certain transitional measures must be adopted to achieve these objectives: the application of a production and investment plan, the establishment of mechanisms to equalize prices, and the creation of a reconversion fund to facilitate the rationalization of production. All customs duties on coal and steel between participating countries will be abolished immediately and the same railway freight rates will be applied. Gradually conditions will be created which will automatically insure the most rational distribution of production and the highest level of productivity.

In contradistinction to an international cartel which tends to divide and exploit national markets by restrictive practices and the maintenance of large profits, the proposed organization would insure the merging of markets and the expansion of production. The basic principles and engagements defined above will be the object of a treaty signed between the states and submitted to the parliaments for ratification. The negotiations necessary to work out the measures of implementation will be carried on with the assistance of an arbiter designated by common agreement. It will be the arbiter's responsibility to see to it that the agreements reached are in conformity with the principles and, in case of a deadlock, he will decide upon the solution to be adopted. The common high authority responsible for the functioning of the whole organization will be composed of independent personalities designated on a parity basis by the governments, and its president will be chosen by common agreement of the governments. Its decisions will be enforceable in France, Germany and the other member countries. Appropriate provisions will insure the necessary means of appeal from the decisions of the high authority. A United Nations representative attached to the authority will make a report twice yearly to the United Nations on the functioning of the new organization, especially with respect to the safeguard of its pacific aims. The establishment of the high authority in no way prejudices property rights in the enterprises concerned. In the exercise of its task, the common high authority will take into account the powers conferred upon the International Authority for the Ruhr and the obligations of all kinds imposed upon Germany, as long as these obligations subsist.

# 19. European Union: An English View

*The author of the following selection is Sir Alfred Zimmern, one of the great modern English scholars of politics. In analyzing the problem of European Union, he draws upon the accumulated experience of England, his own researches and writing upon ancient and modern politics, and the facts, as he sees them, of the twentieth century. His remarks are contained in an address given at the Third Annual Conference on American Foreign Policy, Colgate University, Hamilton, New York, July 24, 1959. At that time, Sir Alfred was Director, Greater Hartford Council for the United Nations Economic, Scientific and Cultural Organization. In the course of his remarks, he refers to observations which had been made, a few weeks earlier,*

*by Dwight D. Eisenhower, Supreme Allied Commander, Europe,
concerning the urgency of the problem of European integration.*

## SIR ALFRED ZIMMERN*

Let me begin by thanking the organizers of this Conference
for giving me an opportunity to address you on the subject of
European Union and by explaining why it is that, though a
consistent opponent of European Union in the past, I found
myself able to accept their invitation.

Two reasons determined that acceptance. The first is that,
in a conference such as this, we Europeans can learn to deepen
our understanding of the United States in the persons of some
of its most thoughtful leaders and, as a good friend of mine,
who is equally at home on each side of the Atlantic, is never
tired of repeating: "A real understanding of the United States
is the best guarantee of peace."

The second reason is that European Union has ceased to
be a Continental question and has become an Atlantic question. For me Europe, looked at by itself, never made sense:
indeed, the more closely one looked at it, the more diligently
one studied it and turned it about and about, the less sense
it made. But Europe looked at from the Atlantic angle, Europe
closely associated with the United States within the framework
of the United Nations, is quite another matter. It not only
makes sense: it makes peace and law and order—European
order and world order.

Why was I opposed to European Union in the past? I was
opposed to it both as a political thinker and as an Englishman.

I was opposed to it as a political thinker, because I saw no
possibility of the establishment of a United Europe on a basis
of constitutional freedom—the very term "Free Europe" is of
quite recent coinage—and a United Europe established on any
other basis seemed to me to spell reaction, perhaps even barbarism, rather than progress. In holding this view, which separated me from many European scholars and public men for

---

* From Sir Alfred Zimmern, "How Can Europe Unite?" *Vital Speeches
of the Day,* XVII (September 1, 1959), pp. 677–680. Reprinted by
permission of the editor of *Vital Speeches.*

whom I entertain esteem, I found myself at one with the deep-
rooted feelings of the two oldest and most experienced exponents of freedom among the European peoples, the people of
Great Britain and the people of Switzerland. For them, too,
European union never made political sense.

And I was opposed to European union as an Englishman,
because I believed that it would diminish the power of my
country and thus lessen the influence of the political values
for which it stands.

So long as the United States was not in the picture, so long
as a particle of doubt existed in the minds of Europeans as to
the acceptance of full responsibility by the people of the United
States for the future of freedom in Europe, the concept of
European union faced Englishmen with a question to which
it was impossible for them to give a straight answer: for we
could not honestly answer "yes," and diplomatic courtesy prevented us from answering with a plain "no." These matters
belong now to a past age, so there is no reason why I should
not explain why we found the question so embarrassing or how
our persistent policy of evasion helped to create the legend of
*Perfide Albion.*

British statesmen with their feet on the ground—I need only
mention Castlereagh, who clipped the wings of the Holy Alliance, and Canning, who called in a New World to redress
the balance of the Old, have always known, ever since Britain
became a Great Power in the 16th century, that she was committed to a role to which her physical resources were not equal,
that we, in our little island, were living dangerously, with only
a small margin of reserve power to draw upon. The only way
in which we could meet this situation was by keeping our potential enemies divided amongst themselves. Thus we were
driven to practice the policy of the Balance of Power. Had the
Powers which we thus strove to divide been consistent friends
of freedom, had Switzerland and Holland, for instance, been
preponderant in the Chancelleries of Europe, the Balance of
Power would have been a purely selfish policy and, I do not
hesitate to add, a wicked policy. But, in the Europe of that
time, a Europe steeped in the traditions and methods of Mac-

chiavelli, what else could we do? I ask you, as freedom-loving Americans, for an answer that would have made better sense.

Today Freedom is no longer a minority force in international relations, driven to use stratagems in self-protection. Freedom is the major force. It is she who has the big battalions on her side. For as far ahead as political thought can see, the United States will occupy a preponderant position in the world, and the people of the United States, who might have set the crown of world empire on their brows, have decided to share their power in a constitutional partnership of free nations. Thus free nations everywhere are called, at a moment in world history corresponding to the moment of 1787 in your own constitutional annals, to a task of political construction.

European union occupies a very special place in this worldwide constructive task, in which Europeans and North Americans are destined to be pioneers together. It is fitting that in this great enterprise Europe, so long the center of the world's political life and thought, should be the scene of an experiment which will determine the character of the Atomic Age. Will it mark the inauguration of the Rule of Law for the world? Or will it usher in a dark epoch of perpetual fear? The issue lies with us Europeans: for you Americans, in so far as it concerns you, have surely already made up your minds. . . .

Let us then begin by situating the problem of European union in the general pattern of the free world, as it is being unfolded almost month by month in these eventful years.

In its completed pattern the free world, as we can already clearly see, will be a world divided into five distinct political zones or regions.

It is just over a quarter of a century ago since the Locarno Agreements were signed within the framework of the Old League of Nations. They marked the first conscious attempt to use the regional method as part of a general plan of world order. The controversy which this provoked between the Universalists and the Regionalists, between the supporters of the Geneva Protocol and the supporters of Locarno, seems far distant now. Nevertheless, as we look back, we can see that, in spite of some faults of design, for which Europeans later paid dear, Locarno was conceived on sound lines. Man is a small-scale creature, and we must beware of asking the ordinary citizen, even in a free and enlightened world, to promise more than he instinctively feels that he can perform. Certain peoples have indeed, as a result of their history or their geographical situation or their particular cast of mind, enlarged the range of their habitual outlook. I am thinking particularly of the people of the United States in their spacious North American abode, of the people of Great Britain, at home in every ocean and in many lands beyond them, and of the people of France, for whom, at a great moment in their history, it seemed more natural to frame a Declaration of the Rights of Man than a Declaration of the Rights of Frenchmen. These three peoples are among those who can be described as *responsible*. In a regionalized world, in which local interests may tend to occupy an undue place in the public mind, such peoples are likely to be called upon for political service in regions other than that of their homelands. Their contribution will take the form of a steel framework, strengthening and preserving the entire structure of world order.

Let us now briefly survey these zones or regions as they are being disclosed to us.

We can discern the outlines of five regions. Of these, two, the region covered by the Rio Treaty and the North Atlantic Region, have already reached an advanced stage of organization: between them they now cover the whole of the American Continent and the territory of ten Western and Central European States. A third region, covering Australasia and Southeastern Asia, is staked out in the proposed Pacific Security Pact between the United States, Australia and New Zealand. . . . It contains a provision for a Pacific Council "authorized to maintain a consultative relationship with states, regional organizations, associations of states or other authorities in the Pacific area in a position to contribute to the security of that area."

A fourth area, embracing the Near East, South Asia and Africa, is already being envisaged. It will be based on the Eastern Mediterranean, a concept which, in the hands of the planners, is becoming as elastic as the kindred concept

"North Atlantic." In spite of certain local difficulties affecting some of the minor States in the region, its organization is now getting under way. A start is being made with the African section of the area. . . .

There is, as I need not remind you, one large gap in this pattern of the free world—the territory under the control of the Soviet Union in Northern Europe and Northern and Northeastern Asia. This also has its representation in the United Nations. It has, too, a regional organization of its own: but this does not fall into the process which I have been describing, since the peoples of that region do not belong to the free world.

It is time to leave geography behind us and to pass to our main subject, the internal organization of the Union. Here we are in the territory of political science, ground familiar to Americans from *The Federalist,* but ground which has not been so carefully cultivated by European exponents of the concept of union, owing to the romantic haze in which the subject has too often been enveloped and its details obscured.

Political science is concerned with Power. Power is inherent in the concept of government: it is, so to speak, the coinage which statesmen employ: that is why we speak of a government being "in power."

European Union, in the full sense of the term, involves the establishment of a new Power: for any union of States involves the withdrawal of certain powers from existing states, previously independent or, as some say, sovereign, and the placing of these powers in the hands of a new authority, equipped with superior power.

The first question to be asked in connection with European Union is: what are the powers that must be thus handed over if the new union is to be . . . "workable"? The answer is: all the powers needed in order to enable the Union to provide for the common defense. Nothing more but nothing less.

Note what I am here omitting from the preamble of your Constitution. It is not for the new union to "establish justice, insure domestic tranquility, promote the general welfare and secure the blessings of liberty." In a union of free peoples this is not necessary and, in a union of peoples as diverse as those in the North Atlantic area, it would also be impracticable, as I need not pause to explain in detail.

By thus concentrating on essentials and sternly ruling out non-essentials, we clear out of our way much that has hitherto complicated the discussion of European Union. We can ignore social, economic and cultural problems as such, and also political problems in the narrower sense, only dealing with them when they form part of the problem of defense.

The second question to be asked is: does the establishment of European Union involve the framing of a new Constitution by means of the processes which normally accompany the creation of a new State or Power? The answer is in the negative. Nothing so elaborate is required. As for the general constitutional framework of the Union, it exists already in the shape of the United Nations Charter. As for the particular regional framework, it is also already largely provided for in the organization set up under the North Atlantic Treaty. Our task is therefore relatively simple. It is to take that organization as our basis and to strengthen it at the points where more power is needed in order to construct a workable defense union.

The third question to be asked is: what method should we adopt in this work of constitutional construction? Should we plan to proceed by gradual stages over a period of years or should we aim at reaching our objective, so to speak, at one blow?

General Eisenhower in his London speech gave a direct answer to this question. European Union for him is not an academic question or a matter for leisurely parliamentary debate. It is an immediate and urgent need for the accomplishment of the task entrusted to him by the North Atlantic peoples. He stands as a soldier in full view of the enemy, exposed to all the dangers entailed by such a position: and this is what he tells us: "Any soldier contemplating this problem will be moved to express an opinion that it cannot be attacked successfully by slow infiltration, but only by direct and decisive assault with all available means."

What does General Eisenhower mean by these words: "direct and decisive assault with all available means"? They were evidently chosen with care. Let us try to be faithful to him in interpreting them.

Let us consider General Eisenhower's position in the chain of command. From whom does he hold his authority? To whom is he responsible?

General Eisenhower, in his position of Commander in Chief of the North Atlantic Treaty Forces, is the servant of twelve independent governments, responsible respectively to twelve sovereign and equal peoples. So far as their external affairs are concerned, these governments are bound by the terms of the Charter of the United Nations and by the North Atlantic Treaty. This commits them to adhere to certain common principles of policy. The North Atlantic Treaty, however, contains a clause which crosses the boundary between common principles and common action. It establishes, in Article 9, "a Council on which each" of the twelve governments is "represented, to consider matters concerning the implementation of" the Treaty and goes on to order this Council to "set up such subsidiary bodies as may be necessary." "In particular," says the concluding sentence of the Article, "it shall establish immediately a Defense Committee which shall recommend measures for the implementation of Articles 3 and 5"—the articles laying down the obligation of mutual aid.

How does the Council, which we may describe, in constitutional terms, as the North Atlantic Executive, function? The Article prescribes, in language modeled on Article 28 of the United Nations Charter, dealing with the Security Council, that "it shall be so organized as to be able to meet promptly at any time." It has now been in operation for about two years, during which it has normally been attended by the Foreign Ministers of the twelve Powers and occasionally, in case of need, by their Prime Ministers. Under the Council, in the administrative chain, there is a secretariat, known as the Permanent Commission, with its seat in London. It is composed of officials engaged in dealing with day to day problems of common interest to the twelve Powers.

Parallel in the administrative chain with the Permanent Commission is the Defense Committee which, as I have just said, is expressly provided for in the Treaty. It consists, not of professional soldiers, but of the Defense Ministers of the twelve governments. This is essential in order to preserve the control of the military by the civil power, implicit in the philosophy of the United Nations Charter. This is the authority immediately above General Eisenhower in the chain of command. It was the Defense Ministers in Council who, formally speaking, recommended his appointment, which was then acted on by the Foreign Ministers' Council and the individual governments.

Thus General Eisenhower's chain of command runs upward through the Defense Committee and through the body which I have termed the North Atlantic Executive to the twelve governments and their peoples.

It was at General Eisenhower's express wish that, when he decided to set up his headquarters in France, the civilian body parallel with his own, the so-called Permanent Commission, remained in London—a decision which caused some surprise at the time. It would seem that General Eisenhower purposely wished to emphasize the distinction between the military and the civil domains.

In this brief analysis I have omitted to mention a number of other bodies in this field, such as that dealing with military supplies and similar economic matters: but I think I have said enough to enable you to understand what General Eisenhower must have had in mind, in relation to his own particular work, when he spoke of "the deadly danger of procrastination, timid measures, slow steps and cautious stages," and of how "the negative is always happy in lethargy, contemplating, almost with complacent satisfaction, the difficulties of the other courses."

Americans went through, between 1776 and 1787, the experience of delay and obstruction which General Eisenhower brings before us so vividly out of his own experience. Your statesmen found a way out, or rather, they *cut* their way out. Can we cut a way out for General Eisenhower?

I think that we can, if we apply the knife at the right point. That point is the Council of Prime Ministers or Foreign Ministers—the body which corresponds, in the North Atlantic Treaty, to the Security Council in the United Nations Charter.

The suggestion which I wish to put before you, in the present grave emergency, is that the Prime Ministers' Council be made the point of departure for the creation of a true Executive in the North Atlantic area. The twelve Prime Ministers should meet and choose five men, whether from within or without their own ranks, who together would exercise, in the domain of defense, full executive powers over a certain period of time.

I will not pause to discuss the length of their tenure. In the case of the Swiss Federal Councillors, who form the nearest present-day parallel to the kind of executive that I am proposing, appointment is virtually for life; in the case of the Presidency of the United States which, like the Swiss Federal Council, is not responsible to a popular assembly, it is four years, once renewable; for a dictator under the Roman republican constitution it was six months.

As to the choice of the men best fitted to work closely with General Eisenhower in his tremendous task, can we doubt that the Prime Ministers, with their close knowledge of the personalities and problems of the area, would make—I will not say a perfect, but at least a wise choice?

The Five would not represent the individual countries of which they are nationals. They would form a single organic body, as close-knit as a cabinet. They would take no individual decisions. All their public dealings—in particular, their relations with the Press and public opinion—would be in common. However, it is a reasonable supposition, that of the five, one would normally be an American citizen, another would be French and a third drawn either from Great Britain or Canada, the remaining two places going to nationals of the other nine Powers.

This proposal may startle you, especially when you begin to realize what it would mean in concrete cases, as, for instance in the fields in which military needs impinge on domestic policy and local interest—on the "web of customs barriers interlaced with bilateral agreements, multilateral cartels, local shortages and economic monstrosities"—to quote General

Eisenhower again. But before you dismiss it as Utopian or unrealistic, as it certainly would have been in the pre-atomic age, I would beg of you to consider it carefully in the light of the organic development, which, as I have tried to put before you, has already taken place in the North Atlantic area and to ask yourselves how else we can respond to General Eisenhower's grave and forceful appeal, how else we can hope to secure either the thoroughly effective organization or the unfettered leadership which are indispensable if we are to overcome the present danger and enable our civilization to survive.

In the old Roman days the cry of danger was "the enemy is at the gates," and the duty expected of the public authority was to provide against the republic sustaining damage. Today the enemy is above us and all around us and the danger that we have to face is that of the extinction of all our values, public and private alike. Is it not the duty of all good citizens to raise their minds to the height of our circumstances and of our problems—the problems which this conference has come together to discuss, and with God's help, to play its part in solving?

◇◇◇◇◇◇◇◇◇◇◇◇◇◇◇◇◇◇◇◇◇◇◇◇◇◇◇◇◇◇◇◇◇◇◇◇◇◇◇◇◇◇◇◇◇◇◇◇◇◇◇◇

# 20. European Union: A German View

*The prospects for European Union depend decisively on the position of Germany, the most powerful and most feared state in Western Europe. On the one hand, a Union without Germany is unthinkable; on the other hand, a Union with Germany poses the opposite problem of whether the Union would not be dominated by Germany. Hence, the issue of the evils resulting from sovereignty merges into the issue of what kind of Union has a chance to succeed. The following analysis is by the venerable former Chancellor of the West German Republic, Konrad Adenauer. It reflects an acute awareness of the key problems; and it reviews the major steps that had been taken by 1953*

*towards Union. It is significant to read such a statement a dec-
ade later, for it reveals that even so sober an observer as
Adenauer was greatly over-optimistic concerning the rate and
ease with which the development toward Union might take
place. To mention only one point, his confidence that the
European Defence Community organization—which was intended to integrate German troops with others for the NATO
alliance—would bring about a "common foreign policy" has
proved to be unrealistic. In fact, in August of 1954, the French
National Assembly decisively rejected the EDC, thereby block-
ing, for a time, the re-armament of Germany.*

*Chancellor Adenauer's statements were made in an address
delivered, April 16, 1953, to a luncheon given in his honor by
the American Committee on United Europe.*

## KONRAD ADENAUER*

I am particularly grateful to your Chairman, General Donovan,
for affording me this opportunity to make your acquaintance
and to exchange a few ideas with you. We Europeans consider
it very encouraging to know that on the other side of the ocean
there exists a group of influential citizens who are so devoted
to the concept of a United Europe. In Europe we are very well
aware of the fact that we can reach the aim which we have
set ourselves only with the active assistance of our American
friends. You who are gathered here today are already ac-
quainted with the problems we have to face. Therefore, I may
expect on your part a great measure of understanding and I
shall be able to limit myself to commenting on a few problems
in the field of European unification, problems which, as far as
I am aware, have not so far become the property of the American public.

*I.* In the first place, may I once more clarify the motives
which underlie our endeavors toward European unification.

1. The most acute of these motives is obviously the constant
and ever growing menace from the East. Recently, for special

* From Konrad Adenauer, "The Political Unification of Europe,"
*Vital Speeches of the Day,* XIX (June 1, 1953), pp. 489–492. Reprinted by permission of the editor of *Vital Speeches.*

reasons, I have been led to communicate figures concerning
Russian armaments to my colleagues, the Ministers of Foreign
Affairs of the other Schuman Plan states. These figures form
a threatening picture of the comparative military power existing
within the Soviet power area including the satellite states and
that part of Germany under Soviet occupation, on the one
hand, and that of the free nations of Europe on the other. On
one side is a total of over 200 complete divisions with modern
equipment, mobile, and possessing a comparatively very strong
firepower; on the other side are the NATO forces stationed in
Europe which do not, so long as Germany does not participate,
exhaust the manpower potentialities of free Europe and which,
moreover, until such time as the European Defense Community comes into existence, will continue to evince the weakness of a coalition army. The necessity of balancing this difference in power is obvious. It is equally obvious that, in view
of the depth of modern military operations—consider for example, jet fighters and the extreme mobility of armored divisions—
military planning and operations limited to the small area of
European states has lost every significance. It was therefore,
logically, almost inevitable that the development of events led,
as early as December 1950, to the conclusion by the Council
of the North Atlantic Treaty Organization that Germany should
contribute to the defense of Europe. When it came to determine the *form* of such a contribution on the part of Germany,
the idea was conceived of a completely integrated European
Army. This means that advantage was taken of the solutions in the field of organization which had been developed
for the implementation of the Schuman Plan. Again, the main
thought was that the member states participating in the Defense Community would *give up their sovereignty* in the field
of defense and hand that sovereignty to the Community.

When he took that road, we were fully aware, as the French
Foreign Minister Robert Schuman has acknowledged, that the
European solutions were developing in a somewhat unnatural
chronological order. If we had had enough time at our disposal to develop the various elements of European unification
one by one, it is certain that the field of defense would have

been the last to be lifted from the national sphere of the individual states into the supra-national sphere of a United Europe. For the right and the power of self-defense have always been those elements of state sovereignty which have been most strongly guarded. But if we lacked time, it was precisely because of that menace from the East to which I have referred— that is the reason why unification in this field has progressed more quickly than in the political field.

However, I must stress that this acute menace is not the only reason for the policies of European defense.

2. The second of these reasons is the necessity to help balance and stabilize the relative power of East and West. It will be enough to recall the relative power situation which existed before World War I and to a certain degree also in the period between the first and the second World War. The great European powers then represented an economic, military, and political potential so great that the independent policies of these great powers by themselves formed a stabilizing factor in the world situation. Before World War I the economic and military potential of Russia was far from being developed as it is today and Russia's ideology and political system was not a latent danger for world peace as it is today. Today, the defense center against the dangers of the fantastic power accumulated by the Oriental bloc is situated outside Europe. It is situated in your country, which has assumed the heavy and self-sacrificing responsibility of leading the free world in its endeavors for the maintenance of freedom. If measured by modern power standards, the present political structure of Europe appears as made up of small states. Europe may be considered as doomed if it continues to be divided into a great number of states and exposed to the suction of the power system of Soviet Russia. Power works as a magnet on weaker bodies. But Europe must not be destroyed. Europe is the heart of Western Christian culture. It has done infinite good for the development of mankind. Its spiritual, cultural, religious, economic and political strength is not exhausted. Mankind would be considerably poorer if this old Europe of ours were one day to be vanquished by the assault of Asian barbarism. That is why Europe must unite to

save itself from such a fate, from being in any way absorbed by the Eastern bloc. Only through union can it again become economically healthy and live without having constantly to accept grants from America. It is the only way leading to higher standards of living sufficient for it to keep pace with the scientific and cultural achievements of the rest of the world. Only through union can Europe achieve a political weight of its own which will enable it to be a really useful and healthy partner in the free world.

And then there is a third concrete reason for the policy of a United Europe, which in itself justifies that policy—the unification of Europe would in the future render European wars impossible. Why is it that the most concrete and the most intensive unification movement so far achieved is in the field of coal and steel production? In the first place, because the unification of these heavy industries, whose production may be considered the very symbol of armaments, excludes any possibility of one of the participating countries arming against any other. Millions of Europeans will in future times be spared untold misery if the unification of the coal and steel industries, the defense community and all the other plans implemented or blueprinted lead to but one result—the end of wars among European peoples and the end of wars between France and Germany in particular.

*II.* Such therefore are our most important motives. Our task is not completed. Nevertheless, important things have been done and it is not weakness nor indecision that are to blame if we have not achieved more—it is the dimension of the obstacles we have to overcome.

1. At first sight, the picture of European organization seems complicated. First we have the Council of Europe in Strasbourg with its fourteen member states. That Council was the first symptom of European consciousness after the Second World War. It is not complete because its parliamentary organ has only *consultative* authority and is not entitled to make decisions. Moreover, its Committee of Ministers functions under the rule of unanimity which confers a right of veto on any one of its members. We have also created the Organization for

European Economic Cooperation, as a counterweight to the extraordinary economic assistance which your country afforded Europe after the war—an effort which for all times will be connected with the name Marshall. Perhaps this organization has not fulfilled all the expectations which were aroused at the time of its creation, particularly because here again the principle of unanimity exists and has led in many instances to compromise solutions. Nevertheless, the OEEC, like the Council of Europe, has exercised a considerable educational influence. Through this organization, European statesmen, economists, administrators, ministers and public opinion have learned, more than at any previous time, to think not within a narrow national framework but rather in terms of wide European organization, that of supra-national communities, the first being the Coal and Steel Community. More and more the creative energy of European statesmen is concentrating on this line of development. These plans are the first that led us to think in federal terms. All these plans—the Coal and Steel Community, the Defense Community and the now envisaged political community—have this in common: that the member states transfer part of their sovereignty to the larger whole. Therefore, there is in principle no need for unanimity; rather, these communities are constructed somewhat like a federal state. They have their own executive, they have their own parliamentary organ and also their own judiciary. In addition, the particular interests of the individual member states are represented in a Council of Ministers.

As I have said, the co-existence of these three types of organizations may appear rather complex. But should we not feel encouraged by the very fact that a United Europe is being approached from so many different angles? All these systems represent, after all, various strata of an historic evolution and I have no doubt that in a not too distant future they will be welded together in a closely unified structure. Even today it may be said that great care has been taken to arrange for coordination and mutual interaction. A strong liaison has been established through joint meetings, mutual information services, deputation of permanent observers. This is demonstrated

by the only supra-national community so far set up, the Coal
and Steel Community. That organization has organic connection
with both the Council of Europe and the Organization for
European Economic Cooperation.

2. There is a possibility that criticism will be leveled at our
efforts to unify Europe from another angle. It may be alleged
that our work is done piecemeal in a double sense. In the first
place, it may be said that our efforts do not encompass the
totality of the nations' life, but are limited to certain aspects
of it. True, what has been achieved so far or what has been
written into signed treaties are only limited aspects—economic
policies in the matter of coal and steel, then the military policies which, through the treaty for the European Defense Community, are leading to the creation of a European army. Yet
it would be completely wrong to perceive in this temporary
limitation a permanent defect in the organization of Europe.
The fields in which we have been active have such importance
for the economic and political life of the participating countries that they had to be dealt with first. These developments
will, through their very nature, lead to further progress in the
integration of Europe. The European Defense Community will
necessarily lead to a common foreign policy. Therefore, it is
mere coincidence that the draft of the treaty on the European
Defense Community contained Article 38 which envisaged a
political community as an outgrowth of the defense community. A decision to draft a charter for a political community
was made even before the treaty on the defense community
has come into force. It was a happy occasion in my political
career when, in my capacity as Chairman of the Council of
Ministers of the European Coal and Steel Community, I was able
to acquaint the parliament of that Community in September of
last year with the decision, taken by the Council of Ministers
in Luxembourg, that the parliamentary Assembly was requested
to undertake forwith the drafting of a treaty for a political
community. The Assembly of the Coal and Steel Community
immediately set up an Ad Hoc commission to draft such a
treaty for a political community within six months. One month
ago, the Council of Ministers of the six participating countries

received that draft, and we shall open our discussions on it on the 12th of May. I hope that we shall be successful in working with equal speed and energy in the Council of Ministers so that it will soon be possible for the governments of the six countries concerned to sign the treaty and submit it for ratification to their parliaments. We shall then witness, for the first time in history, common elections to a European parliament. A European Executive based on the confidence of this European parliament will then be created and this will be the first step towards the United States of Europe. This political community is not supposed to encompass all aspects of the life of its member nations. Participating states will always retain certain tasks relating to their individual territories, in which they will remain completely sovereign.

Our aim is not to set up a central power which will absorb the total existence of European states, rather it will be a community of a federal character, meaning that wide sectors of national life will be left to member states. This is particularly true in respect of their cultural life, to the extent that this cultural life is the concern of the government, and the same applies to various other matters. Above all, Europeans must avoid one mistake for which our American friends have so often blamed us—perfectionism. We must proceed step by step. We must gather experience. We must let things ripen. We must take due account of public opinion in our various countries. That public opinion must be convinced by the success of our efforts at unification in the various fields. Wisdom and moderation are just as important as power of decision and energetic progress.

3. We are further criticized for working piecemeal in a geographic sense. There is a biased sort of slogan according to which all we are creating is a "Little Europe" and preventing a great Europe from coming into existence. That slogan is wrong. It is true that the supra-national communities which we have set up, decided on or planned, comprise only six European countries; France, Italy, the Netherlands, Belgium, Luxembourg and the Federal Republic of Germany.

a. But in the first place we have always said and we shall

tirelessly repeat, that this is just a beginning. Participation in these supra-national communities is open to all countries that wish to join. There are several reasons why no more than these six countries have so far joined up. A number of European countries are today under Soviet domination. These countries have no authority to decide in favor of participation, but naturally we are thinking of these very countries as future members of the European community. Need I say expressly that this applies also and in particular to that part of Germany which is at present, and against the will of its population, under Soviet dictatorship?

True, there are also countries west of the Iron Curtain that hesitate to join us at this time. We request these countries—and this is explicitly written into our treaties—not to ignore our permanent invitation to join us. The community of the six countries is in no way exclusive. Once more, this is just the beginning. If we are successful—and we shall be successful—the community will automatically expand.

b. There is another answer we can give to this criticism and this concerns in particular a problem which has been of more concern to us than to many others—our relations with Great Britain. Great Britain has not responded to our suggestion to join us because of her position within the British Commonwealth. It is not for us to enter into a discussion with the British Government on the validity of this argument. But we sincerely desire to see England participate in our community as closely as possible. Yet it would be a great mistake, both from the point of view of method and of policy, were we to raise the question in such a way that Great Britain would have no other choice than to become a full member of the European community or not to join at all. The truth is that between full membership in the European Community and absolute non-participation there are intermediate stages, possibilities of organic links between the continental European community and Great Britain. What I have in mind is a partial and relative participation in our federative community—we have come to designate such participation by the name "association."

Let me give an example of what I have in mind: Great Britain has a permanent mission to the Coal and Steel Community. The executive organ of the Coal and Steel Community, that is, the High Authority, has already set up, through a joint commission, a liaison between the Coal and Steel Community and Great Britain. Moreover, the interaction between the Coal and Steel Community, the Council of Europe and the Organization for European Economic Cooperation, to which I have referred—and I am thinking of the exchange of information, joint meetings, etc.—works for a close relationship with Great Britain. Here is another example: The European Defense Community, as you know, is linked even more closely with Great Britain than with the other NATO states through an automatic treaty of assistance. Apart from this mutual assistance agreement, we have had the great satisfaction of seeing the British Government offer particularly close military cooperation with the European Defense Community.

All this goes to show how wrong, how foolish even, is this slogan about "little Europe." I should like to suggest a comparison in the realm of chemistry: the creation of the intensive core of the supra-national community is a process of crystallization, the effect of which is not limited to the core which achieves the most complete integration. Around this core the other political elements gather, under the compulsion of nature, as it were. And so there comes into being a system of communities of various grades, including the largest of these communities which encompasses the free nations of the West and which is the Atlantic Community.

*III.* This is what I invite my American friends and godfathers of European unification to consider whenever they are tempted to become impatient with the slow pace at which United Europe is developing. I fully understand your impatience. I myself am often impatient. But let us not forget that in the course of two thousand years of European history, dams have been erected within Europe which it is impossible to tear down in a few months. What is happening in Europe at this time is indeed revolutionary. Deep rooted concepts must be abandoned. The whole political education of the peoples of

Europe, which was oriented toward the idea of the nation as the ultimate value in political decision, must now be reversed.

That cannot be accomplished in a day. That is why it is so important for us to have the youth of the peoples of Europe on our side. There lies all our hope. Our hope lies in the creative energy of unbiased young people who are not hindered by heavily weighted memories and who look to the future rather than to the past.

Our efforts shall not abate. But if we are to keep up our courage there is one thing we need and I shall now conclude with one request. What we need is the certainty that the most powerful nation in the world, a nation which believes in freedom more strongly than any other, that your nation with its sympathy, its moral and material strength, is on our side. I repeat what I said before, and if I do so it is not as a bon mot—the Americans are the best Europeans. Your history offers the most impressive example of what people can achieve if they have the earnest will to unite. Do help us as well in our quest to find ourselves. If you do that, then I have not the slighest doubt that we shall succeed in our efforts.

# Part Two

◇◇◇◇◇◇◇◇◇◇◇

# PURPOSES

*Part One of these readings emphasized the common attri-
butes of states and the implications of those attributes for
the nature of international relations. In Parts Two and Three,
the emphasis shifts. The common attributes are taken for
granted, and two different, closely related questions, are
posed: What is the purpose of the state in relation to other
states? What form of government is most likely to achieve
that purpose?*

*Like most basic political questions, these are ancient ones,
to which different answers have been and continue to be
given. The antiquity and interdependence of the questions,
as well as the variety of the answers, can be illustrated by
looking at the views of three great political theorists, ranging
from classical Greece to the modern world.*

*Plato, in the* Republic, *makes Socrates and a group of
friends try to discover the nature of justice. Early in the discussion, the nature of the question appears to require a treatment of the best political society, for it is in such a society,
if anywhere, that justice would be realized. Now Socrates
and his friends agree that even the best* polis *will need soldiers to defend it. A critical problem, then, is how to ensure
that the soldiers will bravely defend the* polis *when it is necessary, but never engage in aggressive, expansionist war.*

129

*The answer which Socrates gives is that the form of govern-
ment—an elite of specially selected and educated men, called
philosopher-kings—will ensure this. It will do so by creating
and maintaining good general institutions for the* polis; *by
careful selection of the soldiers and by giving them thorough
moral as well as physical and military training; and by sub-
jecting them, in the final analysis, to the political direction
of the philosopher-kings. The conclusion is that this form of
government, and only this form, is adequate to the task.*

*Eighteen centuries later, Niccolo Machiavelli, in his* The
Prince *and* Discourses on Livy, *disputed Plato's premises
and conclusions. Machiavelli argues that since even Plato is
forced to make Socrates admit the virtual impossibility, in
practice, of realizing the one truly necessary form of government, he is also forced to admit the virtual impossibility of
restraining man's natural tendency to aggrandizement.
Machiavelli's conclusion is, then, the opposite of Plato's: the
best form of government is not one which—foolishly—attempts to restrain that tendency, but one which builds upon
it by making the state capable of harnessing it to external
expansion. Hence, according to Machiavelli, the best form
of government will be one which is consciously modelled on
both the internal and external practices of ancient Rome, the
greatest empire which has ever existed.*

*A third variation on the theme is provided by the great
modern German philosopher, Immanuel Kant (1724–1804).
In a famous little book,* Perpetual Peace; A Philosophical
Sketch *(1795), Kant sets forth a hypothetical scheme by
which the perennial conflict and war among states might
be permanently altered. Kant starts from the premise that men
are naturally in a war-like "state of nature," much as Hobbes
had done. But Kant, in contrast to Hobbes, and in a way
quite paradoxically, given his premise, concludes very differently: he concludes that if all states were to possess a "republican" constitution, the hypothetical condition of perpetual*

*peace might become a reality. By a "republican" constitution he means one based on the general, clarified or educated "will" of all the people; and one which is organized on the basis of a separation of the legislative and executive powers. His reasoning is that under such a form of government, the state's policies will constantly be guided by the shrewd self-interest of all the citizens: they will appreciate the dangers and burdens of war vastly better than any nonrepublican "rulers" possibly could, for they will realize that they must suffer the dangers and bear the burdens of war.*

*It will be noticed that in each of these three cases, a connection is made between the understanding of the purpose of the state and the* kind *of government which is recommended. One could say, on the basis of these three examples, that there is general agreement that at the core of the purpose of the state, in its external relations, is the defense of the existence of the state against external destruction. But beyond this, there is wide disagreement. There is disagreement on how exactly to understand the relation of this defensive purpose to possible offensive purposes. There is disagreement on the kind of government which might achieve even the purpose of defense in an adequate manner. And there is even more basic disagreement on the necessary internal means, such as education and political institutions.*

*These disagreements on purposes and forms constitute the focus in this and the following part of the readings. In this part, the emphasis is on the side of the analysis of purposes; in Part Three, it is on the side of the form of government. The two aspects of the problem are, as I have already indicated by the three sketches above, intertwined; but for reasons of clarity in treatment, they are separated into different parts.*

*This part is divided into five sections. VII, The Fundamental Nature of the Problem, contains a selection from Classical Greece—by the historian Thucydides. It illustrates the continuing nature of the problem of the purpose of the state in its external relations. VIII, The Continuum of Alternatives: Classical Theories, then provides four alternative interpretations of that problem. The interpretations, by Aristotle, John Locke, Machiavelli and Treitschke, range along a wide continuum. They are intended to provide the student with a detailed, if concise, treatment of "classical" theories of the purpose of the state in its external relations. Finally, in IX, X and XI, a parallel continuum of views in the twentieth century is provided; but in this case, the emphasis is upon the views of political actors rather than that of theorists. It is for the student, then, to think of the problem at different levels, aided by the arguments of men of theory and men of practice.*

# VII. The Fundamental Nature of the Problem

## 21. The Contest of Might and Right

*Ancient Greece was a relatively small area within a larger "world." But in the fifth century* B.C., *this small area contained several hundred poleis, of which the most prominent were places such as Athens, Sparta, Corinth and Megara. The relations among these poleis were as intricate, in their own way, as the relations among modern nation-states. It is essentially for this reason, in addition to the fact that a very high level of political and intellectual development was reached within the most prominent of the poleis, that the Greek world remains to this day a fascinating historical laboratory for the comparative study of international relations.*

*Early in the fifth century* B.C., *Athens and Sparta led the Greeks in a series of wars against the invading Persians. In famous battles at Marathon (490), Thermopylae (480), and Plataea (479), the citizens of both showed great intrepidity in repulsing their common enemy. But once victory was secure, the alliance against the Persians disintegrated—not the first, nor the last time in history that such an event has taken place. The Greek world soon divided into what today might be called two "spheres of influence." The first was the Athenian Empire, an agglomeration of poleis which, in one way or another, had come progressively under Athenian control. The second was the Peloponnesian League, headed by Sparta.*

*By the middle of the century, the conflict between Athens and Sparta erupted in the first of a series of Peloponnesian Wars. The greatest of these wars is the one treated by Thucydides (c. 466* B.C.*–c. 400* B.C.*). The war began in 431 and, after an interlude from 421–414, ended in 404 with the crushing defeat of Athens. This devastating war marked the beginning of the end of the world of the Greek polis. Its significance seems to have been understood from the very outset by Thucydides. He says, at the beginning of his work, that he began to*

write the history of the war from the moment it broke out, so
convinced was he that it was the greatest war the Greeks would
ever experience. Furthermore, when he later sets forth the basic
causes of the war, he says, in a somber mood: "The Peloponnesian war was prolonged to an immense length, and long as it
was it was short without parallel for the misfortunes that it
brought upon Hellas."

The selection from Thucydides which follows is often called
the "Melian Dialogue." It took place in the sixteenth year of the
war, at a time when Athens still confidently expected to defeat
the Spartans. The exchange between the Athenians and the leaders of the little polis of Melos starkly presents the tension between the purpose of the Athenians—to preserve their empire—
and the purpose of the Melians—to defend their independence.
The chilling terms in which Thucydides so briefly describes
the aftermath of this discussion—the eventual annihilation of
the Melian polis by the Athenians because of the refusal of the
Melian leaders to capitulate—provide a sober, but baffling
commentary on the power relations of political societies. Is
Thucydides simply recording the facts? Is he insensitive to the
irony of this kind of use of power by the brilliant Athenian
polis? Is he indicating that it is necessarily thus in the relations
of independent political societies? Does he mean that, as the
Athenians seem to claim at one point, the greater power is the
greater right? If so, what is the implication for the purpose of
all political societies in their external relations?

It is impossible, here, to answer such questions. They are
stated simply to indicate to the student the ambiguity of Thucydides' presentation of this elemental situation. It is almost as
though he deliberately draws our attention to the ambiguity of
the reality by his own terse handling of the problem. It is for
the student, then, to reflect upon the reality through the help
of the eloquent words which Thucydides attributes to these de-
parted speakers.

## THUCYDIDES*

The Melians are a colony of Lacedæmon that would not submit
to the Athenians like the other islanders, and at first remained

* From *The History of The Peloponnesian War* by Thucydides, trans-
lated by Richard Crawley, revised by Feetham. Everyman's Library.
Bk. V, sects. 86–116. Reprinted by permission of E. P. Dutton and
Co., Inc.

neutral and took no part in the struggle, but afterwards upon the Athenians using violence and plundering their territory, assumed an attitude of open hostility. Cleomedes, son of Lycomedes, and Tisias, son of Tisimachus, the generals, encamping in their territory with the above armament, before doing any harm to their land, sent envoys to negotiate. These the Melians did not bring before the people, but bade them state the object of their mission to the magistrates and the few; upon which the Athenian envoys spoke as follows:—

*Athenians.*—'Since the negotiations are not to go on before the people, in order that we may not be able to speak straight on without interruption, and deceive the ears of the multitude by seductive arguments which would pass without refutation (for we know that this is the meaning of our being brought before the few), what if you who sit there were to pursue a method more cautious still! Make no set speech yourselves, but take us up at whatever you do not like, and settle that before going any farther. And first tell us if this proposition of ours suits you.'

The Melian commissioners answered:—

*Melians.*—'To the fairness of quietly instructing each other as you propose there is nothing to object; but your military preparations are too far advanced to agree with what you say, as we see you are come to be judges in your own cause, and that all we can reasonably expect from this negotiation is war, if we prove to have right on our side and refuse to submit, and in the contrary case, slavery.'

*Athenians.*—'If you have met to reason about presentiments of the future, or for anything else than to consult for the safety of your state upon the facts that you see before you, we will give over; otherwise we will go on.'

*Melians.*—'It is natural and excusable for men in our position to turn more ways than one both in thought and utterance. However, the question in this conference is, as you say, the safety of our country; and the discussion, if you please, can proceed in the way which you propose.'

*Athenians.*—'For ourselves, we shall not trouble you with specious pretences—either of how we have a right to our empire because we overthrew the Mede, or are now attacking you because of wrong that you have done us—and make a long speech which would not be believed; and in return we hope that you, instead of thinking to influence us by saying that you did not join the Lacedæmonians, although their colonists, or that you have done us no wrong, will aim at what is feasible, holding in view the real sentiments of us both; since you know as well as we do that right, as the world goes, is only in question between equals in power, while the strong do what they can and the weak suffer what they must.'

*Melians.*—'As we think, at any rate, it is expedient—we speak as we are obliged, since you enjoin us to let right alone and talk only of interest—that you should not destroy what is our common protection, the privilege of being allowed in danger to invoke what is fair and right, and even to profit by arguments not strictly valid if they can be got to pass current. And you are as much interested in this as any, as your fall would be a signal for the heaviest vengeance and an example for the world to meditate upon.'

*Athenians.*—'The end of our empire, if end it should, does not frighten us: a rival empire like Lacedæmon, even if Lacedæmon was our real antagonist, is not so terrible to the vanquished as subjects who by themselves attack and overpower their rulers. This, however, is a risk that we are content to take. We will now proceed to show you that we are come here in the interest of our empire, and that we shall say what we are now going to say, for the preservation of your country; as we would fain exercise that empire over you without trouble, and see you preserved for the good of us both.'

*Melians.*—'And how, pray, could it turn out as good for us to serve as for you to rule?'

*Athenians.*—'Because you would have the advantage of submitting before suffering the worst, and we should gain by not destroying you.'

*Melians.*—'So that you would not consent to our being neutral, friends instead of enemies, but allies of neither side.'

*Athenians.*—'No; for your hostility cannot so much hurt us as your friendship will be an argument to our subjects of our weakness, and your enmity of our power.'

*Melians.*—'Is that your subjects' idea of equity, to put those who have nothing to do with you in the same category with peoples that are most of them your own colonists, and some conquered rebels?'

*Athenians.*—'As far as right goes they think one has as much of it as the other, and that if any maintain their independence it is because they are strong, and that if we do not molest them it is because we are afraid; so that besides extending our empire we should gain in security by your subjection; the fact that you are islanders and weaker than others rendering it all the more important that you should not succeed in baffling the masters of the sea.'

*Melians.*—'But do you consider that there is no security in the policy which we indicate? For here again if you debar us from talking about justice and invite us to obey your interest, we also must explain ours, and try to persuade you, if the two happen to coincide. How can you avoid making enemies of all existing neutrals who shall look at our case and conclude from it that one day or another you will attack them? And what is this but to make greater the enemies that you have already, and to force others to become so who would otherwise have never thought of it?'

*Athenians.*—'Why, the fact is that continentals generally give us but little alarm; the liberty which they enjoy will long prevent their taking precautions against us; it is rather islanders like yourselves, outside our empire, and subjects smarting under the yoke, who would be the most likely to take a rash step and lead themselves and us into obvious danger.'

*Melians.*—'Well then, if you risk so much to retain your empire, and your subjects to get rid of it, it were surely great baseness and cowardice in us who are still free not to try everything that can be tried, before submitting to your yoke.'

*Athenians.*—'Not if you are well advised, the contest not being an equal one, with honour as the prize and shame as the penalty, but a question of self-preservation and of not resisting those who are far stronger than you are.'

*Melians.*—'But we know that the fortune of war is sometimes more impartial than the disproportion of numbers might

lead one to suppose; to submit is to give ourselves over to
despair, while action still preserves for us a hope that we may
stand erect.'

*Athenians.*—'Hope, danger's comforter, may be indulged in
by those who have abundant resources, if not without loss at
all events without ruin; but its nature is to be extravagant, and
those who go so far as to put their all upon the venture see
it in its true colours only when they are ruined; but so long
as the discovery would enable them to guard against it, it is
never found wanting. Let not this be the case with you, who
are weak and hang on a single turn of the scale; nor be like
the vulgar, who, abandoning such security as human means
may still afford, when visible hopes fail them in extremity,
turn to invisible, to prophecies and oracles, and other such
inventions that delude men with hopes to their destruction.'

*Melians.*—'You may be sure that we are as well aware as
you of the difficulty of contending against your power and
fortune, unless the terms be equal. But we trust that the gods
may grant us fortune as good as yours, since we are just men
fighting against unjust, and that what we want in power will
be made up by the alliance of the Lacedæmonians, who are
bound, if only for very shame, to come to the aid of their
kindred. Our confidence, therefore, after all is not so utterly
irrational.'

*Athenians.*—'When you speak of the favour of the gods, we
may as fairly hope for that as yourselves; neither our pretensions nor our conduct being in any way contrary to what men
believe of the gods, or practise among themselves. Of the gods
we believe, and of men we know, that by a necessary law of
their nature they rule wherever they can. And it is not as if
we were the first to make this law, or to act upon it when made:
we found it existing before us, and shall leave it to exist for
ever after us; all we do is to make use of it, knowing that you
and everybody else, having the same power as we have,
would do the same as we do. Thus, as far as the gods are
concerned, we have no fear and no reason to fear that we
shall be at a disadvantage. But when we come to your notion
about the Lacedæmonians, which leads you to believe that

shame will make them help you, here we bless your simplicity
but do not envy your folly. The Lacedæmonians, when their
own interests or their country's laws are in question, are the
worthiest men alive; of their conduct towards others much
might be said, but no clearer idea of it could be given than
by shortly saying that of all the men we know they are most
conspicuous in considering what is agreeable honourable, and
what is expedient just. Such a way of thinking does not promise
much for the safety which you now unreasonably count upon.'

*Melians.*—'But it is for this very reason that we now trust
to their respect for expediency to prevent them from betraying
the Melians, their colonists, and thereby losing the confidence
of their friends in Hellas and helping their enemies.'

*Athenians.*—'Then you do not adopt the view that expediency goes with security, while justice and honour cannot be
followed without danger; and danger the Lacedæmonians generally court as little as possible.'

*Melians.*—'But we believe that they would be more likely
to face even danger for our sake, and with more confidence
than for others, as our nearness to Peloponnese makes it easier
for them to act, and our common blood insures our fidelity.'

*Athenians.*—'Yes, but what an intending ally trusts to, is
not the goodwill of those who ask his aid, but a decided superiority of power for action; and the Lacedæmonians look to
this even more than others. At least, such is their distrust of
their home resources that it is only with numerous allies that
they attack a neighbour; now is it likely that while we are
masters of the sea they will cross over to an island?'

*Melians.*—'But they would have others to send. The Cretan
sea is a wide one, and it is more difficult for those who command it to intercept others, than for those who wish to elude
them to do so safely. And should the Lacedæmonians mis-
carry in this, they would fall upon your land, and upon those
left of your allies whom Brasidas did not reach; and instead
of places which are not yours, you will have to fight for your
own country and your own confederacy.'

*Athenians.*—'Some diversion of the kind you speak of you
may one day experience, only to learn, as others have done,

that the Athenians never once yet withdrew from a siege for fear of any. But we are struck by the fact, that after saying you would consult for the safety of your country, in all this discussion you have mentioned nothing which men might trust in and think to be saved by. Your strongest arguments depend upon hope and the future, and your actual resources are too scanty, as compared with those arrayed against you, for you to come out victorious. You will therefore show great blindness of judgment, unless, after allowing us to retire, you can find some counsel more prudent than this. You will surely not be caught by that idea of disgrace, which in dangers that are disgraceful, and at the same time too plain to be mistaken, proves so fatal to mankind; since in too many cases the very men that have their eyes perfectly open to what they are rushing into, let the thing called disgrace, by the mere influence of a seductive name, lead them on to a point at which they become so enslaved by the phrase as in fact to fall wilfully into hopeless disaster, and incur disgrace more disgraceful as the companion of error, than when it comes as the result of misfortune. This, if you are well advised, you will guard against; and you will not think it dishonourable to submit to the greatest city in Hellas, when it makes you the moderate offer of becoming its tributary ally, without ceasing to enjoy the country that belongs to you; nor when you have the choice given you between war and security, will you be so blinded as to choose the worse. And it is certain that those who do not yield to their equals, who keep terms with their superiors, and are moderate towards their inferiors, on the whole succeed best. Think over the matter, therefore, after our withdrawal, and reflect once and again that it is for your country that you are consulting, that you have not more than one, and that upon this one deliberation depends its prosperity or ruin.'

The Athenians now withdrew from the conference; and the Melians, left to themselves, came to a decision corresponding with what they had maintained in the discussion, and answered, 'Our resolution, Athenians, is the same as it was at first. We will not in a moment deprive of freedom a city that has been inhabited these seven hundred years; but we put our trust in the fortune by which the gods have preserved it until now, and in the help of men, that is, of the Lacedæmonians; and so we will try and save ourselves. Meanwhile we invite you to allow us to be friends to you and foes to neither party, and to retire from our country after making such a treaty as shall seem fit to us both.'

Such was the answer of the Melians. The Athenians now departing from the conference said, 'Well, you alone, as it seems to us, judging from these resolutions, regard what is future as more certain than what is before your eyes, and what is out of sight, in your eagerness, as already coming to pass; and as you have staked most on, and trusted most in, the Lacedæmonians, your fortune, and your hopes, so will you be most completely deceived.'

The Athenian envoys now returned to the army; and the Melians showing no signs of yielding, the generals at once betook themselves to hostilities, and drew a line of circumvallation round the Melians, dividing the work among the different states. Subsequently the Athenians returned with most of their army, leaving behind them a certain number of their own citizens and of the allies to keep guard by land and sea. The force thus left stayed on and besieged the place. . . . Under the command of Philocrates, son of Demeas, the siege was pressed vigorously; and some treachery taking place inside, the Melians surrendered at discretion to the Athenians, who put to death all the grown men whom they took, and sold the women and children for slaves, and subsequently sent out five hundred colonists and inhabited the place themselves.

# VIII. The Continuum of Alternatives: Classical Theories

## 22. The Relation of War and Peace

*Aristotle's* Politics, *from which the following selection is taken, is a treatise on the nature of the* polis—*which the translator has called "state." Its treatment of the relation of war and peace, as purposes of political society, is a systematic extension of Aristotle's fundamental proposition that such society is natural to man. The comparison of the quality of the individual soul to the quality of the* polis *is, of course, strongly reminiscent of Plato's* Republic.

### ARISTOTLE *

Every state is a community of some kind, and every community is established with a view to some good; for mankind always act in order to obtain that which they think good. But, if all communities aim at some good, the state or political community, which is the highest of all, and which embraces all the rest, aims, and in a greater degree than any other, at the highest good. . . .

When several villages are united in a single community, perfect and large enough to be nearly or quite self-sufficing, the state comes into existence, originating in the bare needs of life, and continuing in existence for the sake of a good life. And therefore, if the earlier forms of society are natural, so is the state, for it is the end of them, and the [completed] nature is the end. For what each thing is when fully developed, we call

---

* From Aristotle, *The Politics,* trans. B. Jowett, Bk. I, ch. 1; Bk. VII, chs. 1, 14, 15.

its nature, whether we are speaking of a man, a horse, or a family. Besides, the final cause and end of a thing is the best, and to be self-sufficing is the end and the best.

Hence it is evident that the state is a creation of nature, and that man is by nature a political animal. And he who by nature and not by mere accident is without a state, is either above humanity, or below it; he is the

"Tribeless, lawless, heartless one,"

whom Homer denounces—the outcast who is a lover of war; he may be compared to a bird which flies alone.

Now the reason why man is more of a political animal than bees or any other gregarious animals is evident. Nature, as we often say, makes nothing in vain, and man is the only animal whom she has endowed with the gift of speech. And whereas mere sound is but an indication of pleasure or pain, and is therefore found in other animals (for their nature attains to the perception of pleasure and pain and the intimation of them to one another, and no further), the power of speech is intended to set forth the expedient and inexpedient, and likewise the just and the unjust. And it is a characteristic of man that he alone has any sense of good and evil, of just and unjust, and the association of living beings who have this sense makes a family and a state.

Thus the state is by nature clearly prior to the family and to the individual, since the whole is of necessity prior to the part; for example, if the whole body be destroyed, there will be no foot or hand, except in an equivocal sense, as we might speak of a stone hand; for when destroyed the hand will be no better. But things are defined by their working and power; and we ought not to say that they are the same when they are no longer the same, but only that they have the same name. The proof that the state is a creation of nature and prior to the individual is that the individual, when isolated, is not self-sufficing; and therefore he is like a part in relation to the whole. But he who is unable to live in society, or who has no need because he is sufficient for himself, must be either a beast or a god: he is no part of a state. A social instinct is

implanted in all men by nature, and yet he who first founded
the state was the greatest of benefactors. For man, when perfected, is the best of animals, but, when separated from law
and justice, he is the worst of all; since armed injustice is
the more dangerous, and he is equipped at birth with the
arms of intelligence and with moral qualities which he may
use for the worst ends. Wherefore, if he have not virtue, he is
the most unholy and the most savage of animals, and the most
full of lust and gluttony. But justice is the bond of men in
states, and the administration of justice, which is the determination of what is just, is the principle of order in political
society. . . .

He who would duly inquire about the best form of a State
ought first to determine which is the most eligible life; while
this remains uncertain the best form of the State must also be
uncertain; for, in the natural order of things, those may be
expected to lead the best life who are governed in the best
manner of which their circumstances admit. We ought therefore to ascertain, first of all, which is the most generally eligible
life, and then whether the same life is or is not best for the
State and for individuals.

. . . Certainly no one will dispute the propriety of that
partition of goods which separates them into three classes, viz.,
external goods, goods of the body, and goods of the soul, or
deny that the happy man must have all three. For no one
would maintain that he is happy who has not in him a particle
of courage or temperance or justice or prudence, who is afraid
of every insect which flutters past him, and will commit any
crime, however great, in order to gratify his lust of meat or
drink, who will sacrifice his dearest friend for the sake of half
a farthing, and is as feeble and false in mind as a child or a
madman. These propositions are universally acknowledged as
soon as they are uttered, but men differ about the degree or
relative superiority of this or that good. Some think that a very
moderate amount of virtue is enough, but set no limit to their
desires of wealth, property, power, reputation, and the like.
To whom we reply by an appeal to facts, which easily prove
that mankind do not acquire or preserve virtue by the help of

external goods, but external goods by the help of virtue, and that happiness, whether consisting in pleasure or virtue, or both, is more often found with those who are most highly cultivated in their mind and in their character, and have only a moderate share of external goods, than among those who possess external goods to a useless extent but are deficient in higher qualities; and this is not only matter of experience, but, if reflected upon, will easily appear to be in accordance with reason. For, whereas external goods have a limit, like any other instrument, and all things useful are of such a nature that where there is too much of them they must either do harm, or at any rate be of no use, to their possessors, every good of the soul, the greater it is, is also of greater use, if the epithet useful as well as noble is appropriate to such subjects. No proof is required to show that the best state of one thing in relation to another is proportioned to the degree of excellence by which the natures corresponding to those states are separated from each other: so that, if the soul is more noble than our possessions or our bodies, both absolutely and in relation to us, it must be admitted that the best state of either has a similar ratio to the other. Again, if it is for the sake of the soul that goods external and goods of the body are eligible at all, and all wise men ought to choose them for the sake of the soul, and not the soul for the sake of them.

Let us acknowledge then that each one has just so much of happiness as he has of virtue and wisdom, and of virtuous and wise action. God is a witness to us of this truth, for he is happy and blessed, not by reason of any external good, but in himself and by reason of his own nature. And herein of necessity lies the difference between good fortune and happiness; for external goods come of themselves, and chance is the author of them, but no one is just or temperate by or through chance. In like manner, and by a similar train of argument, the happy State may be shown to be that which is [morally] best and which acts rightly; and rightly it cannot act without doing right actions, and neither individual nor State can do right actions without virtue and wisdom. Thus the courage, justice, and wisdom of a State have the same form and nature as the qualities which give the individual who possesses them the name of just, wise, or temperate.

. . . Since we say that the virtue of the citizen and ruler is the same as that of the good man, and that the same person must first be a subject and then a ruler, the legislator has to see that they become good men, and by what means this may be accomplished, and what is the end of the perfect life.

Now the soul of man is divided into two parts, one of which has reason in itself, and the other, not having reason in itself, is able to obey reason. And we call a man good because he has the virtues of these two parts. In which of them the end is more likely to be found is no matter of doubt to those who adopt our division; for in the world both of nature and of art the inferior always exists for the sake of the better or superior, and the better or superior is that which has reason. The reason too, in our ordinary way of speaking, is divided into two parts, for there is a practical and a speculative reason, and there must be a corresponding division of actions; the actions of the naturally better principle are to be preferred by those who have it in their power to attain to both or to all, for that is always to everyone the most eligible which is the highest attainable by him. The whole of life is further divided into two parts, business and leisure, war and peace, and all actions into those which are necessary and useful, and those which are honorable. And the preference given to one or the other class of actions must necessarily be like the preference given to one or other part of the soul and its actions over the other; there must be war for the sake of peace, business for the sake of leisure, things useful and necessary for the sake of things honorable. All these points the statesman should keep in view when he frames his laws; he should consider the parts of the soul and their functions, and above all the better and the end; he should also remember the diversities of human lives and actions. For men must engage in business and go to war, but leisure and peace are better; they must do what is necessary and useful, but what is honorable is better. In such principles children and persons of every age which requires education should be trained. Whereas even the Hellenes of the present day, who are reputed to be best governed, and the legislators who gave them their constitutions, do not appear to have framed their governments with a regard to the best end, or to have given them laws and education with a view to all the virtues, but in a vulgar spirit have fallen back on those which promised to be more useful and profitable. Many modern writers have taken a similar view: they commend the Lacedæmonian constitution, and praise the legislator for making conquest and war his sole aim, a doctrine which may be refuted by argument and has long ago been refuted by facts. For most men desire empire in the hope of accumulating the goods of fortune; and on this ground Thibron and all those who have written about the Lacedæmonian constitution have praised their legislator, because the Lacedæmonians, by a training in hardships, gained great power. But surely they are not a happy people now that their empire has passed away, nor was their legislator right. How ridiculous is the result, if, while they are continuing in the observance of his laws and no one interferes with them, they have lost the better part of life. These writers further err about the sort of government which the legislator should approve, for the government of freemen is noble, and implies more virtue than despotic government. Neither is a city to be deemed happy or a legislator to be praised because he trains his citizens to conquer and obtain dominion over their neighbors, for there is great evil in this. On a similar principle any citizen who could, would obviously try to obtain the power in his own State—the crime which the Lacedæmonians accuse King Pausanias of attempting, although he had so great honor already. No such principle and no law having this object is either statesmanlike or useful or right. For the same things are best both for individuals and for States, and these are the things which the legislator ought to implant in the minds of his citizens. Neither should men study war with a view to the enslavement of those who do not deserve to be enslaved; but first of all they should provide against their own enslavement, and in the second place obtain empire for the good of the governed, and not for the sake of exercising a general despotism, and in the third place they should seek to be masters only over those who deserve to be slaves. Facts, as well as arguments, prove that the legislator should direct all his military and other measures to the

provision of leisure and the establishment of peace. For most
of these military States are safe only while they are at war, but
fall when they have acquired their empire; like unused iron
they rust in time of peace. And for this the legislator is to
blame, he never having taught them how to lead the life of
peace.

Since the end of individuals and of States is the same, the
end of the best man and of the best State must also be the
same; it is therefore evident that there ought to exist in both
of them the virtues of leisure; for peace, as has been often
repeated, is the end of war, and leisure of toil. But leisure and
cultivation may be promoted, not only by those virtues which
are practised in leisure, but also by some of those which are
useful to business. For many necessaries of life have to be
supplied before we can have leisure. Therefore a city must
be temperate and brave, and able to endure: for truly, as the
proverb says, "There is no leisure for slaves," and those who
cannot face danger like men are the slaves of any invader.
Courage and endurance are required for business and philosophy for leisure, temperance and justice for both, more
especially in times of peace and leisure, for war compels men
to be just and temperate, whereas the enjoyment of good fortune and the leisure which comes with peace tends to make
them insolent. Those then, who seem to be the best-off and
to be in the possession of every good, have special need of
justice and temperance—for example, those (if such there be,
as the poets say) who dwell in the Islands of the Blest; they
above all will need philosophy and temperance and justice,
and all the more the more leisure they have, living in the
midst of abundance. There is no difficulty in seeing why the
State that would be happy and good ought to have these virtues. If it be disgraceful in man not to be able to use the goods
of life, it is peculiarly disgraceful not to be able to use them
in time of peace—to show excellent qualities in action and
war, and when they have peace and leisure to be no better
than slaves. Wherefore we should not practice virtue after the
manner of the Lacedæmonians. For they, while agreeing with
other men in their conception of the highest goods, differ from

the rest of mankind in thinking that they are to be obtained by the practice of a single virtue. . . .

◇◇◇◇◇◇◇◇◇◇◇◇◇◇◇◇◇◇◇◇◇◇◇◇◇◇◇◇◇◇◇◇◇◇◇◇◇◇◇◇◇◇◇◇◇◇◇◇◇◇◇

# 23. The Necessity to Expand

*As has been indicated in the general introduction of this part, Machiavelli took issue with the view of Plato—and Aristotle, for that matter—that the purpose of political society is to make virtuous men. Or to be more exact now, Machiavelli tries to redefine the nature of political virtue. He emphasizes the decisive importance of the external relations of states, thereby shifting the purpose of the state in the process. The first selection here is from his most famous book,* The Prince, *Ch. 14. It states, in uncompromising terms, the proper weight to be given, in Machiavelli's view, to the art of war. The second selection is really an elaborate amplification of that view, and is taken from his longer, less well known book,* Discourses on Livy. *The connection, in this selection, between the purpose of external expansion, and the tripartite governmental form of ancient Rome, is a good example of the interdependence of these aspects of the problem of the state in its external relations. The comparison of the attitudes of Machiavelli and Aristotle to Sparta is particularly instructive for the student of international relations.*

**NICCOLO MACHIAVELLI***

## THE PRINCE

A prince should have no other aim or thought, nor take up any other thing for his study, but war and its organisation

---

* The selection from *The Prince*, ch. 14, is translated by L. Ricci and revised by E. R. P. Vincent. It is reprinted by permission of the Oxford University Press. The selection from *Discourses on the First Ten Books of Titus Livius*, Bk. 1, Chs. 2, 4, 6, is translated by Christian E. Detmold; it is reprinted from the Modern Library edition of *The Prince and The Discourses*.

and discipline, for that is the only art that is necessary to one who commands, and it is of such virtue that it not only maintains those who are born princes, but often enables men of private fortune to attain to that rank. And one sees, on the other hand, that when princes think more of luxury than of arms, they lose their state. The chief cause of the loss of states, is the contempt of this art, and the way to acquire them is to be well versed in the same.

Francesco Sforza, through being well armed, became, from private status, Duke of Milan; his sons, through wishing to avoid the fatigue and hardship of war, from dukes became private persons. For among other evils caused by being disarmed, it renders you contemptible; which is one of those disgraceful things which a prince must guard against. Because there is no comparison whatever between an armed and a disarmed man; it is not reasonable to suppose that one who is armed will obey willingly one who is unarmed; or that any unarmed man will remain safe among armed servants. For one being disdainful and the other suspicious, it is not possible for them to act well together. And therefore a prince who is ignorant of military matters, besides the other misfortunes already mentioned, cannot be esteemed by his soldiers, nor have confidence in them.

He ought, therefore, never to let his thoughts stray from the exercise of war; and in peace he ought to practise it more than in war, which he can do in two ways: by action and by study. As to action, he must, besides keeping his men well disciplined and exercised, engage continually in hunting, and thus accustom his body to hardships; and meanwhile learn the nature of the land, how steep the mountains are, how the valleys debouch, where the plains lie, and understand the nature of rivers and swamps. To all this he should devote great attention. This knowledge is useful in two ways. In the first place, one learns to know one's country, and can the better see how to defend it. Then by means of the knowledge and experience gained in one locality, one can easily understand any other that it may be necessary to observe; for the hills and valleys, plains and rivers of Tuscany, for instance, have a certain resemblance to those of other provinces, so that from a knowledge of the country in one province one can easily arrive at a knowledge of others. And that prince who is lacking in this skill is wanting in the first essentials of a leader; for it is this which teaches how to find the enemy, take up quarters, lead armies, plan battles and lay siege to towns with advantage.

Philopœmen, prince of the Achaei, among other praises bestowed on him by writers, is lauded because in times of peace he thought of nothing but the methods of warfare, and when he was in the country with his friends, he often stopped and asked them: If the enemy were on that hill and we found ourselves here with our army, which of us would have the advantage? How could we safely approach him maintaining our order? If we wished to retire, what ought we to do? If they retired how should we follow them? And he put before them as they went along all the contingencies that might happen to an army, heard their opinion, gave his own, fortifying it by argument; so that thanks to these constant reflections there could never happen any incident when actually leading his armies for which he was not prepared.

But as to exercise for the mind, the prince ought to read history and study the actions of eminent men, see how they acted in warfare, examine the causes of their victories and defeats in order to imitate the former and avoid the latter, and above all, do as some men have done in the past, who have imitated some one, who has been much praised and glorified, and have always kept his deeds and actions before them, as they say Alexander the Great imitated Achilles, Cæsar Alexander, and Scipio Cyrus. And whoever reads the life of Cyrus written by Xenophon, will perceive in the life of Scipio how gloriously he imitated the former, and how, in chastity, affability, humanity, and liberality Scipio conformed to those qualities of Cyrus as described by Xenophon.

A wise prince should follow similar methods and never remain idle in peaceful times, but industriously make good use of them, so that when fortune changes she may find him prepared to resist her blows, and to prevail in adversity.

## DISCOURSES ON THE FIRST TEN BOOKS
## OF TITUS LIVIUS

When there is combined under the same constitution a prince, a nobility, and the power of the people, then these three powers will watch and keep each other reciprocally in check.

Amongst those justly celebrated for having established such a constitution, Lycurgus beyond doubt merits the highest praise. He organized the government of Sparta in such manner that, in giving to the king, the nobles, and the people each their portion of authority and duties, he created a government which maintained itself for over eight hundred years in the most perfect tranquillity, and reflected infinite glory upon this legislator. On the other hand, the constitution given by Solon to the Athenians, by which he established only a popular government, was of such short duration that before his death he saw the tyranny of Pisistratus arise. And although forty years afterwards the heirs of the tyrant were expelled, so that Athens recovered her liberties and restored the popular government according to the laws of Solon, yet it did not last over a hundred years; although a number of laws that had been overlooked by Solon were adopted, to maintain the government against the insolence of the nobles and the license of the populace. The fault he had committed in not tempering the power of the people and that of the prince and his nobles, made the duration of the government of Athens very short, as compared with that of Sparta.

But let us come to Rome. Although she had no legislator like Lycurgus, who constituted her government, at her very origin, in a manner to secure her liberty for a length of time, yet the disunion which existed between the Senate and the people produced such extraordinary events, that chance did for her what the laws had failed to do. Thus, if Rome did not attain the first degree of happiness, she at least had the second. Her first institutions were doubtless defective, but they were not in conflict with the principles that might bring her to perfection. For Romulus and all the other kings gave her many and good laws, well suited even to a free people; but as the object of these princes was to found a monarchy, and not a republic, Rome, upon becoming free, found herself lacking all those institutions that are most essential to liberty, and which her kings had not established. And although these kings lost their empire, . . . yet those who expelled them appointed immediately two consuls in place of the king; and thus it was found that they had banished the title of king from Rome, but not the regal power. The government, composed of Consuls and a Senate, had but two of the three elements of which we have spoken, the monarchical and the aristocratic; the popular power was wanting. In the course of time, however, the insolence of the nobles . . . induced the people to rise against the others. The nobility, to save a portion of their power, were forced to yield a share of it to the people; but the Senate and the Consuls retained sufficient to maintain their rank in the state. It was then that the Tribunes of the people were created, which strengthened and confirmed the republic, being now composed of the three elements of which we have spoken above. Fortune favored her, so that, although the authority passed successively from the kings and nobles to the people, by the same degrees and for the same reasons that we have spoken of, yet the royal authority was never entirely abolished to bestow it upon the nobles; and these were never entirely deprived of their authority to give it to the people; but a combination was formed of the three powers, which rendered the constitution perfect, and this perfection was attained by the disunion of the Senate and the people, as we shall more fully show. . . .

It cannot be denied that the Roman Empire was the result of good fortune and military discipline; but it seems to me that it ought to be perceived that where good discipline prevails there also will good order prevail, and good fortune rarely fails to follow in their train. Let us, however, go into details upon this point. I maintain that those who blame the quarrels of the Senate and the people of Rome condemn that which was the very origin of liberty, and that they were probably more impressed by the cries and noise which these disturbances occasioned in the public places, than by the good effect which

they produced; and that they do not consider that in every
republic there are two parties, that of the nobles and that of
the people; and all the laws that are favorable to liberty result
from the opposition of these parties to each other, as may easily be seen from the events that occurred in Rome. From the
time of the Tarquins to that of the Gracchi, that is to say,
within the space of over three hundred years, the differences
between these parties caused but very few exiles, and cost still
less blood; they cannot therefore be regarded as having been
very injurious and fatal to a republic, which during the course
of so many years saw on this account only eight or ten of its
citizens sent into exile, and but a very small number put to
death, and even but a few condemned to pecuniary fines. Nor
can we regard a republic as disorderly where so many virtues
were seen to shine. For good examples are the result of good
education, and good education is due to good laws; and good
laws in their turn spring from those very agitations which have
been so inconsiderately condemned by many. For whoever will
carefully examine the result of these agitations will find that
they have neither caused exiles nor any violence prejudicial to
the general good, and will be convinced even that they have
given rise to laws that were to the advantage of public liberty.
And if it be said that these are strange means,—to hear constantly the cries of the people furious against the Senate, and
of a Senate declaiming against the people, to see the populace
rush tumultuously through the streets, close their houses, and
even leave the city of Rome,—I reply, that all these things can
alarm only those who read of them, and that every free state
ought to afford the people the opportunity of giving vent, so to
say, to their ambition; and above all those republics which
on important occasions have to avail themselves of this very
people. Now such were the means employed at Rome; when
the people wanted to obtain a law, they resorted to some of
the extremes of which we have just spoken, or they refused to
enroll themselves to serve in the wars, so that the Senate was
obliged to satisfy them in some measure. . . . If the republic
had been more tranquil, it would necessarily have resulted that

she would have been more feeble, and that she would have lost with her energy also the ability of achieving that high degree of greatness to which she attained; so that to have removed the cause of trouble from Rome would have been to deprive her of her power of expansion. And thus it is seen in all human affairs, upon careful examination, that you cannot avoid one inconvenience without incurring another. If therefore you wish to make a people numerous and warlike, so as to create a great empire, you will have to constitute it in such manner as will cause you more difficulty in managing it; and if you keep it either small or unarmed, and you acquire other dominions, you will not be able to hold them, or you will become so feeble that you will fall a prey to whoever attacks you. And therefore in all our decisions we must consider well what presents the least inconveniences, and then choose the best, for we shall never find any course entirely free from objections. Rome then might, like Sparta, have created a king for life, and established a limited senate; but with her desire to become a great empire, she could not, like Sparta, limit the number of her citizens; and therefore a king for life and a limited senate would have been of no benefit to her so far as union was concerned. If any one therefore wishes to establish an entirely new republic, he will have to consider whether he wishes to have her expand in power and dominion like Rome, or whether he intends to confine her within narrow limits. In the first case, it will be necessary to organize her as Rome was, and submit to dissensions and troubles as best he may; for without a great number of men, and these well armed, no republic can ever increase. In the second case, he may organize her like Sparta and Venice; but as expansion is the poison of such republics, he must by every means in his power prevent her from making conquests, for such acquisitions by a feeble republic always prove their ruin, as happened to both Sparta and Venice; the first of which, having subjected to her rule nearly all Greece, exposed its feeble foundations at the slightest accident, for when the rebellion of Thebes occurred, which was led by Pelopidas, the other cities of Greece also rose up and almost ruined Sparta.

In like manner, Venice, having obtained possession of a great part of Italy, and the most of it not by war, but by means of money and fraud, when occasion came for her to give proof of her strength, she lost everything in a single battle. I think, then, that to found a republic which should endure a long time it would be best to organize her internally like Sparta, or to locate her, like Venice, in some strong place; and to make her sufficiently powerful, so that no one could hope to overcome her readily, and yet on the other hand not so powerful as to make her formidable to her neighbors. In this wise she might long enjoy her independence. For there are but two motives for making war against a republic: one, the desire to subjugate her; the other, the apprehension of being subjugated by her. The two means which we have indicated remove, as it were, both these pretexts for war; for if the republic is difficult to be conquered, her defences being well organized, as I presuppose, then it will seldom or never happen that any one will venture upon the project of conquering her. If she remains quiet within her limits, and experience shows that she entertains no ambitious projects, the fear of her power will never prompt any one to attack her; and this would even be more certainly the case if her constitution and laws prohibited all aggrandizement. And I certainly think that if she could be kept in this equilibrium it would be the best political existence, and would insure to any state real tranquillity. But as all human things are kept in a perpetual movement, and can never remain stable, states naturally either rise or decline, and necessity compels them to many acts to which reason will not influence them; so that, having organized a republic competent to maintain herself without expanding, still, if forced by necessity to extend her territory, in such case we shall see her foundations give way and herself quickly brought to ruin. And thus, on the other hand, if Heaven favors her so as never to be involved in war, the continued tranquillity would enervate her, or provoke internal dissensions, which together, or either of them separately, will be apt to prove her ruin. Seeing then the impossibility of establishing in this respect a perfect equilibrium, and that a precise middle course cannot be maintained, it is proper in the organization of a republic to select the most honorable course, and to constitute her so that, even if necessity should oblige her to expand, she may yet be able to preserve her acquisitions. To return now to our first argument, I believe it therefore necessary rather to take the constitution of Rome as a model than that of any other republic, (for I do not believe that a middle course between the two can be found,) and to tolerate the differences that will arise between the Senate and the people as an unavoidable inconvenience in achieving greatness like that of Rome.

◇◇◇◇◇◇◇◇◇◇◇◇◇◇◇◇◇◇◇◇◇◇◇◇◇◇◇◇◇◇◇◇◇◇◇◇◇◇◇◇◇◇◇◇◇◇◇◇

# 24. The Protection of Life, Liberty, and Property

*In 1689, one of the most influential books on politics ever written was first published: John Locke's* Two Treatises *of* Government. *Locke, in the second of his treatises, shows the connection between the internal and external powers of civil society. He defines this power differently than either Aristotle or Machiavelli had done; and he thereby contributes substantially to laying the foundation of the modern, constitutional state. The fact that he was, in earlier times, known as "America's philosopher," because of his influence on a number of the Founding Fathers of the Republic, makes him doubly interesting to American students of international relations.*

**JOHN LOCKE***

§ 3. Political power I take to be a right of making laws with penalties of death, and consequently all less penalties, for the

---

* From John Locke, *Two Treatises of Government,* in *The Works of John Locke* (9 vols.; London, 1824), II, sects. 3, 4, 6, 7, 14, 87, 88, 143–148, 175, 176.

regulating and preserving of property, and of employing the
force of the community, in the execution of such laws, and
in the defence of the commonwealth from foreign injury; and
all this only for the public good.

§ 4. To understand political power right, and derive it from
its original, we must consider what state all men are naturally
in, and that is, a state of perfect freedom to order their actions
and dispose of their possessions and persons, as they think fit,
within the bounds of the law of nature; without asking leave,
or depending upon the will of any other man.

A state also of equality, wherein all the power and jurisdiction is reciprocal, no one having more than another; there
being nothing more evident than that creatures of the same
species and rank, promiscuously born to all the same advantages of nature, and the use of the same faculties, should also
be equal one amongst another without subordination or subjection; unless the Lord and Master of them all should, by
any manifest declaration of his will, set one above another,
and confer on him, by an evident and clear appointment, an
undoubted right to dominion and sovereignty. . . .

§ 6. But though this be a state of liberty, yet it is not a state
of licence: though man in that state have an uncontrollable
liberty to dispose of his person or possessions, yet he has not
liberty to destroy himself, or so much as any creature in his
possession, but where some nobler use than its bare preservation calls for it. The state of nature has a law of nature to
govern it, which obliges every one: and reason, which is that
law, teaches all mankind, who will but consult it, that being
all equal and independent, no one ought to harm another in his
life, health, liberty, or possessions: for men being all the workmanship of one omnipotent and infinitely wise Maker; all the
servants of one sovereign Master, sent into the world by his
order, and about his business; they are his property, whose
workmanship they are, made to last during his, not another's
pleasure: and being furnished with like faculties, sharing all
in one community of nature, there cannot be supposed any
such subordination among us that may authorize us to destroy
another, as if we were made for one another's uses, as the

inferior ranks of creatures are for ours. Every one, as he is bound to preserve himself, and not to quit his station wilfully, so by the like reason, when his own preservation comes not in competition, ought he, as much as he can, to preserve the rest of mankind, and may not, unless it be to do justice to an offender, take away or impair the life, or what tends to the preservation of life, the liberty, health, limb, or goods of another.

§ 7. And that all men may be restrained from invading others' rights, and from doing hurt to one another, and the law of nature be observed, which willeth the peace and preservation of all mankind, the execution of the law of nature is, in that state, put into every man's hands, whereby every one has a right to punish the transgressors of that law to such a degree as may hinder its violation: for the law of nature would, as all other laws that concern men in this world, be in vain, if there were nobody that in the state of nature had a power to execute that law, and thereby preserve the innocent, and restrain offenders. And if any one in the state of nature may punish another for any evil he has done, every one may do so: for in that state of perfect equality, where naturally there is no superiority or jurisdiction of one over another, what any may do in prosecution of that law every one must needs have a right to do. . . .

§ 14. It is often asked, as a mighty objection, "where are or ever were there any men in such a state of nature?" To which it may suffice as an answer at present, that since all princes and rulers of independent governments, all through the world, are in a state of nature, it is plain the world never was, nor ever will be, without numbers of men in that state. I have named all governors of independent communities, whether they are, or are not, in league with others: for it is not every compact that puts an end to the state of nature between men, but only this one of agreeing together mutually to enter into one community, and make one body politic; other promises and compacts men may make one with another, and yet still be in the state of nature. . . .

§ 87. Man being born, as has been proved, with a title to

perfect freedom, and uncontrolled enjoyment of all the rights and privileges of the law of nature, equally with any other man, or number of men in the world, hath by nature a power, not only to preserve his property, that is, his life, liberty, and estate, against the injuries and attempts of other men; but to judge of and punish the breaches of that law in others, as he is persuaded the offence deserves, even with death itself, in crimes where the heinousness of the fact, in his opinion, requires it. But because no political society can be, nor subsist, without having in itself the power to preserve the property, and, in order thereunto, punish the offences of all those of that society; there, and there only is political society, where every one of the members hath quitted this natural power, resigned it up into the hands of the community in all cases that exclude him not from appealing for protection to the law established by it. And thus all private judgment of every particular member being excluded, the community comes to be umpire, by settled standing rules, indifferent, and the same to all parties; and by men having authority from the community, for the execution of those rules, decides all the differences that may happen between any members of that society concerning any matter of right; and punishes those offences which any member hath committed against the society, with such penalties as the law has established: whereby it is easy to discern who are, and who are not, in political society together. Those who are united into one body, and have a common established law and judicature to appeal to, with authority to decide controversies between them, and punish offenders, are in civil society one with another: but those who have no such common appeal, I mean on earth, are still in the state of nature, each being, where there is no other, judge for himself, and executioner: which is, as I have before showed it, the perfect state of nature.

§ 88. And thus the commonwealth comes by a power to set down what punishment shall belong to the several transgressions which they think worthy of it, committed amongst the members of that society, (which is the power of making laws) as well as it has the power to punish any injury done unto any of its members, by any one that is not of it, (which is the power of war and peace:) and all this for the preservation of the property of all the members of that society, as far as is possible. But though every man who has entered into civil society, and is become a member of any commonwealth, has thereby quitted his power to punish offences against the law of nature, in prosecution of his own private judgment; yet with the judgment of offences, which he has given up to the legislative in all cases, where he can appeal to the magistrate, he has given a right to the commonwealth to employ his force, for the execution of the judgments of the commonwealth, whenever he shall be called to it; which indeed are his own judgments, they being made by himself, or his representative. And herein we have the original of the legislative and executive power of civil society, which is to judge by standing laws, how far offences are to be punished, when committed within the commonwealth; and also to determine, by occasional judgments founded on the present circumstances of the fact, how far injuries from without are to be vindicated; and in both these to employ all the force of all the members, when there shall be need. . . .

§ 143. The legislative power is that, which has a right to direct how the force of the commonwealth shall be employed for preserving the community and the members of it. . . .

§ 144. But because the laws, that are at once, and in a short time made, having a constant and lasting force, and need a perpetual execution, or an attendance thereunto; therefore it is necessary there should be a power always in being, which should see to the execution of the laws that are made, and remain in force. And thus the legislative and executive power come often to be separated.

§ 145. There is another power in every commonwealth, which one may call natural, because it is that which answers to the power every man naturally had before he entered into society: for though in a commonwealth, the members of it are distinct persons still in reference to one another, and as such are governed by the laws of the society; yet in reference to the rest of mankind, they make one body, which is, as every member of it before was, still in the state of nature with the rest of mankind. Hence it is, that the controversies that happen between any man of the society with those that are out of it, are managed by the public; and an injury done to a member of their body engages the whole in the reparation of it. So that, under this consideration, the whole community is one body in the state of nature, in respect of all other states or persons out of its community.

§ 146. This therefore contains the power of war and peace, leagues and alliances, and all the transactions with all persons and communities without the commonwealth; and may be called federative, if any one pleases. So the thing be understood, I am indifferent as to the name.

§ 147. These two powers, executive and federative, though they be really distinct in themselves, yet one comprehending the execution of the municipal laws of the society within itself, upon all that are parts of it; the other the management of the security and interest of the public without, with all those that it may receive benefit or damage from; yet they are always almost united. And though this federative power in the well or ill management of it be of great moment to the commonwealth, yet it is much less capable to be directed by antecedent, standing, positive laws, than the executive; and so must necessarily be left to the prudence and wisdom of those whose hands it is in, to be managed for the public good: for the laws that concern subjects one amongst another, being to direct their actions, may well enough precede them. But what is to be done in reference to foreigners, depending much upon their actions, and the variation of designs, and interests, must be left in great part to the prudence of those who have this power committed to them, to be managed by the best of their skill, for the advantage of the commonwealth.

§ 148. Though, as I said, the executive and federative power of every community be really distinct in themselves, yet they are hardly to be separated, and placed at the same time in the hands of distinct persons: for both of them requiring the force of the society for their exercise, it is almost impracticable to place the force of the commonwealth in distinct, and

not subordinate hands; or that the executive and federative
power should be placed in persons that might act separately,
whereby the force of the public would be under different
commands; which would be apt some time or other to cause
disorder and ruin. . . .

§ 175. Though governments can originally have no other rise
than that before-mentioned, nor politics be founded on any
thing but the consent of the people; yet such have been the
disorders ambition has filled the world with, that in the noise
of war, which makes so great a part of the history of mankind, this consent is little taken notice of: and therefore many
have mistaken the force of arms for the consent of the people,
and reckon conquest as one of the originals of government.
But conquest is as far from setting up any government, as
demolishing a house is from building a new one in the place.
Indeed, it often makes way for a new frame of a commonwealth, by destroying the former; but, without the consent of
the people, can never erect a new one.

§ 176. That the aggressor, who puts himself into the state of
war with another, and unjustly invades another man's right,
can, by such an unjust war, never come to have a right over
the conquered, will be easily agreed by all men, who will not
think that robbers and pirates have a right of empire over
whomsoever they have force enough to master, or that men
are bound by promises which unlawful force extorts from them.
Should a robber break into my house, and with a dagger at
my throat make me seal deeds to convey my estate to him,
would this give him any title? Just such a title, by his sword,
has an unjust conqueror, who forces me into submission. The
injury and the crime are equal, whether committed by the
wearer of the crown or some petty villain. The title of the
offender, and the number of his followers, make no difference
in the offence, unless it be to aggravate it. The only difference
is, great robbers punish little ones, to keep them in their obedience; but the great ones are rewarded with laurels and tri-
umphs, because they are too big for the weak hands of justice
in this world, and have the power in their own possession
which should punish offenders. What is my remedy against

a robber, that so broke into my house? Appeal to the law for justice. But perhaps justice is denied, or I am crippled and cannot stir, robbed and have not the means to do it. If God has taken away all means of seeking remedy, there is nothing left but patience. But my son, when able, may seek the relief of the law, which I am denied: he or his son may renew his appeal, till he recover his right. But the conquered, or their children, have no court, no arbitrator on earth to appeal to. Then they may appeal, as Jephthah did, to heaven, and repeat their appeal till they have recovered the native right of their ancestors, which was, to have such a legislative over them as the majority should approve, and freely acquiesce in. If it be objected, this would cause endless trouble; I answer, no more than justice does, where she lies open to all that appeal to her. He that troubles his neighbour without a cause, is punished for it by the justice of the court he appeals to; and he that appeals to heaven must be sure he has right on his side, and a right too that is worth the trouble and cost of the appeal, as he will answer at a tribunal that cannot be deceived, and will be sure to retribute to every one according to the mischiefs he hath created to his fellow-subjects; that is, any part of mankind: from whence it is plain, that he that "conquers in an unjust war, can thereby have no title to the subjection and obedience of the conquered."

◇◇◇◇◇◇◇◇◇◇◇◇◇◇◇◇◇◇◇◇◇◇◇◇◇◇◇◇◇◇◇◇◇◇◇◇◇◇◇◇◇◇◇◇◇◇◇◇◇◇◇

# 25. The Value of War

*When Treitschke, whom we have encountered already in considering the concepts of "independence" and "sovereignty," wrote his* Politics *in the nineteenth century, he provided fuel for those who attacked the basic idea of the limited, "constitutional" state. His ideas are reminiscent of those of Machiavelli,*

*but with the difference that Treitschke tends to single out war,
as such, as being a fundamental purpose of the state; whereas
Machiavelli seems to accept war as part of the necessitous
character of political life. The difference is important, especially in trying to understand how it is that, in the twentieth
century, ideas of the value of war could be traced to influential
thinkers of the preceding century.*

## HEINRICH VON TREITSCHKE*

Theoretically, . . . no limit can be set to the functions of a
State. It will attempt to dominate the outer life of its members
as far as it is able to do so. A more fruitful subject for specu-
lation will be to fix the theoretic minimum for its activity, and
decide what functions it must at the least fulfil before it can
be given the name of State. When we have set this minimum
we shall come to the further question of how far beyond it the
State may reasonably extend its action. We then see at once
that since its first duty, as we have already said, is the double
one of maintaining power without, and law within, its primary
obligations must be the care of its Army and its Jurisprudence,
in order to protect and to restrain the community of its citizens. The fulfilment of these two functions is attained by certain
material means; therefore some form of fiscal system must
exist, even in the most primitive of States, in order to provide
these means.

No State can endure which can no longer fulfil these ele-
mentary duties. It is only in abnormal circumstances that we
find any exception to this rule, as when an artificial balance
of power protects the smaller States which can no longer protect
themselves.

The functions of the State in maintaining its own internal administration of justice are manifold. It must firstly, in civil law,
place the prescribed limit upon the individual will. It will
nevertheless proportionately restrict its own activity in this
sphere, since no individual is compelled to exercise his own

---

* From Heinrich von Treitschke, *Politics*, trans. B. Dugdale and
T. De Bille (London: Constable and Co., Ltd., 1916), I, 63–66. Reprinted by permission of Constable and Co.

legal rights. Here the State will issue no direct commands, but merely act as mediator, leaving the carrying out of its decrees to the free will of the contracting parties. . . .

The interference of the State is more active in the domain of criminal law. Here it exercises compulsion in order to protect its legal ordinances against the invasion of evil design, and here it lays down what the rights and duties of its citizens should be. In sharp contrast with the principles of civil jurisprudence, the individual is here given no choice whether he will or will not act in full accordance with the law. The principles of common law are so absolutely binding that they are synonymous with duty.

The State decides the measure of the citizen's share in the Constitution. Public servants have no option in the extent to which they will exercise their functions. For instance, if the State refrains from imposing universal suffrage as a duty, it does so only upon grounds of expediency.

The next essential function of the State is the conduct of war. The long oblivion into which this principle had fallen is a proof of how effeminate the science of government had become in civilian hands. . . .

Without war no State could be. All those we know of arose through war, and the protection of their members by armed force remains their primary and essential task. War, therefore, will endure to the end of history, as long as there is multiplicity of States. The laws of human thought and of human nature forbid any alternative, neither is one to be wished for. The blind worshipper of an eternal peace falls into the error of isolating the State, or dreams of one which is universal, which we have already seen to be at variance with reason.

Even as it is impossible to conceive of a tribunal above the State, which we have recognized as sovereign in its very essence, so it is likewise impossible to banish the idea of war from the world. It is a favourite fashion of our time to instance England as particularly ready for peace. But England is perpetually at war; there is hardly an instant in her recent history in which she has not been obliged to be fighting somewhere. The great strides which civilization makes against barbarism and unreason are only made actual by the sword. Between civilized nations also war is the form of litigation by which States makes their claims valid. The arguments brought forward in these terrible law suits of the nations compel as no argument in civil suits can ever do. Often as we have tried by theory to convince the small States that Prussia alone can be the leader in Germany, we had to produce the final proof upon the battlefields of Bohemia and the Main.

Moreover war is a uniting as well as a dividing element among nations; it does not draw them together in enmity only, for through its means they learn to know and to respect each other's peculiar qualities.

It is important not to look upon war always as a judgment from God. Its consequences are evanescent; but the life of a nation is reckoned by centuries, and the final verdict can only be pronounced after the survey of whole epochs.

Such a State as Prussia might indeed be brought near to destruction by a passing phase of degeneracy; but being by the character of its people more reasonable and more free than the French, it retained the power to call up the moral force within itself, and so to regain its ascendancy.[1] Most undoubtedly war is the one remedy for an ailing nation. Social selfishness and party hatreds must be dumb before the call of the State when its existence is at stake. Forgetting himself, the individual must only remember that he is a part of the whole, and realize the unimportance of his own life compared with the common weal.

The grandeur of war lies in the utter annihilation of puny man in the great conception of the State, and it brings out the full magnificence of the sacrifice of fellow-countrymen for one another. In war the chaff is winnowed from the wheat. . . .

It is war which fosters the political idealism which the materialist rejects. What a disaster for civilization it would be if mankind blotted its heroes from memory. The heroes of a nation are the figures which rejoice and inspire the spirit of its youth, and the writers whose words ring like trumpet blasts

---

[1] The reference here is to the Prussian victory over France in the Franco-Prussian War, 1870–1871.

become the idols of our boyhood and our early manhood. He who feels no answering thrill is unworthy to bear arms for his country. To appeal from this judgment to Christianity would be sheer perversity, for does not the Bible distinctly say that the ruler shall rule by the sword, and again that greater love hath no man than to lay down his life for his friend? To Aryan races, who are before all things courageous, the foolish preaching of everlasting peace has always been vain. They have always been men enough to maintain with the sword what they have attained through the spirit. . . .

. . . It did not strike the Ancients as possible that the State could legislate too much. The words of Tacitus, *in pessima republica plurimae leges,* which are so often and so willingly quoted in this context, simply mean that when the morals of a State are bad it may seek in vain to remedy the evil by a multitude of laws.

The modern theory of individualism, decked with its various titles, stands as the poles asunder from these conceptions of antiquity. From it the doctrine emanates that the State should content itself with protection of life and property, and with wings thus clipped be pompously dubbed a Constitutional State.

This teaching is the legitimate child of the old doctrine of Natural Law. According to it the State can only exist as a means for the individual's ends. The more ideal the view adopted of human life, the more certain does it seem that the State should content itself with the purely exterior protective functions. William Humboldt [2] sets forth this belief in its most alluring and intelligent form in one of his early writings, *Suggestions for an Attempt to define the Boundaries of the State's Activity.* The State, he says, should defend the lives and goods of its citizens, and for the rest ensure to them the greatest possible freedom. Without liberty there is no morality; therefore a State-enforced morality is worthless, and the State must abstain from interference in the free life of its members. . . .

. . . But when we probe this theory which has cast its spell over so many distinguished men, we find that it has totally

---

[2] Humboldt (1767–1835) was, by turn, scholar, diplomat, minister of state, and patriot.

overlooked the continuity of history, and the bond which unites the succeeding generations. The State, as we have seen, is enduring; humanly speaking, it is eternal. Its work therefore is to prepare the foundations for the future. If it existed only to protect the life and goods of its citizens it would not dare to go to war, for wars are waged for the sake of honour, and not for protection of property. They cannot therefore be explained by the empty theory which makes the State no more than an Insurance Society. Honour is a moral postulate, not a juridical conception. . . .

. . . It may no doubt be proved that the Constitutional State may discharge all the duties of promoting culture. But all this is mere juggling with phrases. It behoves us to say boldly that the idea of the Constitutional State is not adequate to express the real essence of the State and its functions. The State is a moral community called to positive labours for the improvement of the human race, and its ultimate aim is to build up real national character through and within itself, for this is the highest moral duty of nations as well as individuals. When we have taken this to our hearts we are able to perceive that the Germans are far from having accomplished these great national tasks. National character is exactly what they lack in comparison with their neighbours, for their unity is so young. A sure and certain national instinct is not a universal quality with us, as it is with the French people.

We may, then, shortly call the State the instrument of civilization, and demand of it positive labour for the economic and intellectual welfare of its members. History shows us how the sphere of the State's activity widens with the growth of culture. Everything which we call Government in the strict sense has been created through the progress of civilization. . . .

# IX. The Continuum of Alternatives: Constitutional Democracy in the Twentieth Century

*From 1815 until 1914, no major war took place in Europe. Jack London, writing in 1911, voiced a widely held opinion when he said: "War itself, the old red anarch, is passing. . . . Not only has war, by its own evolution rendered itself futile, but man himself, with greater wisdom and higher ethics, is opposed to war." Since those optimistic words were committed to paper, two devastating world wars and the eruption of Fascism and Communism as political systems have taken place. Twentieth-century conflict among such different political systems reflects, among other factors, different conceptions of the purpose of the state. It is the purpose of this and the next two sections to present a number of statements, by political actors within those different systems, of the purpose of the state in relation to other states. Such statements, because they are largely* ad hoc, *and refer to specific political situations, necessarily lack the systematic quality to be found in the works of the four theorists included in the preceding section. But in one sense, this* ad hoc *quality of the statements is instructive: it reveals, in concrete historical situations, the application of the general concepts and principles shared by different men in different political systems.*

*The spokesmen for constitutional democracy are three great statesmen: Woodrow Wilson, an American President leading his country in war against the autocratic German state; Winston Churchill, a British Prime Minister analyzing British policy towards the continent; and Charles de Gaulle, the French President of the Fifth Republic defining the task of the modern state in a crisis-ridden age. Their statements should be read as* ad hoc *definitions of the purpose of the state by concrete example.*

◇◇◇◇◇◇◇◇◇◇◇◇◇◇◇◇◇◇◇◇◇◇◇◇◇◇◇◇◇◇◇◇◇◇◇◇◇◇◇◇◇◇◇◇◇◇

# 26. An American View

*On April 6, 1917, the United States declared war on Germany. On June 14, President Wilson delivered an address in Washington. Its theme—that dedication to the flag is dedication of a people to its true cause—was to become the rallying cry of the President in leading the American state into the war against Germany.*

## WOODROW WILSON

### "THIS IS A PEOPLE'S WAR"*

We meet to celebrate Flag Day because this flag which we honor and under which we serve is the emblem of our unity, our power, our thought and purpose as a Nation. It has no other character than that which we give it from generation to generation. . . . We are about to carry it into battle, to lift it where it will draw the fire of our enemies. We are about to bid thousands, hundreds of thousands, it may be millions, of our men, the young, the strong, the capable men of the Nation, to go forth and die beneath it on fields of blood far away,—for what? For some unaccustomed thing? For something for which it has never sought the fire before? American armies were never before sent across the seas. Why are they sent now? For some new purpose, for which this great flag has never been carried before, or for some old, familiar, heroic purpose for which it has seen men, its own men, die on every battlefield upon which Americans have borne arms since the Revolution?

---

* From Woodrow Wilson, *War and Peace: Presidential Messages, Addresses, Public Papers (1917–1924)* (New York and London: Harper and Brothers, 1927), Vol. I, pp. 60–67.

These are questions which must be answered. We are Americans. We in our turn serve America, and can serve her with no private purpose. We must use her flag as she has always used it. We are accountable at the bar of history and must plead in utter frankness what purpose it is we seek to serve.

It is plain enough how we were forced into the war. The extraordinary insults and aggressions of the Imperial German Government left us no self-respecting choice but to take up arms in defense of our rights as a free people and of our honor as a sovereign government. The military masters of Germany denied us the right to be neutral. . . .

But that is only part of the story. We know now as clearly as we knew before we were ourselves engaged that we are not the enemies of the German people and that they are not our enemies. They did not originate or desire this hideous war or wish that we should be drawn into it; and we are vaguely conscious that we are fighting their cause, as they will some day see it, as well as our own. They are themselves in the grip of the same sinister power that has now at last stretched its ugly talons out and drawn blood from us. The whole world is at war because the whole world is in the grip of that power and is trying out the great battle which shall determine whether it is to be brought under its mastery or fling itself free. . . .

. . . The great fact that stands out above all the rest is that this is a Peoples' War, a war for freedom and justice and self-government amongst all the nations of the world, a war to make the world safe for the peoples who live upon it and have made it their own, the German people themselves included; and that with us rests the choice to break through all these hypocrisies and patent cheats and masks of brute force and help set the world free, or else stand aside and let it be dominated a long age through by sheer weight of arms, and the arbitrary choices of self-constituted masters, by the nation which can maintain the biggest armies and the most irresistible armaments,—a power to which the world has afforded no parallel and in the face of which political freedom must wither and perish.

For us there is but one choice. We have made it. Woe be

to the man or group of men that seeks to stand in our way
in this day of high resolution when every principle we hold
dearest is to be vindicated and made secure for the salvation
of the nations. We are ready to plead at the bar of history,
and our flag shall wear a new luster. Once more we shall make
good with our lives and fortunes the great faith to which we
were born, and a new glory shall shine in the face of our people.

*More than a year after his Flag Day address, President Wilson,
speaking at Mount Vernon, chose American Independence Day
to set forth a series of four points defining United States purposes in the war. The scope of the commitment which this set
of purposes entails extends the purpose of the state considerably beyond what had traditionally been thought to be true.*

## THE FOUR POINTS*

. . . These are the ends for which the associated peoples
of the world are fighting and which must be conceded them
before there can be peace:

1. The destruction of every arbitary power anywhere that
can separately, secretly, and of its single choice disturb the
peace of the world; or, if it cannot be presently destroyed, at
the least its reduction to virtual impotence.

2. The settlement of every question, whether of territory, of
sovereignty, of economic arrangement, or of political relationship, upon the basis of the free acceptance of that settlement
by the people immediately concerned, and not upon the basis
of the material interest or advantage of any other nation or
people which may desire a different settlement for the sake
of its own exterior influence or mastery.

3. The consent of all nations to be governed in their conduct towards each other by the same principles of honor and
of respect for the common law of civilized society that govern
the individual citizens of all modern states in their relations
with one another; to the end that all promises and covenants
may be sacredly observed, no private plots or conspiracies

---

* From Wilson, *op. cit.,* I, pp. 233–234.

hatched, no selfish injuries wrought with impunity, and a mutual trust established upon the handsome foundation of a mutual respect for right.

4. The establishment of an organization of peace which shall make it certain that the combined power of free nations will check every invasion of right and serve to make peace and justice the more secure by affording a definite tribunal of opinion to which all must submit and by which every international readjustment that cannot be amicably agreed upon by the peoples directly concerned shall be sanctioned.

These great objects can be put into a single sentence. What we seek is the reign of law, based upon the consent of the governed and sustained by the organized opinion of mankind.

These great ends cannot be achieved by debating and seeking to reconcile and accommodate what statesmen may wish, with their projects for balances of power and of national opportunity. They can be realized only by the determination of what the thinking peoples of the world desire, with their longing hope for justice and for social freedom and opportunity.

*When the war ended, Wilson entered upon his great project of binding the United States to its task, as he conceived it, by ensuring its participation in the League of Nations. On September 5, 1919, in one of many speeches given around the country, he talked to a distinguished group of citizens in St. Louis. In defending what he claimed was a "new system" of international politics, he stated, in concise form, his own understanding of what the purpose of the state is: to act so as to make humanity better.*

## WORLD POLITICS *

. . . The politics of the world, the policy of mankind, the concert of the methods by which the world is to be bettered, that concert of will and of action which will make every nation a nobler instrument of Divine Providence—that is world politics.

I have sometimes heard gentlemen discussing the questions

---

* From Wilson, *op. cit.*, I, p. 621.

that are now before us with a distinction drawn between nationalism and internationalism in these matters. It is very difficult for me to follow their distinction. The greatest nationalist
is the man who wants his nation to be the greatest nation, and
the greatest nation is the nation which penetrates to the heart
of its duty and mission among the nations of the world. With
every flash of insight into the great politics of mankind, the
nation that has that vision is elevated to a place of influence
and power which it cannot get by arms, which it cannot get
by commercial rivalry, which it can get by no other way than
by that spiritual leadership which comes from a profound
understanding of the problems of humanity. . . .

◇◇◇◇◇◇◇◇◇◇◇◇◇◇◇◇◇◇◇◇◇◇◇◇◇◇◇◇◇◇◇◇◇◇◇◇◇◇◇◇◇◇◇◇◇◇◇◇◇◇

# 27. A British View

*Sir Winston Churchill's six-volume memoir on World War II
is a rich and exciting source book for those who would study at
first hand the thought, action and speech of one of the great
modern statesmen. His analysis of the fateful events which led
to the outbreak of the war emphasizes the vacillation and lack
of understanding of most British, French and other western
democratic leaders. The first selection here is presented by him
as a statement he had made, already in 1936, of the basic principles to guide British policy.*

## SIR WINSTON CHURCHILL

### PRINCIPLES OF FOREIGN POLICY *

For four hundred years the foreign policy of England has
been to oppose the strongest, most aggressive, most dominating

---

* From Winston S. Churchill, *The Gathering Storm* (Boston: Houghton Mifflin Co., 1948), pp. 207–210. Reprinted by permission of
Houghton Mifflin Co.

Power on the Continent, and particularly to prevent the Low Countries falling into the hands of such a Power. Viewed in the light of history, these four centuries of consistent purpose amid so many changes of names and facts, of circumstances and conditions, must rank as one of the most remarkable episodes which the records of any race, nation, state, or people can show. Moreover, on all occasions England took the more difficult course. Faced by Philip II of Spain, against Louis XIV under William III and Marlborough, against Napoleon, against William II of Germany, it would have been easy and must have been very tempting to join with the stronger and share the fruits of his conquest. However, we always took the harder course, joined with the less strong Powers, made a combination among them, and thus defeated and frustrated the Continental military tyrant whoever he was, whatever nation he led. Thus we preserved the liberties of Europe, protected the growth of its vivacious and varied society, and emerged after four terrible struggles with an ever-growing fame and widening Empire, and with the Low Countries safety protected in their independence. Here is the wonderful unconscious tradition of British foreign policy. All our thoughts rest in that tradition today. I know of nothing which has occurred to alter or weaken the justice, wisdom, valour, and prudence upon which our ancestors acted. I know of nothing that has happened to human nature which in the slightest degree alters the validity of their conclusions. I know of nothing in military, political, economic, or scientific fact which makes me feel that we might not, or cannot, march along the same road. I venture to put this very general proposition before you because it seems to me that if it is accepted, everything else becomes much more simple.

Observe that the policy of England takes no account of which nation it is that seeks the overlordship of Europe. The question is not whether it is Spain, or the French Monarchy, or the French Empire, or the German Empire, or the Hitler régime. It has nothing to do with rulers or nations; it is concerned solely with whoever is the strongest or the potentially dominating tyrant. Therefore, we should not be afraid of being accused of being pro-French or anti-German. If the circumstances were reversed, we could equally be pro-German and anti-French. It is a law of public policy which we are following, and not a mere expedient dictated by accidental circumstances, or likes and dislikes, or any other sentiment.

The question, therefore, arises which is today the Power in Europe which is the strongest, and which seeks in a dangerous and oppressive sense to dominate. Today, for this year, probably for part of 1937, the French Army is the strongest in Europe. But no one is afraid of France. Everyone knows that France wants to be let alone, and that with her it is only a case of self-preservation. Everyone knows that the French are peaceful and overhung by fear. They are at once brave, resolute, peace-loving, and weighed down by anxiety. They are a liberal nation with free parliamentary institutions.

Germany, on the other hand, fears no one. She is arming in a manner which has never been seen in German history. She is led by a handful of triumphant desperadoes. The money is running short, discontents are arising beneath these despotic rulers. Very soon they will have to choose, on the one hand, between economic and financial collapse or internal upheaval, and on the other, a war which could have no other object, and which, if successful, can have no other result, than a Germanised Europe under Nazi control. Therefore, it seems to me that all the old conditions present themselves again, and that our national salvation depends upon our gathering once again all the forces of Europe to contain, to restrain, and if necessary to frustrate, German domination. For, believe me, if any of those other Powers, Spain, Louis XIV, Napoleon, Kaiser Wilhelm II, had with our aid become the absolute masters of Europe, they could have despoiled us, reduced us to insignificance and penury on the morrow of their victory. We ought to set the life and endurance of the British Empire and the greatness of this island very high in our duty, and not be led astray by illusions about an ideal world, which only means that other and worse controls will step into our place, and that the future direction will belong to them.

It is at this stage that the spacious conception and extremely vital organisation of the League of Nations presents itself as a prime factor. The League of Nations is, in a practical sense, a British conception, and it harmonises perfectly with all our past methods and actions. Moreover, it harmonises with those broad ideas of right and wrong, and of peace based upon controlling the major aggressor, which we have always followed. We wish for the reign of law and freedom among nations and within nations, and it was for that, and nothing less than that, that those bygone architects of our repute, magnitude, and civilisation fought, and won. The dream of a reign of international law and of the settlement of disputes by patient discussion, but still in accordance with what is lawful and just, is very dear to the British people. You must not underrate the force which these ideals exert upon the modern British democracy. One does not know how these seeds are planted by the winds of the centuries in the hearts of the working people. They are there, and just as strong as their love of liberty. We should not neglect them, because they are the essence of the genius of this island. Therefore, we believe that in the fostering and fortifying of the League of Nations will be found the best means of defending our island security, as well as maintaining grand universal causes with which we have very often found our own interests in natural accord.

My three main propositions are: First, that we must oppose the would-be dominator or potential aggressor. Secondly, that Germany under its present Nazi régime and with its prodigious armaments, so swiftly developing, fills unmistakably that part. Thirdly, that the League of Nations rallies many countries, and unites our own people here at home in the most effective way to control the would-be aggressor. I venture most respectfully to submit these main themes to your consideration. Everything else will follow from them.

It is always more easy to discover and proclaim general principles than to apply them. First, we ought to count our effective association with France. That does not mean that we should develop a needlessly hostile mood against Germany. It is a part of our duty and our interest to keep the temperature low between these two countries. We shall not have any difficulty in this so far as France is concerned. Like us, they are a parliamentary democracy with tremendous inhibitions against war, and, like us, under considerable drawbacks in preparing their defence. Therefore, I say we ought to regard our defensive association with France as fundamental. Everything else must be viewed in proper subordination now that the times have become so sharp and perilous. Those who are possessed of a definite body of doctrine and of deeply rooted convictions upon it will be in a much better position to deal with the shifts and surprises of daily affairs than those who are merely taking short views, and indulging their natural impulses as they are evoked by what they read from day to day. The first thing is to decide where you want to go. For myself, I am for the armed League of all Nations, or as many as you can get, against the potential aggressor, with England and France as the core of it. Let us neglect nothing in our power to establish the great international framework. If that should prove to be beyond our strength, or if it breaks down through the weakness or wrong-doing of others, then at least let us make sure that England and France, the two surviving free great countries of Europe, can together ride out any storm that may blow with good and reasonable hopes of once again coming safely into port.

*In reflecting upon the "tragedy of Munich," Churchill was struck by the awful responsibility which a statesman had in deciding whether to make war to defend certain principles. This was the occasion for him to set forth, even if only briefly and somewhat elliptically, his view of the moral dimension of state action.*

## THE PRIMACY OF HONOR *

It may be well here to set down some principles of morals and action which may be a guide in the future. No case of this kind can be judged apart from its circumstances. The facts may be unknown at the time, and estimates of them must be

---

* From Winston S. Churchill, *The Gathering Storm* (Boston: Houghton Mifflin Co., 1948), pp. 319–320. Reprinted by permission of Houghton Mifflin Co.

largely guesswork, coloured by the general feelings and aims of whoever is trying to pronounce. Those who are prone by temperament and character to seek sharp and clear-cut solutions of difficult and obscure problems, who are ready to fight whenever some challenge comes from a foreign Power, have not always been right. On the other hand, those whose inclination is to bow their heads, to seek patiently and faithfully for peaceful compromise, are not always wrong. On the contrary, in the majority of instances they may be right, not only morally but from a practical standpoint. How many wars have been averted by patience and persisting good will! Religion and virtue alike lend their sanctions to meekness and humility, not only between men but between nations. How many wars have been precipitated by firebrands! How many misunderstandings which led to wars could have been removed by temporising! How often have countries fought cruel wars and then after a few years of peace found themselves not only friends but allies!

The Sermon on the Mount is the last word in Christian ethics. Everyone respects the Quakers. Still, it is not on these terms that Ministers assume their responsibilities of guiding states. Their duty is first so to deal with other nations as to avoid strife and war and to eschew aggression in all its forms, whether for nationalistic or ideological objects. But the safety of the State, the lives and freedom of their own fellow countrymen, to whom they owe their position, make it right and imperative in the last resort, or when a final and definite conviction has been reached, that the use of force should not be excluded. If the circumstances are such as to warrant it, force may be used. And if this be so, it should be used under the conditions which are most favourable. There is no merit in putting off a war for a year if, when it comes, it is a far worse war or one much harder to win. These are the tormenting dilemmas upon which mankind has throughout its history been so frequently impaled. Final judgment upon them can only be recorded by history in relation to the facts of the case as known to the parties at the time, and also as subsequently proved.

There is, however, one helpful guide, namely, for a nation to keep its word and to act in accordance with its treaty obligations to allies. This guide is called *honour*. It is baffling to reflect that what men call honour does not correspond always to Christian ethics. Honour is often influenced by that element of pride which plays so large a part in its inspiration. An exaggerated code of honour leading to the performance of utterly vain and unreasonable deeds could not be defended, however fine it might look. Here, however, the moment came when Honour pointed the path of Duty, and when also the right judgment of the facts at that time would have reinforced its dictates.

For the French Government to leave her faithful ally, Czechoslovakia, to her fate was a melancholy lapse from which flowed terrible consequences. Not only wise and fair policy, but chivalry, honour, and sympathy for a small threatened people made an overwhelming concentration. Great Britain, who would certainly have fought if bound by treaty obligations, was nevertheless now deeply involved, and it must be recorded with regret that the British Government not only acquiesced but encouraged the French Government in a fatal course.

*During the early part of the war the democratic states went from defeat to defeat. In December of 1939, Churchill, then still Lord of the Admiralty, was greatly concerned by the fact that the Nazis were obtaining iron ore from Norway. The question was how to stop this. Churchill says that he was very reluctant to mine the territorial waters of Norway, which would be a violation of international law; but he concluded that this must be done, and summarized his reasoning in the final section of a memorandum to his colleagues.*

## LAW AND STATE ACTION *

The effect of our action against Norway upon world opinion and upon our own reputation must be considered. We have taken up arms in accordance with the principles of the Covenant of the League in order to aid the victims of German

---

* From Winston S. Churchill, *The Gathering Storm* (Boston: Houghton Mifflin Co., 1948), p. 547. Reprinted by permission of Houghton Mifflin Co.

aggression. No technical infringement of international law, so long as it is unaccompanied by inhumanity of any kind, can deprive us of the good wishes of neutral countries. No evil effect will be produced upon the greatest of all neutrals, the United States. We have reason to believe that they will handle the matter in the way most calculated to help us. And they are very resourceful.

The final tribunal is our own conscience. We are fighting to re-establish the reign of law and to protect the liberties of small countries. Our defeat would mean an age of barbaric violence, and would be fatal, not only to ourselves, but to the independent life of every small country in Europe. Acting in the name of the Covenant, and as virtual mandatories of the League and all it stands for, we have a right, and indeed are bound in duty, to abrogate for a space some of the conventions of the very laws we seek to consolidate and reaffirm. Small nations must not tie our hands when we are fighting for their rights and freedom. The letter of the law must not in supreme emergency obstruct those who are charged with its protection and enforcement. It would not be right or rational that the aggressor Power should gain one set of advantages by tearing up all laws, and another set by sheltering behind the innate respect for law of its opponents. Humanity, rather than legality, must be our guide.

Of all this history must be the judge. We now face events.

◇◇◇◇◇◇◇◇◇◇◇◇◇◇◇◇◇◇◇◇◇◇◇◇◇◇◇◇◇◇◇◇◇◇◇◇◇◇◇◇◇◇◇◇◇◇◇◇◇◇◇◇◇

# 28. A French View

*Charles de Gaulle's leadership of France, at various periods since the dark days of 1939, has proved to be a turbulent affair. As President of the newly constituted Fifth Republic, his major object has been to reestablish French fortunes at home and*

*abroad. In the first selection, de Gaulle speaks on May 31, 1960
to the French nation on the occasion of the sudden, unexpected
failure of a "Summit Conference" of Western and Soviet leaders. His remarks should be compared to those of Wilson for
the implications they contain of the purpose of the state in the
international arena.*

## CHARLES DE GAULLE

### INTERNATIONAL LIFE AS A BATTLE *

Man "limited by his nature" is "infinite in his desires." The
world is thus full of opposing forces. Of course, human wisdom
has often succeeded in preventing these rivalries from degen-
erating into murderous conflicts. But the competition of efforts
is the condition of life. Our country finds itself confronted today
with this law of the species, as it has been for 2,000 years.

The division of the peoples that inhabit Europe and North
America is the main fact and the worst evil of our time. Two
camps are set up, face to face, under conditions such that it
depends solely on Moscow or Washington whether or not a
large part of humanity is wiped out in a few hours.

In the face of such a situation, France deems that there is
no territorial disagreement or ideological dispute that has any
importance by comparison with the necessity of exorcising this
monstrous peril. In France's view, this situation implies three
conditions.

The first is a détente, in other words, the bettering of international relations, putting a stop to provocative actions and
speeches and increasing trade, cultural exchanges and the visits
of tourists in order that a more peaceful atmosphere might be
created. . . .

. . . The second condition is a specific degree of controlled
disarmament, preferably aimed at the devices capable of carrying bombs to strategic distances, in order that the possibility—
and, at the same time—the temptation suddenly to provoke
general destruction might vanish.

---

* From *Major Addresses, Statements and Press Conferences of General
Charles de Gaulle,* (May 19, 1958–January 31, 1964), French Embassy,
Press and Information Division. Pp. 75–78.

The third condition is a beginning of organized cooperation between East and West devoted to the service of man, either by helping in the progress of underdeveloped peoples or by collaborating in the great projects of scientific research, on which depends the future of all. . . .

Yet, until we achieve an organized peace, if that is at all possible, France intends, as far as she is concerned, to be ready to defend herself. This means, first of all, that she shall remain an integral part of the Atlantic Alliance. Moreover, the recent trial has shown the deep-seated solidarity which exists among the Western powers. Of course, President Eisenhower, Prime Minister Macmillan and I each have our own problems and our own temperament. But, when faced with recent events, we three, in view of the friendship which unites us, did not have much trouble in reaching agreement, in wisdom and in firmness. Our alliance appeared a living reality. In order that it become even more so, France must have her own role in it, and her own personality. This implies that she too must acquire a nuclear armament since others have one; that she must be sole mistress of her resources and her territory, in short, that her destiny, although associated with that of her allies, must remain in her own hands. It goes without saying that such an autonomy must be coupled with an ever closer coordination among the Western world powers, regarding their policy and their strategy.

But if the Atlantic Alliance is necessary at present for the security of France and of the other free peoples of our old continent, they must, behind this shield, organize to achieve their joint power and development. The trials they have gone through showed them how much their divisions and conflicts had cost them. Neither the Rhine, nor the Low Countries, nor the Alps, nor the Pyrenees, nor the English Channel nor the Mediterranean, for which they fought so long and so bitterly, any longer set them one against the other. No feeling of hatred remains between them. On the contrary, the nostalgia inspired in each of these lands by its relative downfall in relation to the great new empires, has drawn them closer in the feeling that together they would regain this grandeur for which past centuries had given them the talent and the habit. To this must be added the fact that they constitute an incomparable whole, precisely when our time, which abolishes distances and obstacles, demands large ensembles.

To contribute to build Western Europe into a political, economic, cultural and human group, organized for action, progress and defense—that is what France wants to work toward. Already West Germany, Italy, The Netherlands, Belgium and Luxembourg are cooperating directly with her in several fields. In particular, the Common Market of the Six will, on December 31, become a practical reality. Of course, the participants do not want this organization to injure the other countries of Europe, and we must expect a way to be found of accommodating interests. Also of course, the nations which are becoming associated must not cease to be themselves, and the path to be followed must be that of organized cooperation between states, while waiting to achieve, perhaps, an imposing confederation. But France, as far as she is concerned, has recognized the necessity of this Western Europe, which in former times was the dream of the wise and the ambition of the powerful and which appears today as the indispensable condition of the equilibrium of the world.

Now, in the last analysis and as always, it is only in equilibrium that the world will find peace. On our old continent, the organization of a western group, at the very least equivalent to that which exists in the east, may one day, without risk to the independence and the freedom of each nation and taking into account the probable evolution of political regimes, establish a European entente from the Atlantic to the Urals. Then Europe, no longer split in two by ambitions and ideologies become out-of-date, would again be the heart of civilization. The accession to progress of the masses of Asia, Africa and Latin America would certainly be hastened and facilitated. But also, the cohesion of this great and strong European Community would lead vast countries in other continents, which are advancing toward power, also to take the way of cooperation, rather than to yield to the temptation of war.

Yes, international life, like life in general, is a battle. The battle which our country is waging tends to unite and not to divide, to honor and not to debase, to liberate and not to dominate. Thus it is faithful to its mission, which always was and which remains human and universal. The purpose is great. The task is hard. But in the midst of world alarms you can see, women and men of France, what weight France's will can have again.

*General de Gaulle gave a press conference on May 15, 1962, at which he was asked a number of questions about his government's policy toward European integration. He took the opportunity to clarify his conception of what the European state-system is like and is likely to be in the foreseeable future.*

## STATES AS THE ELEMENTS *

. . . I have never personally, in any of my statements, spoken of a "Europe of nations," although it is always being claimed that I have done so. It is not, of course, that I am repudiating my own; quite on the contrary, I am more attached to France than ever, and I do not believe that Europe can have any living reality if it does not include France and her Frenchmen, Germany and its Germans, Italy and its Italians, and so forth. Dante, Goethe, Chateaubriand belong to all Europe to the very extent that they were respectively and eminently Italian, German and French. They would not have served Europe very well if they had been stateless, or if they had thought and written in some kind of integrated Esperanto or Volapük.

But it is true that the nation is a human and sentimental element, whereas Europe can be built on the basis of active, authoritative and responsible elements. What elements? The states, of course; for, in this respect, it is only the states that are valid, legitimate and capable of achievement. I have already said, and I repeat, that at the present time there cannot be any other Europe than a Europe of states, apart, of course, from myths, stories and parades. What is happening with regard to the Economic Community proves this every day, for it is the states, and only the states, that created this Economic Com-

---

* From *Major Addresses,* pp. 175–177.

munity, that furnished it with funds; that provided it with staff members; and it is the states that give it reality and efficiency, all the more so as it is impossible to take any far-reaching economic measure without committing a political action.

It is a political action, when tariffs are dealt with in common, when coal-mining areas are converted, when wages and social welfare funds are made the same in the six states, when each state allows workers from the five other states to settle on its territory, when decrees are consequently taken and when Parliament is asked to vote necessary laws, funds and sanctions. It is a political action when agriculture is included in the Common Market, and it is the six states, and they alone, that succeeded in doing so last January by means of their political bodies. It is a political action when the association of Greece or of the African states or of the Malagasy Republic is being dealt with. It is a political action when one negotiates with Great Britain on the request that it has made to enter the Common Market. It is again a political action when the applications of other states for participation or association are considered. It is still a political action when one comes to consider the requests that the United States announces that it will make with regard to its economic relations with the Community.

In fact, the economic development of Europe cannot be assured without its political union and, in this regard, I want to point out the arbitrary nature of a certain idea that was voiced during the recent discussions in Paris and that claimed to keep economic matters out of the meetings of the heads of state or government, whereas, for each of them, in their respective countries, economy is the constant and primary issue.

I should like to speak more particularly about the objection to integration. The objection is presented to us with the words, "Let us merge the six states into a supranational entity; this way, things will be quite simple and practical." But such an entity cannot be found without there being in Europe today a federator with sufficient power, authority and skill. That is why one falls back on a type of hybrid, in which the six states would undertake to comply with what will be decided upon by a certain majority. At the same time, although there are already six national parliaments, plus the European Parliament, plus the Consultative Assembly of the Council of Europe—which did, it is true, predate the conception of the Six and which, I am told, is dying on the shore where it was abandoned—we must, it seems, elect yet another parliament, a so-called European one—which would lay down the law for the six states.

These are ideas that may, perhaps, beguile certain minds, but I certainly do not see how they could be carried out in practice, even if there were six signatures on the dotted line. Is there a France, a Germany, an Italy, a Holland, a Belgium, a Luxembourg, that would be ready—in a matter that is important for them from the national or the international point of view—to do something that they would consider bad because this would be dictated to them by others? Would the French people, the German people, the Italian people, the Dutch people, the Belgian people, or the Luxembourg people dream of submitting to laws voted by foreign deputies if these laws were to run contrary to their own deep-seated will? This is not so; there is no way, at the present time, for a foreign majority to be able to constrain recalcitrant nations. It is true that, in this "integrated" Europe, as they say, there would perhaps be no policy at all. This would simplify things a great deal. Indeed, once there would be no France and no Europe, once there would be no policy—since no one policy could be imposed on each of the six states—one would refrain from making any policies at all. But then, perhaps, this world would follow the lead of some outsider who did have a policy. There would perhaps be a federator, but the federator would not be European. And it would not be an integrated Europe, it would be something quite different, much broader and much more extensive with, I repeat, a federator. Perhaps it is this which, sometimes and to a certain degree, is at the basis of some remarks of such or such an advocate of European integration. In that case, it would be best to say so.

You see, when one's mind dwells on matters of great import, it is pleasant to dream of the marvelous lamp that Aladdin had only to rub in order to soar above the real. But there is no magic formula that will make it possible to build something as difficult as a united Europe. Thus, let us place reality at the basis of the edifice and, when we shall have completed the work, this will be the time for us to lull ourselves to sleep with the tales of "The Thousand and One Nights."

*Given his view of states as the true elements of the international system, it is hardly surprising to find de Gaulle vitally concerned with what tasks the state must fulfill. His immediate concern is France, of course; but the remarks which follow— made on January 14, 1963, at a press conference, in reply to questions about the constitutional reforms of the Fifth Republic—are pertinent to other modern states.*

## THE TASK OF THE STATE IN THE TWENTIETH CENTURY *

The striking thing about this constitutional reform is, it seems to me, that it succeeded because it corresponds above all to a truly absolute necessity of modern times. It is commonplace to observe that current developments always make the role of the State more and more vital and already there is no national activity which can take place today without its consent, often its intervention and sometimes its direction. Everything, and even the fate of each and every person, is thus more or less directly bound up with the action of the State, action which is expressed by a national trend, by regulations and by laws. In this action, as in all action, a head is needed and, as this head is a person, it is fitting that this person receive the personal expression of the confidence of all those concerned. We must also take into account the overwhelming factor that, in the political and strategic position in which the world finds itself, there are countries, in particular our own, which are at any moment, one can say it, in danger of sudden death; hence the necessity for these countries to have at the summit a permanent authority who is in a position to take charge of their destiny and, if need be, instantly to take decisions of vast consequence. It is these very conditions which have henceforth excluded the former system of parties—unstable, uncertain, in-

---

* From *Major Addresses*, pp. 209–210.

constant—and it is these same conditions which led the country, following its instinct and its reason, to answer as it did, first by confirming once again the existing institutions, then by choosing its Deputies.

For the first time since its birth, the Republic is established in continuity. Undoubtedly, the problems that confront us mean that free debate remains open, from which can and must emerge a host of ideas, proposals and improvements from those who are not biased. We must not of course expect the old hands at repining, disparagement and bitterness to cease, at least for the moment, to vent their spleen, spit out their bile and distill their vinegar. Only, it is a fact that the old game, the game of continuous intrigues, contrivances, falls, ascents, that was practiced by the specialists, this game cannot be resumed. The mere application of the provisions of the Constitution checks this and, if it were necessary, recourse to the judgment of the country would be there to prevent it.

Thus, for four years, the stability and the effectiveness of the State have made possible the accomplishment of a task which, and I have no reason for hiding this, appears to me to be considerable. I do not wish to fail to mention here the truly outstanding merits of the man whom I had then placed at my side as my Premier, M. Michel Debré, and also of the merits of his colleagues in the Government. Now we must continue the task on a basis of more assured national unity. For this task I called on M. Georges Pompidou and also the other Ministers. The country has given the undertaking its approval and the new National Assembly has expressed its confidence in the men.

What is this undertaking? It is quite simply the transformation of our country in accordance with the dictates of modern civilization. A transformation which applies first to man's condition; all those material and spiritual attributes which each man wishes to attain—it is a matter of making them more and more accessible, first by adding to their number, then by procuring increased resources to obtain them. This transformation also affects our life as a collectivity, a life which we must attempt to make easier and easier and increasingly fruitful—for families, cities, rural areas, occupations—hence the need for those social investments called education, housing, hospitalization, urban and agricultural development and sports. It is a transformation that embraces the entire nation, either through the adaptation of its activity and its administration on its own territory, or through the strengthening of its ties with the other States, in particular with its neighbors, then with those States which are carried by their needs or by their inclinations to cooperate by preference with it.

Finally, this transformation is aimed at setting up the means of defending ourselves. It goes without saying that all this must be rigorously linked with the development of our economy; failing this, payments and expenditures will spiral unchecked and we shall very quickly have inflation again. But, however necessary, just and desirable this progress may be, France knows itself well enough to be aware that there is no theory which can make it abound, suddenly, with the wealth of an El Dorado. All that we desire to have in addition to that which we have already will come only from the regular increase in our national product. There is not a single human society in the world, whatever may be its political, economic and social system, which can nourish progress in any way other than by expansion.

# X. The Continuum of Alternatives: Communism in the Twentieth Century

*In the early stages of the Russian Revolution of 1917, many of the revolutionaries expected the old state-system of Europe simply to collapse as the revolution spread. The failure of the revolution to do so, and the great resilience of the system, led to a series of adjustments in Communist doctrine. The expectation, based on the theories of Karl Marx and Friedrich Engels, that the state would soon wither away, gradually was replaced with the idea of two systems of states, the one headed by the Soviet Union, the other incorporating all "capitalist" states. In the selections which follow, it is important to notice the way in which Communist leaders grow increasingly confident that the system of "socialist" states will defeat the "capitalist" system at the same time that they increasingly defend the continued existence of the state in Communist societies.*

◇◇◇◇◇◇◇◇◇◇◇◇◇◇◇◇◇◇◇◇◇◇◇◇◇◇◇◇◇◇◇◇◇◇◇◇◇◇◇◇◇◇◇◇◇◇◇◇◇◇◇◇

# 29. Two World Centers

*In September of 1927, the first American labor delegation to visit the Soviet Union since the Revolution had an interview with Stalin. In the course of the interview, Stalin clearly stated his view that a world conflict between the capitalist and communist systems was inevitable, and that just as inevitably, the communist system would triumph.*

### JOSEPH STALIN*

. . . With regard to the international conditions necessary for the complete triumph of communist society, these will develop

---

\* From *The Strategy and Tactics of World Communism*, Report of the Subcommittee No. 5 of the House Committee on Foreign Affairs, Washington, 1948. Supplement No. 1, pp. 120–121.

and grow in proportion as revolutionary crises and revolutionary outbreaks of the working class in capitalist countries grow. It must not be imagined that the working class in one country, or in several countries, will march towards socialism, and still more to communism, and that the capitalists of other countries will sit still with folded arms and look on with indifference. Still less must it be imagined that the working class in capitalist countries will agree to be mere spectators of the victorious development of socialism in one or another country. As a matter of fact, the capitalists will do all in their power to crush such countries. As a matter of fact, every important step taken towards socialism, and still more towards communism, in any country will be inevitably accompanied by the unrestrained efforts of the working class in capitalist countries to achieve the dictatorship and socialism in those countries. Thus, in the further progress of development of the international revolution, two world centers will be formed: the socialist center, attracting to itself all the countries gravitating towards socialism, and the capitalist center attracting to itself all the countries gravitating toward capitalism. The fight between these two centers for the conquest of world economy will decide the fate of capitalism and communism throughout the whole world, for the final defeat of world capitalism means the victory of socialism in the arena of world economy. . . .

◇◆◇◆◇◆◇◆◇◆◇◆◇◆◇◆◇◆◇◆◇◆◇◆◇◆◇◆◇◆◇◆◇◆◇◆◇◆◇◆◇◆◇◆◇

# 30. The Aim of World Communism *

*The following statement is taken from the Programme of the Communist International, which was adopted at the Sixth World Congress of the Comintern, September 1, 1928.*

The ultimate aim of the Communist International is to replace world capitalist economy by a world system of Communism.

* From *The Strategy and Tactics of World Communism,* Supplement I, pp. 121–128.

Communist society, the basis for which has been prepared by
the whole course of historical development, is mankind's only
way out, for it alone can abolish the contradictions of the
capitalist system which threaten to degrade and destroy the
human race.

Communist society will abolish the class division of society,
i.e., simultaneously with the abolition of anarchy in production,
it will abolish all forces of exploitation and oppression of man
by man. Society will no longer consist of antagonistic classes in
conflict with each other, but will represent a united commonwealth of labor. For the first time in its history mankind will
take its fate into its own hands. Instead of destroying innumerable human lives and incalculable wealth in struggles between
classes and nations, mankind will devote all its energy to the
struggle against the forces of nature, to the development and
strengthening of its own collective might.

After abolishing private ownership in the means of production and converting them into social property, the world system
of Communism will replace the elemental forces of the world
market, of competition and the blind process of social production, by consciously organized and planned production for the
purpose of satisfying rapidly growing social needs. With the
abolition of competition and anarchy in production, devastating
crises and still more devastating wars will disappear. Instead of
colossal waste of productive forces and spasmodic development
of society—there will be planned utilization of all material
resources and painless economic development on the basis of
unrestricted, smooth and rapid development of productive
forces.

The abolition of private property and the disappearance of
classes will do away with the exploitation of man by man.
Work will cease to be toiling for the benefit of a class enemy:
instead of being merely a means of livelihood it will become a
necessity of life: want and economic inequality, the misery of
enslaved classes, and a wretched standard of life generally will
disappear; the hierarchy created in the division of labor system
will be abolished together with the antagonism between mental
and manual labor; and the last vestige of the social inequality
of sexes will be removed. At the same time, the organs of class

domination, and the State in the first place, will disappear also. The State, being the embodiment of class domination, will die out insofar as classes die out, and with it all measures of coercion will expire.

Having defeated Russian imperialism and liberated all the former colonies and oppressed nations of the Tsarist Empire, and systematically laying a firm foundation for their cultural and political development by industrializing their territories; having guaranteed the juridical position of the Autonomous Territories, Autonomous Republics and Allied Republics in the Constitution of the Union and having granted in full the right of nations to self-determination—the dictatorship of the proletariat in the U. S. S. R., by this guarantees, not only formal, but also real equality for the different nationalities of the Union.

Being the land of the dictatorship of the proletariat and of Socialist construction, the land of great working class achievements, of the union of the workers with the peasants and of a new culture marching under the banner of Marxism—the U. S. S. R. inevitably becomes the base of the world movement of all oppressed classes, the center of international revolution, the greatest factor in world history. In the U. S. S. R., the world proletariat for the first time acquires a country that is really its own, and for the colonial movements the U. S. S. R. becomes a powerful center of attraction.

Thus, the U. S. S. R. is an extremely important factor in the general crisis of capitalism, not only because she has dropped out of the world capitalist system and has created a basis for a new Socialist system of production, but also because she plays an exceptionally great revolutionary role generally; she is the international driving force of proletarian revolution that impels the proletariat of all countries to seize power; she is the living example proving that the working class is not only capable of destroying capitalism, but of building up Socialism as well; she is the prototype of the fraternity of nationalities in all lands united in the World Union of Socialist Republics and of the economic unity of the toilers of all countries in a single world Socialist economic system that the world proletariat must establish when it has captured political power.

The simultaneous existence of two economic systems: the

Socialist system in the U. S. S. R. and the capitalist system in other countries, imposes on the Proletarian State the task of warding off the blows showered upon it by the capitalist world (boycott, blockade, etc.), and also compels it to resort to economic maneuvering with and utilizing economic contacts with capitalist countries (with the aid of the monopoly of foreign trade—which is one of the fundamental conditions for the successful building up of Socialism, and also with the aid of credits, loans, concessions, etc.). The principal and fundamental line to be followed in this connection must be the line of establishing the widest possible contact with foreign countries— within limits determined by their usefulness to the U. S. S. R., i.e., primarily for strengthening industry in the U. S. S. R. for laying the base for her own heavy industry and electrification and finally, for the development of her own Socialist engineering industry. Only to the extent that the economic independence of the U. S. S. R., in the capitalist environment is secured can solid guarantees be obtained against the danger that Socialist construction in the U. S. S. R. may be destroyed and that the U. S. S. R. may be transformed into an appendage of the world capitalist system.

On the other hand, notwithstanding their interest in the markets of the U. S. S. R., the capitalist States continually vacillate between their commercial interests and their fear of growth of the U. S. S. R., which means the growth of international revolution. However, the principal and fundamental tendency in the policy of the imperialist Powers is to encircle the U. S. S. R. and conduct counter-revolutionary war against her in order to strangle her and to establish a world bourgeois terrorist régime.

The systematic imperialist attempts politically to encircle the U. S. S. R. and the growing danger of an armed attack upon her, do not, however, prevent the Communist Party of the Soviet Union—a section of the Communist International and the leader of the proletarian dictatorship in the U. S. S. R.—from fulfilling its international obligations and from rendering support to all the oppressed, to the labor movements in capitalist countries, to colonial movements against imperialism and to the struggle against national oppression in every form.

---

◇◇◇◇◇◇◇◇◇◇◇◇◇◇◇◇◇◇◇◇◇◇◇◇◇◇◇◇◇◇◇◇◇◇◇◇◇◇◇◇◇◇◇◇◇◇◇◇◇◇

# 31. Peaceful Coexistence

*Soviet foreign policy often has changed tactics while maintaining the same goal. This relationship of means to end is illustrated by the contemporary Communist slogan of "peaceful coexistence" with the capitalist states. On the one hand, the aim remains what it always has been: to undermine and destroy the capitalist states. On the other hand, the tactic is now different: emphasize the terrible destructiveness of nuclear weapons and at the same time promote the idea of "ideological" and "economic" competition. A spokesman for this modified version of the thesis of "two camps," the former Soviet Premier, Nikita Khrushchev, published the remarks which follow, in 1959, in the journal* Foreign Affairs.

## NIKITA KHRUSHCHEV*

One does not need to delve deeply into history to appreciate how important it is for mankind to ensure peaceful coexistence. And here it may be said parenthetically that the Europeans might have benefited a great deal in their day if, instead of organizing senseless crusades which invariably ended in failure, they had established peaceful relations with the differently-minded peoples of the Moslem East.

But let us turn to facts concerning the relatively recent past when the watershed between states no longer consisted of different religious creeds and customs, but of much deeper differ-

---

* From Nikita Khrushchev, "On Peaceful Coexistence", *Foreign Affairs,* XXXVIII (October 1959), pp. 1–18. Reprinted by permission of the Council on Foreign Relations, Inc., New York.

ences of principle relating to the choice of social systems. This
new situation arose on the threshold of the 1920s when, to the
booming of the guns of the Russian cruiser *Aurora* which had
joined the rebellious workers and peasants, a new and unpre-
cedented social system, a state of workers and peasants, came
into the world.

Its appearance was met with the disgruntled outcries of those
who naïvely believed the capitalist system to be eternal and
immutable. Some people even made an attempt to strangle the
unwanted infant in the cradle. Everybody knows how this
ended: our people voted with their arms for Soviet power, and
it came to stay. And even then, in 1920, V. I. Lenin, reply-
ing to the question of an American correspondent as to what
basis there could be for peace between Soviet Russia and America, said: "Let the American imperialists not touch us. We
won't touch them."

From its very inception the Soviet state proclaimed peaceful
coexistence as the basic principle of its foreign policy. It was
no accident that the very first state act of the Soviet power was
the decree on peace, the decree on the cessation of the bloody
war.

What, then, is the policy of peaceful coexistence?

In its simplest expression it signifies the repudiation of war
as a means of solving controversial issues. However, this does
not cover the entire concept of peaceful coexistence. Apart from
the commitment to non-aggression, it also presupposes an obligation on the part of all states to desist from violating each
other's territorial integrity and sovereignty in any form and
under any pretext whatsoever. The principle of peaceful coexistence signifies a renunciation of interference in the internal
affairs of other countries with the object of altering their
system of government or mode of life or for any other motives. The doctrine of peaceful coexistence also presupposes
that political and economic relations between countries are to
be based upon complete equality of the parties concerned, and
on mutual benefit.

It is often said in the West that peaceful coexistence is

nothing else than a tactical method of the socialist states. There is not a grain of truth in such allegations. Our desire for peace and peaceful coexistence is not conditioned by any time-serving or tactical considerations. It springs from the very nature of socialist society in which there are no classes or social groups interested in profiting by war or seizing and enslaving other people's territories. The Soviet Union and the other socialist countries, thanks to their socialist system, have an unlimited home market and for this reason they have no need to pursue an expansionist policy of conquest and an effort to subordinate other countries to their influence.

It is the people who determine the destinies of the socialist states. The socialist states are ruled by the working people themselves, the workers and peasants, the people who themselves create all the material and spiritual values of society. And people of labor cannot want war. For to them war spells grief and tears, death, devastation and misery. Ordinary people have no need for war.

Contrary to what certain propagandists hostile to us say, the coexistence of states with different social systems does not mean that they will only fence themselves off from one another by a high wall and undertake the mutual obligation not to throw stones over the wall or pour dirt upon each other. No! Peaceful coexistence does not mean merely living side by side in the absence of war but with the constantly remaining threat of its breaking out in the future. *Peaceful coexistence can and should develop into peaceful competition for the purpose of satisfying man's needs in the best possible way.*

We say to the leaders of the capitalist states: Let us try out in practice whose system is better, let us compete without war. This is much better than competing in who will produce more arms and who will smash whom. We stand and always will stand for such competition as will help to raise the well-being of the people to a higher level.

The principle of peaceful competition does not at all demand that one or another state abandon the system and ideology adopted by it. It goes without saying that the acceptance of this principle cannot lead to the immediate end of disputes and contradictions which are inevitable between countries adhering to different social systems. But the main thing is ensured: the states which decided to adopt the path of peaceful coexistence repudiate the use of force in any form and agree on a peaceful settlement of possible disputes and conflicts, bearing in mind the mutual interests of the parties concerned. In our age of the H-bomb and atomic techniques this is the main thing of interest to every man.

Displaying skepticism about the idea of peaceful competition, Vice President Nixon, in his speech over the Soviet radio and television in August 1959, attempted to find a contradiction between the Soviet people's professions of their readiness to coexist peacefully with the capitalist states and the slogans posted in the shops of our factories calling for higher labor productivity in order to ensure the speediest victory of Communism.

This was not the first time we heard representatives of the bourgeois countries reason in this manner. They say: The Soviet leaders argue that they are for peaceful coexistence. At the same time they declare that they are fighting for Communism and they even say that Communism will be victorious in all countries. How can there be peaceful coexistence with the Soviet Union if it fights for Communism?

People who treat the question in this way confuse matters, wilfully or not, by confusing the problems of ideological struggle with the questions of relations between states. Those indulging in this sort of confusion are most probably guided by a desire to cast aspersions upon the Communists of the Soviet Union and to represent them as the advocates of aggressive actions. This, however, is very unwise.

The Communist Party of the Soviet Union at its Twentieth Congress made it perfectly clear and obvious that the allegations that the Soviet Union intends to overthrow capitalism in other countries by means of "exporting" revolution are absolutely unfounded. I cannot refrain from reminding you of my words at the Twentieth Congress: "It goes without saying that among us Communists there are no adherents of capitalism. But this does not mean that we have interfered or plan to interfere in the internal affairs of countries where capitalism still exists. Romain Rolland was right when he said that 'freedom is not brought in from abroad in baggage trains like Bourbons.' It is ridiculous to think that revolutions are made to order."

We Communists believe that the idea of Communism will ultimately be victorious throughout the world, just as it has been victorious in our country, in China and in many other states. Many readers of FOREIGN AFFAIRS will probably disagree with us. Perhaps they think that the idea of capitalism will ultimately triumph. It is their right to think so. We may argue, we may disagree with one another. *The main thing is to keep to the positions of ideological struggle, without resorting to arms in order to prove that one is right.* The point is that with military techniques what they are today, there are no inaccessible places in the world. Should a world war break out, no country will be able to shut itself off from a crushing blow.

We believe that ultimately that system will be victorious on the globe which will offer the nations greater opportunities for improving their material and spiritual life. It is precisely socialism that creates unprecedentedly great prospects for the inexhaustible creative enthusiasm of the masses, for a genuine flourishing of science and culture, for the realization of man's dream of a happy life, a life without destitute and unemployed people, of a happy childhood and tranquil old age, of the realization of the most audacious and ambitious human projects, of man's right to create in a truly free manner in the interests of the people.

But when we say that in the competition between the two systems, the capitalist and the socialist, our system will win, this does not mean, of course, that we shall achieve victory by interfering in the internal affairs of the capitalist countries. Our confidence in the victory of Communism is of a different kind. It is based on a knowledge of the laws governing the development of society. Just as in its time capitalism, as the more progressive system, took the place of feudalism, so will capitalism be inevitably superseded by Communism—the more progressive and more equitable social system. We are confident of the victory of the socialist system because it is a more progressive system than the capitalist system. Soviet power has been in existence for only a little more than 40 years, and during these years we have gone through two of the worst wars, repulsing the attacks of enemies who attempted to strangle us. Capitalism in the United States has been in existence for more than a century and a half, and the history of the United States has developed in such a way that never once have enemies landed on American territory.

Yet the dynamics of the development of the U. S. S. R. and the U. S. A. are such that the 42-year-old land of the Soviets is already able to challenge the 150-year-old capitalist state to economic competition; and the most farsighted American leaders are admitting that the Soviet Union is fast catching up with the United States and will ultimately outstrip it. Watching the progress of this competition, anyone can judge which is the better system, and we believe that in the long run all the peoples will embark on the path of struggle for the building of socialist societies.

You disagree with us? Prove by facts that your system is superior and more efficacious, that it is capable of ensuring a higher degree of prosperity for the people than the socialist system, that under capitalism man can be happier than under socialism. It is impossible to prove this. I have no other explanation for the fact that talk of violently "rolling back" Communism never ceases in the West. Not long ago the U. S. Senate and House of Representatives deemed it proper to pass a resolution calling for the "liberation" of the socialist countries allegedly enslaved by Communism and, moreover, of a number of union republics constituting part of the Soviet Union. The authors of the resolution call for the "liberation" of the Ukraine, Byelorussia, Lithuania, Latvia, Estonia, Armenia, Azerbaijan, Georgia, Kazakhstan, Turkmenistan and even a certain "Ural Area."

I would not be telling the full truth if I did not say that the adoption of this ill-starred resolution was regarded by the

Soviet people as an act of provocation. Personally I agree with this appraisal.

It would be interesting to see, incidentally, how the authors of this resolution would have reacted if the parliament of Mexico, for instance, had passed a resolution demanding that Texas, Arizona and California be "liberated from American slavery." Apparently they have never pondered such a question, which is very regrettable. Sometimes comparisons help to understand the essence of a matter.

Travelling through the Soviet Union, leading American statesmen and public figures have had full opportunity to convince themselves that there is no hope of sowing strife between the Soviet people and the Communist Party and the Soviet Government, and of influencing them to rebel against Communism. How, then, are we to explain the unceasing attempts to revive the policy of "rolling back" Communism? What do they have in mind? Armed intervention in the internal affairs of the socialist countries? But in the West as well as in the East people are fully aware that under the conditions of modern military technique such actions are fraught with immediate and relentless retaliation.

So we come back to what we started with. In our day there are only two ways: peaceful coexistence or the most destructive war in history. There is no third choice.

The problem of peaceful coexistence between states with different social systems has become particularly pressing in view of the fact that since the Second World War the development of relations between states has entered a new stage, that now we have approached a period in the life of mankind when there is a real chance of excluding war once and for all from the life of society. The new alignment of international forces which has developed since the Second World War offers ground for the assertion that a new world war is no longer a fatal inevitability, that it can be averted. . . .

Peaceful coexistence is the only way which is in keeping with the interests of all nations. To reject it would mean under existing conditions to doom the whole world to a terrible and destructive war at a time when it is fully possible to avoid it.

Is it possible that when mankind has advanced to a plane where it has proved capable of the greatest discoveries and of making its first steps into outer space, it should not be able to use the colossal achievements of its genius for the establishment of a stable peace, for the good of man, rather than for the preparation of another war and for the destruction of all that has been created by its labor over many millenniums? Reason refuses to believe this. It protests.

The Soviet people have stated and declare again that they do not want war. If the Soviet Union and the countries friendly to it are not attacked, we shall never use any weapons either against the United States or against any other countries. We do not want any horrors of war, destruction, suffering and death for ourselves or for any other peoples. We say this not because we fear anyone. Together with our friends, we are united and stronger than ever. But precisely because of that do we say that war can and should be prevented. Precisely because we want to rid mankind of war, we urge the Western powers to peaceful and lofty competition. We say to all: Let us prove to each other the advantages of one's own system not with fists, not by war, but by peaceful economic competition in conditions of peaceful coexistence.

As for the social system in some state or other, that is the domestic affair of the people of each country. We always have stood and we stand today for non-interference in the internal affairs of other countries. We have always abided, and we shall abide, by these positions. The question, for example, what system will exist in the United States or in other capitalist countries cannot be decided by other peoples or states. This question can and will be decided only by the American people themselves, only by the people of each country.

# XI. The Continuum of Alternatives:
## Fascism in the Twentieth Century

*The Fascist concept of the state contains a negative and a positive element. The negative element is a virulent criticism of both the constitutional-democratic and Communist states. The positive element is a glorification of violence, warrior heroism, and the total subordination of the individual to the purposes of the state. This combination of elements proved, in the 1920's and 1930's, to be a potent brew.*

◇◇◇◇◇◇◇◇◇◇◇◇◇◇◇◇◇◇◇◇◇◇◇◇◇◇◇◇◇◇◇◇◇◇◇◇◇◇◇◇◇◇◇◇◇◇◇◇◇◇

## 32. Italian Fascism

*In 1932, Benito Mussolini, the leader of the Italian Fascist movement, contributed an article to the* Enciclopedia Italiana. *That article contained the kernel of Mussolini's conception of what the Fascist state is.*

**BENITO MUSSOLINI***

Fascism is now a completely individual thing, not only as a regime but as a doctrine. And this means that to-day Fascism, exercising its critical sense upon itself and upon others, has formed its own distinct and peculiar point of view, to which

* From Benito Mussolini, *The Political and Social Doctrine of Fascism,* trans. Jane Soames, (London: The Hogarth Press, 1933), pp. 11–15, 21, 25–26. Reprinted by permission of The Hogarth Press.

it can refer and upon which, therefore, it can act in the face of all problems, practical or intellectual, which confront the world.

And above all, Fascism, the more it considers and observes the future and the development of humanity quite apart from political considerations of the moment, believes neither in the possibility nor the utility of perpetual peace. It thus repudiates the doctrine of Pacifism—born of a renunciation of the struggle and an act of cowardice in the face of sacrifice. War alone brings up to its highest tension all human energy and puts the stamp of nobility upon the peoples who have the courage to meet it. All other trials are substitutes, which never really put men into the position where they have to make the great decision—the alternative of life or death. Thus a doctrine which is founded upon this harmful postulate of peace is hostile to Fascism. And thus hostile to the spirit of Fascism, though accepted for what use they can be in dealing with particular political situations, are all the international leagues and societies which, as history will show, can be scattered to the winds when once strong national feeling is aroused by any motive—sentimental, ideal, or practical. This anti-Pacifist spirit is carried by Fascism even into the life of the individual; the proud motto of the *Squadrista,* "Me ne frego," written on the bandage of the wound, is an act of philosophy not only stoic, the summary of a doctrine not only political—it is the education to combat, the acceptation of the risks which combat implies, and a new way of life for Italy. Thus the Fascist accepts life and loves it, knowing nothing of and despising suicide: he rather conceives of life as duty and struggle and conquest, life which should be high and full, lived for oneself, but above all for others—those who are at hand and those who are far distant, contemporaries, and those who will come after.

This "demographic" policy of the regime is the result of the above premise. Thus the Fascist loves in actual fact his neighbour, but this "neighbour" is not merely a vague and undefined concept, this love for one's neighbour puts no obstacle in the way of necessary educational severity, and still less to differentiation of status and to physical distance. Fascism repudiates any universal embrace, and in order to live worthily in the community of civilized peoples watches its contemporaries with vigilant eyes, takes good note of their state of mind and, in the changing trend of their interests, does not allow itself to be deceived by temporary and fallacious appearances.

Such a conception of life makes Fascism the complete opposite of that doctrine, the base of so-called scientific and Marxian Socialism, the materialist conception of history; according to which the history of human cvilization can be explained simply through the conflict of interests among the various social groups and by the change and development in the means and instruments of production. That the changes in the economic field—new discoveries of raw materials, new methods of working them, and the inventions of science—have their importance no one can deny; but that these factors are sufficient to explain the history of humanity excluding all others is an absurd delusion. Fascism, now and always, believes in holiness and in heroism; that is to say, in actions influenced by no economic motive, direct or indirect. And if the economic conception of history be denied, according to which theory men are no more than puppets, carried to and fro by the waves of chance, while the real directing forces are quite out of their control, it follows that the existence of an unchangeable and unchanging class-war is also denied—the natural progeny of the economic conception of history. And above all Fascism denies that class-war can be the preponderant force in the transformation of society. These two fundamental concepts of Socialism being this refuted, nothing is left of it but the sentimental aspiration—as old as humanity itself—towards a social convention in which the sorrows and sufferings of the humblest shall be alleviated. But here again Fascism repudiates the conception of "economic" happiness, to be realized by Socialism and, as it were, at a given moment in economic evolution to assure to everyone the maximum of well-being. Fascism denies the materialist conception of happiness as a possibility, and abandons it to its inventors, the economists of the first half of the nineteenth century: that is to say, Fascism denies the validity of the equation, well-being-happiness, which would reduce men to the level of animals, caring for one thing only—to be fat and well-fed—and would thus degrade humanity to a purely physical existence.

After Socialism, Fascism combats the whole complex system of democratic ideology, and repudiates it, whether in its theoretical premises or in its practical application. Fascism denies that the majority, by the simple fact that it is a majority, can direct human society; it denies that numbers alone can govern by means of a periodical consultation, and it affirms the immutable, beneficial and fruitful inequality of mankind, which can never be permanently levelled through the mere operation of a mechanical process such as universal suffrage. The democratic regime may be defined as from time to time giving the people the illusion of sovereignty, while the real effective sovereignty lies in the hands of other concealed and irresponsible forces. Democracy is a regime nominally without a king, but it is ruled by many kings—more absolute, tyrannical and ruinous than one sole king, even though a tyrant. . . .

The foundation of Fascism is the conception of the State, its character, its duty, and its aim. Fascism conceives of the State as an absolute, in comparison with which all individuals or groups are relative, only to be conceived of in their relation to the State. The conception of the Liberal State is not that of a directing force, guiding the play and development, both material and spiritual, of a collective body, but merely a force limited to the function of recording results: on the other hand, the Fascist State is itself conscious, and has itself a will and a personality—thus it may be called the "ethic" State. . . .

The Fascist State is an embodied will to power and government: the Roman tradition is here an ideal of force in action. According to Fascism, government is not so much a thing to be expressed in territorial or military terms as in terms of morality and the spirit. It must be thought of as an Empire— that is to say, a nation which directly or indirectly rules other nations, without the need for conquering a single square yard of territory. For Fascism, the growth of Empire, that is to say the expansion of the nation, is an essential manifestation of vitality, and its opposite a sign of decadence. Peoples which are rising, or rising again after a period of decadence, are always imperialist; any renunciation is a sign of decay and of death. Fascism is the doctrine best adapted to represent the tendencies and the aspirations of a people, like the people of Italy, who are rising again after many centuries of abasement and foreign servitude. But Empire demands discipline, the co-ordination of all forces and a deeply-felt sense of duty and sacrifice: this fact explains many aspects of the practical working of the regime, the character of many forces in the State, and the necessarily severe measures which must be taken against those who would oppose this spontaneous and inevitable movement of Italy in the twentieth century, and would oppose it by recalling the outworn ideology of the nineteenth century—repudiated wheresoever there has been the courage to undertake great experiments of social and political transformation: for never before has the nation stood more in need of authority, of direction and of order. If every age has its own characteristic doctrine, there are a thousand signs which point to Fascism as the characteristic doctrine of our time. For if a doctrine must be a living thing, this is proved by the fact that Fascism has created a living faith; and that this faith is very powerful in the minds of men, is demonstrated by those who have suffered and died for it.

Fascism has henceforth in the world the universality of all those doctrines which, in realizing themselves, have represented a stage in the history of the human spirit.

# 33. National Socialism

*Adolf Hitler's* Mein Kampf *was written while he served a prison term for attempting to take over power in the State of Bavaria in 1924. It contains so blatant and frank a program for terror, war, and revolution that few people could believe*

*he was serious when it was first published. The critical distin-*
*guishing mark of his conception of the state, as compared to*
*that of Mussolini, is the Nazi doctrine that the totalitarian state*
*is meant to be the vehicle by which the German "nation" ac-*
*complishes its historical mission.*

## ADOLF HITLER*

*The state is a means to an end. Its end lies in the preservation*
*and advancement of a community of physically and psychically*
*homogeneous creatures. This preservation itself comprises first*
*of all existence as a race and thereby permits the free develop-*
*ment of all the forces dormant in this race. Of them a part will*
*always primarily serve the preservation of physical life, and*
*only the remaining part the promotion of a further spiritual*
*development. Actually the one always creates the precondition*
*for the other.*

*States which do not serve this purpose are misbegotten, mon-*
*strosities in fact. The fact of their existence changes this no*
*more than the success of a gang of bandits can justify robbery.*

We National Socialists as champions of a new philosophy of
life must never base ourselves on so-called 'accepted facts'—
and false ones at that. If we did, we would not be the champions of a new great idea, but the coolies of the present-day lie.
We must distinguish in the sharpest way between the state as a
vessel and the race as its content. This vessel has meaning
only if it can preserve and protect the content; otherwise it is
useless.

*Thus, the highest purpose of a folkish state is concern for the*
*preservation of those original racial elements which bestow cul-*
*ture and create the beauty and dignity of a higher mankind.*
*We, as Aryans, can conceive of the state only as the living or-*
*ganism of a nationality which not only assures the preservation*
*of this nationality, but by the development of its spiritual and*
*ideal abilities leads it to the highest freedom.*

---

* From Adolf Hitler, *Mein Kampf*, trans. Ralph Mannheim (Boston: Houghton Mifflin Co., 1943), pp. 393–394, 395–396, 397–398. Reprinted by permission of Houghton Mifflin Co.

But what they try to palm off on us as a state today is usually nothing but a monstrosity born of deepest human error, with untold misery as a consequence.

We National Socialists know that with this conception we stand as revolutionaries in the world of today and are also branded as such. But our thoughts and actions must in no way be determined by the approval or disapproval of our time, but by the binding obligation to a truth which we have recognized. Then we may be convinced that the higher insight of posterity will not only understand our actions of today, but will also confirm their correctness and exalt them. . . .

[If] we speak of a higher mission of the state, we must not forget that the higher mission lies essentially in the nationality whose free development the state must merely make possible by the organic force of its being.

Hence, if we propound the question of how the state which we Germans need should be constituted, we must first clearly understand what kind of people it is to contain and what purpose it is to serve.

Our German nationality, unfortunately, is no longer based on a unified racial nucleus. The blending process of the various original components has advanced so far that we might speak of a new race. On the contrary, the poisonings of the blood which have befallen our people, especially since the Thirty Years' War, have led not only to a decomposition of our blood, but also of our soul. The open borders of our fatherland, the association with un-German foreign bodies along these frontier districts, but above all the strong and continuous influx of foreign blood into the interior of the Reich itself, due to its continuous renewal, leaves no time for an absolute blending. No new race is distilled out, the racial constituents remain side by side, with the result that, especially in critical moments in which otherwise a herd habitually gathers together, the German people scatters to all the four winds. Not only are the basic racial elements scattered territorially, but on a small scale within the same territory. Beside Nordic men Easterners, beside Easterners Dinarics, beside both of these Westerners, and mixtures in between. On the one hand, this is a great disadvantage:

the German people lack that sure herd instinct which is based on unity of the blood and, especially in moments of threatening danger, preserves nations from destruction in so far as all petty inner differences in such peoples vanish at once on such occasions and the solid front of a unified herd confronts the common enemy. This co-existence of unblended basic racial elements of the most varying kind accounts for what is termed *hyper-individualism* in Germany. In peaceful periods it may sometimes do good services, but taking all things together, it has robbed us of world domination. If the German people in its historic development had possessed that herd unity which other peoples enjoyed, the German Reich today would doubtless be mistress of the globe. World history would have taken a different course, and no one can distinguish whether in this way we would not have obtained what so many blinded pacifists today hope to gain by begging, whining, and whimpering: *a peace, supported not by the palm branches of tearful, pacifist female mourners, but based on the victorious sword of a master people, putting the world into the service of a higher culture. . . .*

*Anyone who speaks of a mission of the German people on earth must know that it can exist only in the formation of a state which sees its highest task in the preservation and promotion of the most noble elements of our nationality, indeed of all mankind, which still remain intact.*

Thus, for the first time the state achieves a lofty inner goal. Compared to the absurd catchword about safeguarding law and order, thus laying a peaceable groundwork for mutual swindles, the task of preserving and advancing the highest humanity, given to this earth by the benevolence of the Almighty, seems a truly high mission.

From a dead mechanism which only lays claim to existence for its own sake, there must be formed a living organism with the exclusive aim of serving a higher idea.

*The German Reich as a state must embrace all Germans and has the task, not only of assembling and preserving the most valuable stocks of basic racial elements in this people, but slowly and surely of raising them to a dominant position.*

# 34. The Political Soldier and the State

*In 1921, even before he was sentenced to prison for the attempt to seize power in the State of Bavaria, Hitler had organized the Nazi "storm troopers" (the S.A., or Sturm Abteilung). This political-military army was a powerful device to wage war on the Weimar Republic; and after the Nazis came to power in 1933, it was used by the party as one means of maintaining totalitarian control. In the selection which follows, Victor Lutze, chief of staff of the S.A., speaks to the diplomatic corps and the deputies of the foreign press on January 24, 1936.*

## VICTOR LUTZE*

The tasks of the S. A. are those of the party and vice-versa. They are therefore of an internally political nature.

In his sole function of political soldier of the Fuehrer, the S. A. man has paved the way for the new Germany. He has rid himself of all the political-philosophy rubbish of the past and made himself the supporting pillar of the state. . . .

You are familiar with the origin of the national socialist movement, when the Fuehrer, with only a few supporters, declared war on a tremendous turmoil of opinions and outlooks, on Marxism with all its shades on liberalism, on political confessionalism and reaction. First sneered at and mocked, later hated and beaten down.

The propaganda measures taken by the new popular movement which naturally was opposed by the state, necessitated the creation of protective and propaganda troops. The order to this effect was given by the Fuehrer on August 3, 1921.

* From Office of the U.S. Chief Counsel for the Prosecution of Axis Criminals, *Nazi Conspiracy and Aggression* (Washington, D.C.: U.S. Govt. Printing Office, 1946), Vol. 5, pp. 212–218.

And so, in contrast with the military organizations rising
everywhere at that time, the establishment of the S. A. created for the first time a type of soldier whose duties were of a
purely world political-philosophical nature; the political soldier!

## THE DIFFERENCE BETWEEN BEARERS OF
## IDEAS AND BEARERS OF ARMS

And today too, after the attainment and the subsequent sta-
bilization and coordination of the power of the state, the political soldiery of Germany continues to exist. For now as before
we distinguish fundamentally between the soldier as the bearer
of National Socialist ideology, the ideology of the German people, and the soldier as the bearer of arms of the nation. This
difference becomes especially obvious by the fact that every
German male adult who is physically and mentally qualified,
is required by law to undergo military training. Thus, military
service has its foundation in a compulsory state measure—dis-
regarding the German's psychological attitude towards it and
various other factors—while the political soldier voluntarily
serves national socialist ideology.

On one side, therefore, we have *compulsory service,* while
on the other *voluntary service.*

In judging these two types of soldiers, it is necessary that we
keep in mind the fact that soldier like qualities have from the
very early Germanic times been an outstanding characteristic
of the German people. Here again I do not refer to the soldier
as a military man, but as a fighter.

*THE ARMED FORCES: a state necessity*

The soldier as a military man is more or less a public necessity, a statement which can be justified by the fact that those
states with a favorable political and geographical location risk
less the endangering of their existence by doing without the
maintenance of strong armed forces than states located politically and geographically less favorably.

*THE POLITICAL SOLDIER: a national necessity*

The soldier as a fighting man, however, represents a national
necessity, as proven by the history of our people and as recog-

nized by the Fuehrer in its full significance. That means for us: every man who belongs by blood to the great community of the German people is primarily a soldier, a fighter for his people! Out of him and his soldierly qualities the state constructs the soldier, the man who is put into the purely technical position of answering for the needs of his people with the weapon in his hands. . . .

[However], soldierly spirit alone, without an ideological basis, is unable to carry out a political change.

The best soldierly striving remains a technique without spirit if it lacks an ideological basis!

The political leaders of the German people cannot afford to disregard these historical facts. In them originates the national socialist conception.

The states of the past collapsed not essentially because of a lack in factors of political might, but because of a faulty ideological basis and its instrument.

An ideological instrument, which represents in the people the idea on which the state is formed, is in a positive disposition towards the state and on military foundation. They collapsed because they failed to understand that the primary factor was not the state and state form—whether a monarchy or republic—, but the ideological fundamentals of this state.

The national and public necessity for the political soldier is best demonstrated by the above examples.

## NO RIVALRY BETWEEN THE BEARERS OF IDEAS AND BEARERS OF ARMS

But we also learn from them that no rivalry of any sort may exist between organizations of political soldiers and those of military soldiers. (In spite of the operation of a certain foreign press under such impossibilities!) The party and the armed forces are not the end, but the means to the end. Their fields of operation may differ but their aim is the same: Germany!

The political soldier is judged and formed the same way as every other soldier: by the weapon which he bears.

His weapon is his ideology!

But ideologies do not commonly depend on bayonets and
hand grenades, but on the spiritual strength and the unified
political will which this spiritual strength determines!

This function, determining exclusively the character of the
political soldier, excludes from the very first the evaluation of
the S. A. as an armed and technical unit! . . .

The political soldier represents the national living strength of
the German people. This quality fulfills its purpose and meets
its obligations. Living strength, however, is an ability and not
an intention!

## PACIFISM

[The S. A. man, the] political soldier of the new Germany, sees in pacifism only an enemy. Life in itself signifies
struggle, whether seen from an individual point of view or from
one of a national community. Only that which is strong is able
to survive, while that which is weak is ruined by its own lack of
strength. That is the law of nature, which can be changed by
neither human thinking nor knowledge.

Thus, pacifism, the absolute denial of struggle, of initiative,
of heroic thinking, can only be the ideal of uprooted visionaries and weaklings. In Germany, political soldiery has done
away with that negative form of ideology, and thus removed a
cause for international conflict which sooner or later—depending on the rights of the strong over the weak—would have
proved fatal to the German people. Further consideration of
pacifist aims shows that it is of little consequence whether
they are being nurtured in a state which technically possesses
the arms of all times or in one which is in a state of complete
demobilization as was the case with Germany barely three years
ago.

For its primary effect is not a state of technical disarmament, but one of spiritual defenselessness and helplessness.

The political soldier of the new Germany will see to it that
in case of attack, Germany will no longer stay behind us an
easily contaminated body, but be the powerful backbone of the
front, immune against all kinds of political plagues.

For, it is beyond doubt that, had Germany possessed a political soldiery during the prewar period, the outcome of the war would have been decided at the front and not in the homeland!

# Part Three

◇◇◇◇◇◇◇◇◇◇◇◇◇◇

# FORMS

*Since ancient times, the question of the best form of government has tended to be answered in one of two ways. The first answer is that the best form is the rule of the one, or at most the few, most virtuous, or most privileged, or most interested, men. This answer we may call the "oligarchic" position, using the term to mean "rule of few." The second answer is that the best form is the rule of most or all men. This answer we may call the "democratic" position, using the term to mean "rule of all." Finally, there is what we may call the compromise answer: it argues for a combination of qualities from the "few" and the "many" to achieve a "mixed form."*

*Whatever the particular form, the arguments in support of each tend to emphasize advantages to be obtained, both in the internal and external conduct of affairs. It is possible, for limited analytical purposes, to separate the internal and external dimensions; but both theoretically and practically the two are at bottom one and the other side of the same phenomenon. Thus in the United States Constitution, the power of the Congress both to pass laws and to declare war derives from the same fundamental premise: that it is the people's representatives who have the ultimate power to determine the major policies of the society. This premise, in turn, is derived from a complex set of modern theoretical and historical developments, including, for example, the impact of John Locke's conception of the purpose of the state on peoples and governments. The intention of this last part of the readings is to illustrate, first, the continuing character of the problem from antiquity to the present; and second, the kinds of considerations and arguments which have typically been advanced. No attempt is made to represent all shades of opinion; rather, the emphasis is on the core positions, for the other positions tend to be combinations of these.*

*The readings fall into two sections: one on the confrontation of oligarchy and democracy in ancient Greece; the other on the modern confrontation of monarchy and republican government or democracy.*

# XII. The Ancient Greek Conflict of Forms

## 35. Athens versus Sparta

*The selection which follows is Thucydides' record of a series of public speeches which were delivered at a Conference at Sparta in 432 B.C. The background of the speeches is this: Beginning in about 436, a number of political and military skirmishes took place between members of the Athenian and Spartan coalitions. Thus "episodes" involving Corcyra, Potidaea, Epidamnus, and other* poleis *referred to by the speakers, were the occasion for charges and counter-charges which preceded the actual full-scale outbreak of war. Athens and Sparta, as the two leaders, were increasingly prevailed upon to intervene, to lend aid, and, as these speeches indicate, to declare war.*

*By the time the Conference at Sparta took place, Corinth had emerged as one of the chief advocates of war, on the grounds that Athenian power was becoming intolerable. Furthermore, Thucydides himself, in a brief but weighty statement early in the history, says that in addition to the immediate causes of the war, the continued growth of Athenian power and "the alarm which this inspired in Lacedæmon made war inevitable."*

*The connection between the form of government in the two leading* poleis *and the causes of the war is of critical importance, but it is a complex relationship. Athens, beginning with the reforms of Solon in about 594 B.C., had become increasingly democratic in form; and this process was hastened by developments during the war against the Persians. At the time the Conference at Sparta took place, Athens was a democracy, yet was under the leadership of its most famous man, Pericles. Sparta, by contrast, had retained its ancient oligarchic form of government for several hundred years.*

*These differences in form were in part responsible for dif-*

221

*ferences in modes of military organization: Athens was basi-
cally a naval power, Sparta a land power. And these differences
help to account for the way in which, on the one hand, the
Athenians developed their empire, whereas the Spartans, on the
other hand, retained leadership of a somewhat more loosely
controlled confederation. Thus, for example, the Athenians
used their navy, which was based on the democracy, to extort
tribute in the form of grain, gold and other materials from far-
flung satellites. The Spartans, not having this flexibility of
naval power, were content to utilize their reputation as a formidable land power to maintain their leadership. They did so
by being able to offer the prospect of ravaging the lands either
of members of the other coalition, or of their own allies. Finally,
both Athens and Sparta used their respective kinds of power to
try to establish and maintain forms of government similar to
their own in the poleis of their coalition.*

*The main interest, for present purposes, of the speeches ren-
dered at Sparta, is the way in which they reveal the similarities
and differences of the two leading powers, above all, the differences derivative of the fundamentally different forms of government. Thucydides' technique for pointing up this contrast—
and it is a technique of his, for he tells us that he has presented
the speeches so as to make the speakers "say what was in my
opinion demanded of them by the various occasions"—is twofold: He presents the Corinthians' analysis of both powers; and
he then presents spokesmen for the powers who respond both
to the Corinthians and to each other. The resultant inter-play
is a brilliant and profound dramatization of the way in which
these two Greek poleis, as a result, ultimately, of differences in
their internal forms, engaged in actions which lead to the great
war itself.*

*One illustration of this must suffice. When the Athenians pres-
ent at Sparta hear the charges of the Corinthians, they respond
with an audacious public avowal of their right to rule over
others. It is highly probable that such audacity was itself a
factor in causing the deliberate Spartans at last to conclude that
Athenian power must be met. And the audacity of the Athenians is consistent with, indeed a reflection of, that very democratic government which had also produced the empire. Such
an interaction of form and substance is the heart of political*

*history as Thucydides presents it; and it is with this in mind*
*that we turn to the speakers, the first being a man of Corinth.*

## THUCYDIDES*

'Lacedæmonians! the confidence which you feel in your constitution and social order, inclines you to receive any reflexions
of ours on other powers with a certain scepticism. Hence springs
your moderation, but hence also the rather limited knowledge
which you betray in dealing with foreign politics. Time after
time was our voice raised to warn you of the blows about to
be dealt us by Athens, and time after time, instead of taking
the trouble to ascertain the worth of our communications, you
contented yourselves with suspecting the speakers of being inspired by private interest. And so, instead of calling these
allies together before the blow fell, you have delayed to do so
till we are smarting under it; allies among whom we have not
the worst title to speak, as having the greatest complaints to
make, complaints of Athenian outrage and Lacedæmonian
neglect. Now if these assaults on the rights of Hellas had been
made in the dark you might be unacquainted with the facts,
and it would be our duty to enlighten you. As it is, long speeches
are not needed where you see servitude accomplished for some
of us, meditated for others—in particular for our allies—and
prolonged preparations in the aggressor against the hour of
war. Or what, pray, is the meaning of their reception of Corcyra by fraud, and their holding it against us by force? what
of the siege of Potidæa?—places one of which lies most con-
veniently for any action against the Thracian towns; while the
other would have contributed a very large navy to the Peloponnesians?

'For all this you are responsible. You it was who first allowed them to fortify their city after the Median war, and
afterwards to erect the long walls,—you who, then and now,
are always depriving of freedom not only those whom they

* From *The History of the Peloponnesian War* by Thucydides, translated by Richard Crawley, revised by Feetham. Everyman's Library. Bk.
I, sects. 68–88. Reprinted by permission of E. P. Dutton and Co., Inc.

have enslaved, but also those who have as yet been your allies. For the true author of the subjugation of a people is not so much the immediate agent, as the power which permits it having the means to prevent it; particularly if that power aspires to the glory of being the liberator of Hellas. We are at last assembled. It has not been easy to assemble, nor even now are our objects defined. We ought not to be still inquiring into the fact of our wrongs, but into the means of our defence. For the aggressors with matured plans to oppose to our indecision have cast threats aside and betaken themselves to action. And we know what are the paths by which Athenian aggression travels, and how insidious is its progress. A degree of confidence she may feel from the idea that your bluntness of perception prevents your noticing her; but it is nothing to the impulse which her advance will receive from the knowledge that you see, but do not care to interfere. You, Lacedæmonians, of all the Hellenes are alone inactive, and defend yourselves not by doing anything but by looking as if you would do something; you alone wait till the power of an enemy is becoming twice its original size, instead of crushing it in its infancy. And yet the world used to say that you were to be depended upon; but in your case, we fear, it said more than the truth. The Mede, we ourselves know, had time to come from the ends of the earth to Peloponnese, without any force of yours worthy of the name advancing to meet him. But this was a distant enemy. Well, Athens at all events is a near neighbour, and yet Athens you utterly disregard; against Athens you prefer to act on the defensive instead of on the offensive, and to make it an affair of chances by deferring the struggle till she has grown far stronger than at first. And yet you know that on the whole the rock on which the barbarian was wrecked was himself, and that if our present enemy Athens has not again and again annihilated us, we owe it more to her blunders than to your protection. Indeed, expectations from you have before now been the ruin of some, whose faith induced them to omit preparation.

'We hope that none of you will consider these words of remonstrance to be rather words of hostility; men remonstrate with friends who are in error, accusations they reserve for enemies who have wronged them. Besides, we consider that we have as good a right as any one to point out a neighbour's faults, particularly when we contemplate the great contrast between the two national characters; a contrast of which, as far as we can see, you have little perception, having never yet considered what sort of antagonists you will encounter in the Athenians, how widely, how absolutely different from yourselves. The Athenians are addicted to innovation, and their designs are characterised by swiftness alike in conception and execution; you have a genius for keeping what you have got, accompanied by a total want of invention, and when forced to act you never go far enough. Again, they are adventurous beyond their power, and daring beyond their judgment, and in danger they are sanguine; your wont is to attempt less than is justified by your power, to mistrust even what is sanctioned by your judgment, and to fancy that from danger there is no release. Further, there is promptitude on their side against procrastination on yours; they are never at home, you are never from it: for they hope by their absence to extend their acquisitions, you fear by your advance to endanger what you have left behind. They are swift to follow up a success, and slow to recoil from a reverse. Their bodies they spend ungrudgingly in their country's cause; their intellect they jealously husband to be employed in her service. A scheme unexecuted is with them a positive loss, a successful enterprise a comparative failure. The deficiency created by the miscarriage of an undertaking is soon filled up by fresh hopes; for they alone are enabled to call a thing hoped for a thing got, by the speed with which they act upon their resolutions. Thus they toil on in trouble and danger all the days of their life, with little opportunity for enjoying, being ever engaged in getting: their only idea of a holiday is to do what the occasion demands, and to them laborious occupation is less of a misfortune than the peace of a quiet life. To describe their character in a word, one might truly say that they were born into the world to take no rest themselves and to give none to others.

'Such is Athens, your antagonist. And yet, Lacedæmonians,

you still delay, and fail to see that peace stays longest with those, who are not more careful to use their power justly than to show their determination not to submit to injustice. On the contrary, your ideal of fair dealing is based on the principle that if you do not injure others, you need not risk your own fortunes in preventing others from injuring you. Now you could scarcely have succeeded in such a policy even with a neighbour like yourselves; but in the present instance, as we have just shown, your habits are old-fashioned as compared with theirs. It is the law as in art, so in politics, that improvements ever prevail; and though fixed usages may be best for undisturbed communities, constant necessities of action must be accompanied by the constant improvement of methods. Thus it happens that the vast experience of Athens has carried her further than you on the path of innovation.

'Here, at least, let your procrastination end. For the present, assist your allies and Potidæa in particular, as you promised, by a speedy invasion of Attica, and do not sacrifice friends and kindred to their bitterest enemies, and drive the rest of us in despair to some other alliance. Such a step would not be condemned either by the gods who received our oaths, or by the men who witnessed them. The breach of a treaty cannot be laid to the people whom desertion compels to seek new relations, but to the power that fails to assist its confederate. But if you will only act, we will stand by you; it would be unnatural for us to change, and never should we meet with such a congenial ally. For these reasons choose the right course, and endeavour not to let Peloponnese under your supremacy degenerate from the prestige that it enjoyed under that of your ancestors.'

Such were the words of the Corinthians. There happened to be Athenian envoys present at Lacedæmon on other business. On hearing the speeches they thought themselves called upon to come before the Lacedæmonians. Their intention was not to offer a defence on any of the charges which the cities brought against them, but to show on a comprehensive view that it was not a matter to be hastily decided on, but one that demanded further consideration. There was also a wish to call attention to the great power of Athens, and to refresh the memory of the old and enlighten the ignorance of the young, from a notion that their words might have the effect of inducing them to prefer tranquillity to war. So they came to the Lacedæmonians and said that they too, if there was no objection, wished to speak to their assembly. They replied by inviting them to come forward. The Athenians advanced, and spoke as follows:—

'The object of our mission here was not to argue with your allies, but to attend to the matters on which our State despatched us. However, the vehemence of the outcry that we hear against us has prevailed on us to come forward. It is not to combat the accusations of the cities (indeed you are not the judges before whom either we or they can plead), but to prevent your taking the wrong course on matters of great importance by yielding too readily to the persuasions of your allies. We also wish to show on a review of the whole indictment that we have a fair title to our possessions, and that our country has claims to consideration. We need not refer to remote antiquity: there we could appeal to the voice of tradition, but not to the experience of our audience. But to the Median war and contemporary history we must refer, although we are rather tired of continually bringing this subject forward. In our action during that war we ran great risk to obtain certain advantages: you had your share in the solid results, do not try to rob us of all share in the good that the glory may do us. However, the story shall be told not so much to deprecate hostility as to testify against it, and to show, if you are so ill-advised as to enter into a struggle with Athens, what sort of an antagonist she is likely to prove. We assert that at Marathon we were at the front, and faced the barbarian single-handed. That when he came the second time, unable to cope with him by land we went on board our ships with all our people, and joined in the action at Salamis. This prevented his taking the Peloponnesian states in detail, and ravaging them with his fleet; when the multitude of his vessels would have made any combination for self-defence impossible. The best proof of this was furnished by the invader himself. Defeated at sea, he considered his power to be no longer what it had been, and retired as speedily as possible with the greater part of his army.

'Such, then, was the result of the matter, and it was clearly proved that it was on the fleet of Hellas that her cause depended. Well, to this result we contributed three very useful elements, vis. the largest number of ships, the ablest commander, and the most unhesitating patriotism. Our contingent of ships was little less than two-thirds of the whole four hundred; the commander was Themistocles, through whom chiefly it was that the battle took place in the straits, the acknowledged salvation of our cause. Indeed, this was the reason of your receiving him with honours such as had never been accorded to any foreign visitor. While for daring patriotism we had no competitors. Receiving no reinforcements from behind, seeing everything in front of us already subjugated, we had the spirit, after abandoning our city, after sacrificing our property (instead of deserting the remainder of the league or depriving them of our services by dispersing), to throw ourselves into our ships and meet the danger, without a thought of resenting your neglect to assist us. We assert, therefore, that we conferred on you quite as much as we received. For you had a stake to fight for; the cities which you had left were still filled with your homes, and you had the prospect of enjoying them again; and your coming was prompted quite as much by fear for yourselves as for us; at all events, you never appeared till we had nothing left to lose. But we left behind us a city that was a city no longer, and staked our lives for a city that had an existence only in desperate hope, and so bore our full share in your deliverance and in ours. But if we had copied others, and allowed fears for our territory to make us give in our adhesion to the Mede before you came, or if we had suffered our ruin to break our spirit and prevent us embarking in our ships, your naval inferiority would have made a sea-fight unnecessary, and his objects would have been peaceably attained.

'Surely, Lacedæmonians, neither by the patriotism that we displayed at that crisis, nor by the wisdom of our counsels, do we merit our extreme unpopularity with the Hellenes, not at

least unpopularity for our empire. That empire we acquired
by no violent means, but because you were unwilling to prosecute to its conclusion the war against the barbarian, and because the allies attached themselves to us and spontaneously
asked us to assume the command. And the nature of the case
first compelled us to advance our empire to its present height;
fear being our principal motive, though honour and interest
afterwards came in. And at last, when almost all hated us,
when some had already revolted and had been subdued, when
you had ceased to be the friends that you once were, and
had become objects of suspicion and dislike, it appeared no
longer safe to give up our empire; especially as all who left
us would fall to you. And no one can quarrel with a people
for making, in matters of tremendous risk, the best provision
that it can for its interest.

'You, at all events, Lacedæmonians, have used your supremacy to settle the states in Peloponnese as is agreeable to you.
And if at the period of which we were speaking you had per-
severed to the end of the matter, and had incurred hatred in
your command, we are sure that you would have made yourselves just as galling to the allies, and would have been forced
to choose between a strong government and danger to yourselves. It follows that it was not a very wonderful action, or
contrary to the common practice of mankind, if we did accept
an empire that was offered to us, and refused to give it up
under the pressure of three of the strongest motives, fear, honour, and interest. And it was not we who set the example, for
it has always been the law that the weaker should be subject to the stronger. Besides, we believed ourselves to be
worthy of our position, and so you thought us till now, when
calculations of interest have made you take up the cry of
justice—a consideration which no one ever yet brought forward to hinder his ambition when he had a chance of gaining
anything by might. And praise is due to all who, if not so
superior to human nature as to refuse dominion, yet respect
justice more than their position compels them to do.

'We imagine that our moderation would be best demonstrated by the conduct of others who should be placed in our

position; but even our equity has very unreasonably subjected us to condemnation instead of approval. Our abatement of our rights in the contract trials with our allies, and our causing them to be decided by impartial laws at Athens, have gained us the character of being litigious. And none care to inquire why this reproach is not brought against other imperial powers, who treat their subjects with less moderation than we do; the secret being that where force can be used, law is not needed. But our subjects are so habituated to associate with us as equals, that any defeat whatever that clashes with their notions of justice, whether it proceeds from a legal judgment or from the power which our empire gives us, makes them forget to be grateful for being allowed to retain most of their possessions, and more vexed at a part being taken, than if we had from the first cast law aside and openly gratified our covetousness. If we had done so, not even would they have disputed that the weaker must give way to the stronger. Men's indignation, it seems, is more excited by legal wrong than by violent wrong; the first looks like being cheated by an equal, the second like being compelled by a superior. At all events they contrived to put up with much worse treatment than this from the Mede, yet they think our rule severe, and this is to be expected, for the present always weighs heavy on the conquered. This at least is certain. If you were to succeed in overthrowing us and in taking our place, you would speedily lose the popularity with which fear of us has invested you, if your policy of to-day is at all to tally with the sample that you gave of it during the brief period of your command against the Mede. Not only is your life at home regulated by rules and institutions incompatible with those of others, but your citizens abroad act neither on these rules nor on those which are recognised by the rest of Hellas.

'Take time then in forming your resolution, as the matter is of great importance; and do not be persuaded by the opinions and complaints of others to bring trouble on yourselves, but consider the vast influence of accident in war, before you are engaged in it. As it continues, it generally becomes an affair of chances, chances from which neither of us is exempt, and whose event we must risk in the dark. It is a common mistake in going to war to begin at the wrong end, to act first, and wait for disaster to discuss the matter. But we are not yet by any means so misguided, nor, so far as we can see, are you; accordingly, while it is still open to us both to choose aright, we bid you not to dissolve the treaty, or to break your oaths, but to have our differences settled by arbitration according to our agreement. Or else we take the gods who heard the oaths to witness, and if you begin hostilities, whatever line of action you choose, we will try not to be behindhand in repelling you.'

Such were the words of the Athenians. After the Lacedæmonians had heard the complaints of the allies against the Athenians, and the observations of the latter, they made all withdraw, and consulted by themselves on the question before them. The opinions of the majority all led to the same conclusion, the Athenians were open aggressors, and war must be declared at once. But Archidamus, the Lacedæmonian king, came forward, who had the reputation of being at once a wise and a moderate man, and made the following speech:—

'I have not lived so long, Lacedæmonians, without having had the experience of many wars, and I see those among you of the same age as myself, who will not fall into the common misfortune of longing for war from inexperience or from a belief in its advantage and its safety. This, the war on which you are now debating, would be one of the greatest magnitude, on a sober consideration of the matter. In a struggle with Peloponnesians and neighbours our strength is of the same character, and it is possible to move swiftly on the different points. But a struggle with a people who live in a distant land, who have also an extraordinary familiarity with the sea, and who are in the highest state of preparation in every other department; with wealth private and public, with ships, and horses, and heavy infantry, and a population such as no one other Hellenic place can equal, and lastly a number of tributary allies—what can justify us in rashly beginning such a struggle? wherein is our trust that we should rush on it unprepared? Is it in our ships? There we are inferior; while if we

are to practise and become a match for them, time must intervene. Is it in our money? There we have a far greater deficiency. We neither have it in our treasury, nor are we ready
to contribute it from our private funds. Confidence might possibly be felt in our superiority in heavy infantry and population,
which will enable us to invade and devastate their lands. But
the Athenians have plenty of other land in their empire,
and can import what they want by sea. Again, if we are to
attempt an insurrection of their allies, these will have to be
supported with a fleet, most of them being islanders. What then
is to be our war? For unless we can either beat them at sea,
or deprive them of the revenues which feed their navy, we
shall meet with little but disaster. Meanwhile our honour will
be pledged to keeping on, particularly if it be the opinion that
we began the quarrel. For let us never be elated by the fatal
hope of the war being quickly ended by the devastation of
their lands. I fear rather that we may leave it as a legacy to
our children; so improbable is it that the Athenian spirit will
be the slave of their land, or Athenian experience be cowed
by war.

'Not that I would bid you be so unfeeling as to suffer them
to injure your allies, and to refrain from unmasking their intrigues; but I do bid you not to take up arms at once, but to
send and remonstrate with them in a tone not too suggestive
of war, nor again too suggestive of submission, and to employ
the interval in perfecting our own preparations. The means
will be, first, the acquisition of allies, Hellenic or barbarian it
matters not, so long as they are an accession to our strength
naval or pecuniary—I say Hellenic or barbarian, because the
odium of such an accession to all who like us are the objects
of the designs of the Athenians is taken away by the law of
self-preservation—and secondly the development of our home
resources. If they listen to our embassy, so much the better; but
if not, after the lapse of two or three years our position will
have become materially strengthened, and we can then attack
them if we think proper. Perhaps by that time the sight of
our preparations, backed by language equally significant, will
have disposed them to submission, while their land is still

untouched, and while their counsels may be directed to the retention of advantages as yet undestroyed. For the only light in which you can view their land is that of a hostage in your hands, a hostage the more valuable the better it is cultivated. This you ought to spare as long as possible, and not make them desperate, and so increase the difficulty of dealing with them. For if while still unprepared, hurried away by the complaints of our allies, we are induced to lay it waste, have a care that we do not bring deep disgrace and deep perplexity upon Peloponnese. Complaints, whether of communities or individuals, it is possible to adjust; but war undertaken by a coalition for sectional interests, whose progress there is no means of foreseeing, does not easily admit of creditable settlement.

'And none need think it cowardice for a number of confederates to pause before they attack a single city. The Athenians have allies as numerous as our own, and allies that pay tribute, and war is a matter not so much of arms as of money, which makes arms of use. And this is more than ever true in a struggle between a continental and a maritime power. First, then, let us provide money, and not allow ourselves to be carried away by the talk of our allies before we have done so: as we shall have the largest share of responsibility for the consequences be they good or bad, we have also a right to a tranquil inquiry respecting them.

'And the slowness and procrastination, the parts of our character that are most assailed by their criticism, need not make you blush. If we undertake the war without preparation, we should by hastening its commencement only delay its conclusion: further, a free and a famous city has through all time been ours. The quality which they condemn is really nothing but a wise moderation; thanks to its possession, we alone do not become insolent in success and give way less than others in misfortune; we are not carried away by the pleasure of hearing ourselves cheered on to risks which our judgment condemns; nor, if annoyed, are we any the more convinced by attempts to exasperate us by accusation. We are both warlike and wise, and it is our sense of order that makes us so. We are warlike, because self-control contains honour as a chief constituent, and honour bravery. And we are wise, because we are educated with too little learning to despise the laws, and with too severe a self-control to disobey them, and are brought up not to be too knowing in useless matters,—such as the knowledge which can give a specious criticism of an enemy's plans in theory, but fails to assail them with equal success in practice,—but are taught to consider that the schemes of our enemies are not dissimilar to our own, and that the freaks of chance are not determinable by calculation. In practice we always base our preparations against an enemy on the assumption that his plans are good; indeed, it is right to rest our hopes not on a belief in his blunders, but on the soundness of our provisions. Nor ought we to believe that there is much difference between man and man, but to think that the superiority lies with him who is reared in the severest school. These practices, then, which our ancestors have delivered to us, and by whose maintenance we have always profited, must not be given up. And we must not be hurried into deciding in a day's brief space a question which concerns many lives and fortunes and many cities, and in which honour is deeply involved,—but we must decide calmly. This our strength peculiarly enables us to do. As for the Athenians, send to them on the matter of Potidæa, send on the matter of the alleged wrongs of the allies, particularly as they are prepared with legal satisfaction; and to proceed against one who offers arbitration as against a wrongdoer, law forbids. Meanwhile do not omit preparation for war. This decision will be the best for yourselves, the most terrible to your opponents.' . . .

The Lacedæmonians voted that the treaty had been broken, and that war must be declared, not so much because they were persuaded by the arguments of the allies, as because they feared the growth of the power of the Athenians, seeing most of Hellas already subject to them.

# XIII. The Modern Conflict of Forms

# 36. Monarchy

*Jean Bodin, whom we have already encountered as the first formulator of the concept of "sovereignty," was so concerned with the dispute over the different forms of government that he devoted the whole of Book VI, Ch. 4 of his work to a consideration of it. After a lengthy discourse on all the other forms, in each case stating the advantages and disadvantages, he at length concludes that on all crucial points monarchy is the necessarily best form. His argument is a combination of an appeal to authority and reasoning on the basis of certain key premises, such as the premise that a monarch is a "microcosm" of the "whole." It is against the background of arguments such as those provided by Bodin that the later attack on all forms of autocratic government was launched.*

## JEAN BODIN*

There remains monarchy to be considered. All great men have preferred it to any other form. Nevertheless it is beset by many dangers, for even when the succession of a new king means a change from a bad king to a good, or from a good king to a better, there is necessarily a change in the seat of sovereignty, and such a change is critical in all kinds of commonwealth. It is a manner of common experience that when a new prince succeeds, all sorts of new plans, new laws, new officials, new friends, new enemies, new customs, new social habits spring up. Most princes are pleased to introduce novelties of all sorts, just to get themselves talked about. This often entails the most serious consequences, not only for their individual subjects, but for the

---

* From Jean Bodin, *Six Books of the Commonwealth*, trans. M. J. Dooley (Oxford: Basil Blackwell), Book VI, Ch. 4, pp. 195–200. Reprinted by permission of Basil Blackwell.

whole body of the commonwealth. Even when a prince is the wisest of men, and does not behave in this manner, the alliances and peace settlements made by his predecessor are dissolved by his death. That being so, neighbouring princes take up arms, and the stronger attacks, or dictates terms to the weaker. This cannot happen to the undying sovereigns of popular and aristocratic states, for they can make perpetual alliances . . . The other drawback to monarchy is the danger of civil war between aspirants to the crown, especially where it is selective. This has often brought ruin on the state. Even when the crown is hereditary there is no little danger when there is a dispute between claimants of the same degree of relationship. Assassinations follow, and divisions among the subjects, and often the legitimate heir is expelled by the man with the worse title. We have had only too many examples of this before our eyes. Even when the succession is not in question, if the king is under age there are conflicts about the regency, either between the Queen Mother and Princes of the Blood, or among the Princes themselves. When God intended to punish the sins of the people, he threatened them with women and children as rulers . . . Even if a people enjoys the greatest blessing it can hope for—and this seldom happens—and the prince on his accession is of mature years and experienced in affairs, nevertheless the enjoyment of sovereign power too often has the unhappy effect of making fools of wise men, cowards of brave ones, wicked men of honest. There have been too many instances for any examples to be necessary. . . .

Such are the dangers inherent in the monarchical form of government. They are great enough. But they are not so great as those which threaten an aristocracy, and even less than those that threaten popular states. Most of these dangers are avoided when the monarchy passes by hereditary succession, as we shall show in its proper place. Sedition, faction, civil war are a perpetual threat to all types of commonwealth, and the struggle for power in aristocracies and popular states is frequently much more bitter than in a monarchy. In a monarchy conflict over office and over political power only breaks out openly on the death of the prince, and then not very often.

The principal mark of a commonwealth, that is to say the

existence of a sovereign power, can hardly be established except in a monarchy. There can only be one sovereign in the commonwealth. If there are two, three or more, not one of them is sovereign, since none of them can either impose a law on his companions or submit to one at their instance. Though one can imagine a collective sovereign power, vested in a ruling class, or a whole people, there is no true subject nor true protector if there is not some head of the state in whom sovereign power is vested, who can unite all the rest. A simple magistrate, not endowed with sovereign authority, cannot perform this function. Moreover if the ruling class, or the people are, as often happens, divided, the dispute can only be settled by force, and by one taking up arms against another. Even when the majority is agreed, it can easily happen with a people that the minority have considerable resources, and choose a leader whom they force upon the majority, and so carry all before them. We have plenty of evidence of the difficulties that arise in aristocracies and popular states when there is a divergence of opinion and diverse views taken by the magistrates. Some want peace, some war; some want this law, some another; some this president, some that, some alliance with the King of France, others with the King of Spain . . . Again, in a popular or aristocratic state numbers always carry the day. But the wise and virtuous are only a small minority in any community, so that for the most part the more reasonable and discrete are compelled to give way to the majority, at the dictation of some impudent tribune or envious demagogue. But the sovereign monarch can seek the support of the smaller and wiser part, and choose expert advisers, experienced in affairs of state. In popular and aristocratic states, wise and foolish alike have to be admitted to the estates and to the councils.

It is impossible for a people or an aristocracy themselves to issue sovereign commands, or give effect to any project which requires a single person to undertake it, such as the command of an army and such like matters. They have to appoint magistrates or commissaires to this end, and these have neither the sovereign power, the authority, nor the majesty of a king. Whatever powers they have in virtue of their sovereignty, when popular or aristocratic states find themselves engaged in a perilous war either with a foreign enemy, or with one another, or in difficulty in bringing some overmighty subject to justice, in securing public order in times of calamity, in instituting magistrates, or undertaking any other weighty matter, they set up a dictator as sovereign ruler. They thereby recognize that monarchy is the sacred anchor on which of necessity, all must in the last instance rely. . . .

There are many who make the mistake of thinking that an aristocracy is the best kind of state because many heads are better than one in all matters requiring judgement, experience, and good counsel. But there is a great difference between counsel and command. It is better to take the opinion of many than of one in all matters of counsel, for it is said that many understand better than one. But for taking a decision and issuing an order, one is always better than many. He can think over the advice that each has given and then reach a decision without being challenged. Many cannot achieve this so easily. Moreover ambition is unavoidable where there are several rulers sharing power equally, and there are always some who would rather see the commonwealth ruined than recognize that another was wiser than they. Others recognize it well enough, but pride, and fear for their reputation, prevents them from changing their opinions. In fact it is necessary that there should be a sovereign prince with power to make decisions upon the advice of his council. It is impossible that the commonwealth, which is one body, should have many heads, as the Emperor Tiberius pointed out to the Senate.

It is said that new princes run after novelties. If it is true that some, in order to make their power felt, published new laws with and without reason, this evil is much more characteristic of popular and aristocratic states. Magistrates who are in the place of kings in such commonwealths, but have only a very short term of office, are consumed with anxiety lest their year of authority should pass by without anything having been accomplished for which they could be well or ill spoken of. More laws were published in Rome and Athens than all the rest of the world put together. From jealousy of their predecessors magistrates continually undid their work, and always to get credit for themselves, and to steal honour from their compatriots at the expense of the commonwealth. In order to circumvent such dangerous and insatiate ambition, in popular and aristocratic states the name of the magistrate proposing it should not be prefixed to a law, as was the practice in Rome and Athens. This was the cause of such an excess of law-making.

It is not true to say that alliances and treaties of peace perish with the prince who made them. This does not always happen, for the terms may include a clause relating expressly to the lifetime of the prince, and for a certain number of years after his death. In the treaties between the Kings of France and the Confederates it is always laid down that the alliance shall continue for the lifetime of the prince and for five years after his death. Moreover as we have already said, it is better that alliances should not be perpetual. For this reason even aristocracies and popular states frequently limit their alliances to a certain term of years. . . .

There is no need to insist further that monarchy is the best form, seeing that the family, which is the true image of the commonwealth has only one head, as we have shown. All the laws of nature point towards monarchy, whether we regard the microcosm of the body, all of whose members are subject to a single head on which depend will, motion, and feeling, or whether we regard the macrocosm of the world, subject to the one Almighty God. If we look at the heavens we see only one sun. We see that even gregarious animals never submit to many leaders, however good they may be . . . Moreover we may observe that all the peoples of this world since the most ancient times adopted the monarchical form of commonwealth by the light of natural reason. One hears nothing of aristocracies, much less of popular states among the Assyrians, Medes, Persians, Egyptians, Indians, Parthians, Macedonians, Celts, Gauls, Scythians, Arabs, Turks, Muscovites, Tartars, Poles, Danes, Spaniards, English, Africans, and inhabitants of Persia. Even the ancient inhabitants of Greece and Italy were ruled by kings alone until they were corrupted and degraded by ambition. It is a matter of wonder that the popular state of the Romans and the aristocracies of Sparta and Venice have endured for so long as four hundred years. There is reason to wonder how it came about that two or three republics among a hundred others managed to survive for several centuries, seeing that their form is contrary to the course and order of nature. But no one is surprised to see many great and powerful monarchies maintain themselves in all their glory for a thousand or twelve hundred years, for they are ordered according to the laws of nature. . . .

It seems to me that for these reasons, and for others that one need not go in to, it is clear that of the three types of commonwealth monarchy is the most excellent. Among those that are not so well regulated, democracy is the most perverted. The true monarchical state, like a strong and healthy body, can easily maintain itself. But the popular state and the aristocracy are weak and subject to many ills, and must be supported by strict diet and discipline. It is not however always in the power of even wise men, and those practised in affairs of state, either to choose the best or avoid the worst . . . The statesmen, the philosophers, theologians, and historians who have praised monarchy above every other form of state, have not done so to flatter the prince, but to secure the safety and happiness of the subject. But if the authority of the monarch is to be limited, and subjected to the popular estates or to the senate, sovereignty has no sure foundations, and the result is a confused form of popular state, or a wretched condition of anarchy which is the worst possible condition of any commonwealth. These matters should be weighed carefully, and the deceptive arguments of those who would persuade subjects to subordinate the king to their own pleasure, and impose laws on him, should be exposed as leading to the ruin not only of the monarchy, but of the subject. . . .

# 37. Republic

*Tom Paine (1737–1809), had he just read the excerpt from Bodin printed above, no doubt would have snorted and produced still one more lively pamphlet of retort. Indeed, the selection which follows might almost have been written as a direct reply to the kinds of arguments advanced by Bodin in support of monarchy: it attacks the premises, the reasoning and the appeal to authority on which his French predecessor had grounded the* Six Books of the Commonwealth. *In so doing, Paine helped to contribute in no small measure to the wars of the French Revolution, to which we shall turn in following selections.*

## TOM PAINE*

Reason and ignorance, the opposites of each other, influence the great bulk of mankind. If either of these can be rendered sufficiently extensive in a country, the machinery of government goes easily on. Reason shows itself, and ignorance submits to whatever is dictated to it.

The two modes of government which prevail in the world, are, 1st, government by election and representation; 2d, government by hereditary succession. The former is generally known by the name of republic; the latter by that of monarchy and aristocracy.

Those two distinct and opposite forms, erect themselves on the two distinct and opposite bases of reason and ignorance. As the exercise of government requires talents and abilities, and as talents and abilities cannot have hereditary descent, it is evident that hereditary succession requires a belief from man, to which his reason cannot subscribe, and which can only be established upon his ignorance; and the more ignorant any country is, the better it is fitted for this species of government.

On the contrary, government in a well constituted republic, requires no belief from man beyond what his reason authorizes. He sees the *rationale* of the whole system, its origin, and its operation; and as it is best supported when best understood, the human faculties act with boldness, and acquire, under this form of government, a gigantic manliness. . . .

From the revolutions of America and France, and the symptoms that have appeared in other countries, it is evident that

---

* From Tom Paine, *The Rights of Man,* in Thomas Paine, *The Political Writings of Thomas Paine* (New York: Solomon King, 1830), Vol. II, pp. 137–144.

the opinion of the world is changing with respect to systems of government, and that revolutions are not within the compass of political calculations. The progress of time and circumstances, which men assign to the accomplishment of great changes, is too mechanical to measure the force of the mind, and the rapidity of reflection, by which revolutions are generated; all the old governments have received a shock from those that already appear, and which were once more improbable, and are a greater subject of wonder, than a general revolution in Europe would be now.

When we survey the wretched condition of man, under the monarchical and hereditary systems of government, dragged from his home by one power, or driven by another, and impoverished by taxes more than by enemies, it becomes evident that those systems are bad, and that a general revolution in the principle and construction of governments is necessary.

What is government more than the management of the affairs of a nation? It is not, and from its nature cannot be, the property of any particular man or family, but of the whole community, at whose expense it is supported; and though by force or contrivance it has been usurped into an inheritance, the usurpation cannot alter the right of things. Sovereignty, as a matter of right, appertains to the nation only, and not to any individual; and a nation has at all times an inherent, indefeasible right to abolish any form of government it finds inconvenient, and establish such as accords with its interest, disposition, and happiness. The romantic and barbarous distinctions of men into kings and subjects, though it may suit the condition of courtiers cannot that of citizens; and is exploded by the principle upon which governments are now founded. Every citizen is a member of the sovereignty, and as such can acknowledge no personal subjection; and his obedience can be only to the laws.

When men think of what government is, they must necessarily suppose it to possess a knowledge of all the objects and matters upon which its authority is to be exercised. In this view of government, the republican system, as established by America and France, operates to embrace the whole of a nation:

and the knowledge necessary to the interest of all the parts, is to be found in the centre, which the parts by representation form: but the old governments are on a construction that excludes knowledge as well as happiness; government by monks, who know nothing of the world beyond the walls of a convent, is as consistent as government by kings.

What were formerly called revolutions, were little more than a change of persons, or an alteration of local circumstances. They rose and fell like things of course, and had nothing in their existence or their fate that could influence beyond the spot that produced them. But what we now see in the world, from the revolutions of America and France, are a renovation of the natural order of things, a system of principles as universal as truth and the existence of man, and combining moral with political happiness and national prosperity.

"I. Men are born, and always continue, free and equal, in respect to their rights. Civil distinctions, therefore, can be founded only on public utility.

"II. The end of all political associations is the preservation of the natural and imprescriptible rights of man, and these rights are liberty, property, security, and resistance of oppression.

"III. The nation is essentially the source of all sovereignty; nor can any individual, or any body of men, be entitled to any authority which is not expressly derived from it."

In these principles there is nothing to throw a nation into confusion, by inflaming ambition. They are calculated to call forth wisdom and abilities, and to exercise them for the public good, and not for the emolument or aggrandizement of particular descriptions of men or families. Monarchical sovereignty, the enemy of mankind and the source of misery, is abolished; and sovereignty itself is restored to its natural and original place, the nation.—Were this the case throughout Europe, the cause of wars would be taken away.

It is attributed to Henry IV. of France, a man of an enlarged and benevolent heart, that he proposed, about the year 1620, a plan for abolishing war in Europe. The plan consisted in constituting an European congress, or, as the French authors style

it, a pacific republic; by appointing delegates from the several
nations, who were to act, as a court of arbitration, in any disputes that might arise between nation and nation.

Had such a plan been adopted at the time it was proposed, the
taxes of England and France, as two of the parties, would
have been at least ten millions sterling annually, to each nation,
less than they were at the commencement of the French revolution.

To conceive a cause why such a plan has not been adopted,
(and that instead of a congress for the purpose of preventing
war, it has been called only to *terminate* a war, after a fruitless
expense of several years,) it will be necessary to consider the
interest of governments as a distinct interest to that of nations.

Whatever is the cause of taxes to a nation, becomes also the
means of revenue to a government. Every war terminates with
an addition of taxes, and consequently with an addition of
revenue; and in any event of war, in the manner they are now
commenced and concluded, the power and interest of governments are increased. War, therefore, from its productiveness, as
it easily furnishes the pretence of necessity for taxes and ap-
pointments to places and offices, becomes the principal part of
the system of old governments; and to establish any mode to
abolish war, however advantageous it might be to nations, would
be to take from such government the most lucrative of its
branches. The frivolous matters upon which war is made, show
the disposition and avidity of governments to uphold the system of war, and betray the motives upon which they act.

Why are not republics plunged into war, but because the
nature of their government does not admit of an interest distinct
from that of the nation? Even Holland, though an ill-constructed
republic, and with a commerce extending over the world, existed nearly a century without war: and the instant the form of
government was changed in France, the republican principles of
peace, and domestic prosperity and economy, arose with the
new government; and the same consequences would follow the
same causes in other nations.

As war is the system of government on the old construction,

the animosity which nations reciprocally entertain, is nothing more than what the policy of their governments excite, to keep up the spirit of the system. Each government accuses the other of perfidy, intrigue and ambition, as a means of heating the imagination of their respective nations, and incensing them to hostilities. Man is not the enemy of man, but through the medium of a false system of government. Instead, therefore, of exclaiming against the ambition of kings, the exclamation should be directed against the principle of such governments; and instead of seeking to reform the individual, the wisdom of a nation should apply itself to reform the system.

Whether the forms and maxims of governments which are still in practice, were adapted to the condition of the world at the period they were established, is not in this case the question. The older they are the less correspondence can they have with the present state of things. Time, and change of circumstances and opinions have the same progressive effect in rendering modes of government obsolete, as they have upon customs and manners. Agriculture, commerce, manufactures, and the tranquil arts, by which the prosperity of nations is best promoted, require a different system of government, and a different species of knowledge to direct its operations, to what might have been the former condition of the world.

As it is not difficult to perceive, from the enlightened state of mankind, that the hereditary governments are verging to their decline, and that revolutions on the broad basis of national sovereignty, and government by representation, are making their way in Europe, it would be an act of wisdom to anticipate their approach, and produce revolutions by reason and accommodation, rather than commit them to the issue of convulsions.

From what we now see, nothing of reform in the political world ought to be held improbable. It is an age of revolutions, in which every thing may be looked for. The intrigue of courts, by which the system of war is kept up, may provoke a confederation of nations to abolish it: and an European congress to patronize the progress of free government, and promote the civilization of nations with each other is an event nearer in probability, than once were the revolutions and alliance of France and America.

◇◇◇◇◇◇◇◇◇◇◇◇◇◇◇◇◇◇◇◇◇◇◇◇◇◇◇◇◇◇◇◇◇◇◇◇◇◇◇◇◇◇◇◇◇◇◇◇◇◇◇◇◇

# 38. Democracy

*Woodrow Wilson's twentieth-century categorical denunciation of "autocratic" governments, and his complementary praise of "democracy," form the basis of the popular—if oversimplified— conception that the United States entered World War I simply "to make the world safe for democracy." In the selection which follows, Wilson formulates principles which, if they could be applied universally, would mean universal peace, by his own premises. The selection is taken from his address to a joint session of Congress, April 2, 1917, in which the President asked the Congress to declare war on Germany.*

## WOODROW WILSON*

. . . Our object . . . is to vindicate the principles of peace and justice in the life of the world as against selfish and autocratic power and to set up amongst the really free and self-governed peoples of the world such a concert of purpose and of action as will henceforth insure the observance of those principles. . . .

We have no quarrel with the German people. We have no feeling towards them but one of sympathy and friendship. It was not upon their impulse that their government acted in entering this war. It was not with their previous knowledge or approval. It was a war determined upon as wars used to be

* From Woodrow Wilson, *War and Peace: Presidential Messages, Addresses, and Public Papers (1917–1924)* (New York and London: Harper and Brothers, 1927), Vol. I, pp. 11–14.

determined upon in the old, unhappy days when peoples were nowhere consulted by their rulers and wars were provoked and waged in the interest of dynasties or of little groups of ambitious men who were accustomed to use their fellow men as pawns and tools. Self-governed nations do not fill their neighbor states with spies or set the course of intrigue to bring about some critical posture of affairs which will give them an opportunity to strike and make conquest. Such designs can be successfully worked out only under cover and where no one has the right to ask questions. Cunningly contrived plans of deception or aggression, carried, it may be, from generation to generation, can be worked out and kept from the light only within the privacy of courts or behind the carefully guarded confidences of a narrow and privileged class. They are happily impossible where public opinion commands and insists upon full information concerning all the nation's affairs.

A steadfast concert for peace can never be maintained except by a partnership of democratic nations. No autocratic government could be trusted to keep faith within it or observe its covenants. It must be a league of honor, a partnership of opinion. Intrigue would eat its vitals away; the plottings of inner circles who could plan what they would and render account to no one would be a corruption seated at its very heart. Only free peoples can hold their purpose and their honor steady to a common end and prefer the interests of mankind to any narrow interest of their own.

Does not every American feel that assurance has been added to our hope for the future peace of the world by the wonderful and heartening things that have been happening within the last few weeks in Russia? [1] Russia was known by those who knew it best to have been always in fact democratic at heart, in all the vital habits of her thought, in all the intimate relationships of her people that spoke their natural instinct, their habitual attitude towards life. The autocracy that crowned the summit of her political structure, long as it had stood and terrible as was the reality of its power, was not in fact Russian in

---

[1] President Wilson refers here to the Russian Revolution.

origin, character, or purpose; and now it has been shaken off and the great, generous Russian people have been added in all their naïve majesty and might to the forces that are fighting for freedom in the world, for justice, and for peace. Here is a fit partner for a League of Honor.

One of the things that has served to convince us that the Prussian autocracy was not and could never be our friend is that from the very outset of the present war it has filled our unsuspecting communities and even our offices of government with spies and set criminal intrigues everywhere afoot against our national unity of counsel, our peace within and without, our industries and our commerce. Indeed, it is now evident that its spies were here even before the war began; and it is unhappily not a matter of conjecture but a fact proved in our courts of justice that the intrigues which have more than once come perilously near to disturbing the peace and dislocating the industries of the country have been carried on at the instigation, with the support, and even under the personal direction of official agents of the Imperial Government accredited to the Government of the United States. Even in checking these things and trying to extirpate them we have sought to put the most generous interpretation possible upon them because we knew that their source lay not in any hostile feeling or purpose of the German people towards us (who were no doubt as ignorant of them as we ourselves were), but only in the selfish designs of a Government that did what it pleased and told its people nothing. But they have played their part in serving to convince us at last that that Government entertains no real friendship for us and means to act against our peace and security at its convenience. That it means to stir up enemies against us at our very doors the intercepted note to the German Minister at Mexico City is eloquent evidence.

We are accepting this challenge of hostile purpose because we know that in such a Government, following such methods, we can never have a friend; and that in the presence of its organized power, always lying in wait to accomplish we know not what purpose, there can be no assured security for the democratic Governments of the world. We are now about to accept gage of battle with this natural foe to liberty and shall, if necessary, spend the whole force of the Nation to check and nullify its pretensions and its power. We are glad, now that we see the facts with no veil of false pretense about them, to fight thus for the ultimate peace of the world and for the liberation of its peoples, the German peoples included: for the rights of nations great and small and the privilege of men everywhere to choose their way of life and of obedience. The world must be made safe for democracy. Its peace must be planted upon the tested foundations of political liberty. We have no selfish ends to serve. We desire no conquest, no dominion. We seek no indemnities for ourselves, no material compensation for the sacrifices we shall freely make. We are but one of the champions of the rights of mankind. We shall be satisfied when those rights have been made as secure as the faith and the freedom of nations can make them.

# 39. The French Revolutionary Wars

*The French Revolution had a profound effect on international relations. Indeed, the wars which accompanied the internal revolution, and which lasted until the famous settlement at the Congress of Vienna in 1815, were in many respects but an extension of the internal revolution. Prior to the fall of 1792, the internal aspect was dominant; but after that, the revolution also took on the form of a crusade to demolish all existing European monarchies. The first selection in this section is the text of a "propagandist decree" issued by the National Convention on November 19, 1792. The second selection is from a famous pamphlet by perhaps the most brilliantly polemical opponent of the Revolution, the English statesman, Edmund Burke. In remarkably brief compass, Burke juxtaposes the traditional mode of state relations, a mode in which the form of*

*government played only a minor role, to the new, revolution-
ary mode, in which the question of form of government itself
becomes the ground of war and peace. Burke's pamphlet, the*
Thoughts on French Affairs, *was first published in 1791, and
thus in effect predicted the intention of the revolutionaries as
embodied in the propagandist decrees of 1792.*

## SECOND PROPAGANDIST DECREE *

The National Convention declares, in the name of the French
nation, that it will grant fraternity and aid to all peoples who
wish to recover their liberty; and it charges the executive power
with giving the generals the orders necessary for bringing aid
to such peoples and for defending citizens who have been, or
who might be, harassed for the cause of liberty. . . .

## EDMUND BURKE†

### THOUGHTS ON FRENCH AFFAIRS

There have been many internal revolutions in the government
of countries, both as to persons and forms, in which the neighboring states have had little or no concern. Whatever the government might be with respect to those persons and those forms,
the stationary interests of the nation concerned have most commonly influenced the new governments in the same manner
in which they influenced the old; and the revolution, turning
on matter of local grievance or of local accommodation, did not
extend beyond its territory.

The present Revolution in France seems to me to be quite
of another character and description, and to bear little resemblance or analogy to any of those which have been brought
about in Europe, upon principles merely political. *It is a Revolution of doctrine and theoretic dogma.* It has a much greater

---

* From J. H. Stewart, ed., *A Documentary Survey of the French
Revolution,* (New York: Macmillan Co., 1959), Doc. 375, p. 381. Reprinted by permission of the Macmillan Co.

† From Edmund Burke, *Thoughts on French Affairs* in *The Writings
and Speeches of Edmund Burke* (12 Vols.; London: Bickers & Son.,
Ltd.), Vol. 4, pp. 318–323, 327–329, 333.

resemblance to those changes which have been made upon religious grounds, in which a spirit of proselytism makes an essential part.

The last revolution of doctrine and theory which has happened in Europe is the Reformation. It is not for my purpose to take any notice here of the merits of that revolution, but to state one only of its effects.

That effect was, *to introduce other interests into all countries than those which arose from their locality and natural circumstances.* The principle of the Reformation was such as, by its essence, could not be local or confined to the country in which it had its origin. For instance, the doctrine of "Justification by Faith or by Works," which was the original basis of the Reformation, could not have one of its alternatives true as to Germany and false as to every other country. Neither are questions of theoretic truth and falsehood governed by circumstances any more than by places. On that occasion, therefore, the spirit of proselytism expanded itself with great elasticity upon all sides: and great divisions were everywhere the result.

These divisions, however in appearance merely dogmatic, soon became mixed with the political; and their effects were rendered much more intense from this combination. Europe was for a long time divided into two great factions, under the name of Catholic and Protestant, which not only often alienated state from state, but also divided almost every state within itself. The warm parties in each state were more affectionately attached to those of their own doctrinal interest in some other country than to their fellow-citizens or to their natural government, when they or either of them happened to be of a different persuasion. These factions, wherever they prevailed, if they did not absolutely destroy, at least weakened and distracted the locality of patriotism. The public affections came to have other motives and other ties.

It would be to repeat the history of the two last centuries to exemplify the effects of this revolution.

Although the principles to which it gave rise did not operate with a perfect regularity and constancy, they never wholly ceased to operate. Few wars were made, and few treaties were entered into, in which they did not come in for some part. They gave a color, a character, and direction to all the politics of Europe.

These principles of internal as well as external division and coalition are but just now extinguished. But they who will examine into the true character and genius of some late events must be satisfied that other sources of faction, combining parties among the inhabitants of different countries into one connection, are opened, and that from these sources are likely to arise effects full as important as those which had formerly arisen from the jarring interests of the religious sects. The intention of the several actors in the change in France is not a matter of doubt. It is very openly professed.

In the modern world, before this time, there has been no instance of this spirit of general political faction, separated from religion, pervading several countries, and forming a principle of union between the partisans in each. But the thing is not less in human nature. The ancient world has furnished a strong and striking instance of such a ground for faction, full as powerful and full as mischievous as our spirit of religious system had ever been, exciting in all the states of Greece (European and Asiatic) the most violent animosities and the most cruel and bloody persecutions and proscriptions. These ancient factions in each commonwealth of Greece connected themselves with those of the same description in some other states; and secret cabals and public alliances were carried on and made, not upon a conformity of general political interests, but for the support and aggrandizement of the two leading states which headed the aristocratic and democratic factions. For as, in later times, the king of Spain was at the head of a Catholic, and the king of Sweden of a Protestant interest, (France, though Catholic, acting subordinately to the latter,) in the like manner the Lacedæmonians were everywhere at the head of the aristocratic interests, and the Athenians of the democratic. The two leading powers kept alive a constant cabal and conspiracy in every state, and the political dogmas concerning the constitution of a republic were the great instruments by which these leading states chose to aggrandize themselves. Their choice was not unwise; because the interest in opinions, (merely as opinions, and without any experimental reference to their effects) when once they take strong hold of the mind become the most operative of all interests and indeed very often supersede every other.

I might further exemplify the possibility of a political sentiment running through various states, and combining factions in them, from the history of the Middle Ages in the Guelfs and Ghibellines. These were political factions originally in favor of the Emperor and the Pope, with no mixture of religious dogmas: or if anything religiously doctrinal they had in them originally, it very soon disappeared; as their first political objects disappeared also, though the spirit remained. They became no more than names to distinguish factions: but they were not the less powerful in their operation, when they had no direct point of doctrine, either religious or civil, to assert. For a long time, however, those factions gave no small degree of influence to the foreign chiefs in every commonwealth in which they existed. I do not mean to pursue further the track of these parties. I allude to this part of history only as it furnishes an instance of that species of faction which broke the locality of public affections, and united descriptions of citizens more with strangers than with their countrymen of different opinions.

The political dogma, which, upon the new French system, is to unite the factions of different nations, is this: "That the majority, told by the head, of the taxable people in every country, is the perpetual, natural, unceasing, indefeasible sovereign; that this majority is perfectly master of the form as well as the administration of the state, and that the magistrates, under whatever names they are called, are only functionaries to obey the orders (general as laws or particular as decrees) which that majority may make; that this is the only natural government; that all others are tyranny and usurpation."

In order to reduce this dogma into practice, the republicans in France, and their associates in other countries, make it always their business, and often their public profession, to destroy all traces of ancient establishments, and to form a new commonwealth in each country, upon the basis of the French

*Rights of Men.* On the principle of these rights, they mean to institute in every country, and as it were the germ of the whole, parochial governments, for the purpose of what they call equal representation. From them is to grow, by some media, a general council and representative of all the parochial governments. In that representative is to be vested the whole national power,—totally abolishing hereditary name and office, levelling all conditions of men (except where money *must* make a difference,) breaking all connection between territory and dignity, and abolishing every species of nobility, gentry, and Church establishments: all their priests and all their magistrates being only creatures of election and pensioners at will. . . .

This system, as it has first been realized, dogmatically as well as practically, in France, makes France the natural head of all factions formed on a similar principle, wherever they may prevail, as much as Athens was the head and settled ally of all democratic factions, wherever they existed. The other system has no head. . . .

What direction the French spirit of proselytism is likely to take and in what order it is likely to prevail in the several parts of Europe, it is not easy to determine. . . .

All those countries in which several states are comprehended under some general geographical description, and loosely united by some federal constitution,—countries of which the members are small, and greatly diversified in their forms of government, and in the titles by which they are held,—these countries, as it might be well expected, are the principal objects of their hopes and machinations. . . .

As to Germany, (in which, from their relation to the Emperor, I comprehend the Belgic Provinces,) it appears to me to be, from several circumstances, internal and external, in a very critical situation; and the laws and liberties of the Empire are by no means secure from the contagion of the French doctrines and the effect of French intrigues, or from the use which two of the greater German powers may make of a general derangement to the general detriment. I do not say that the French do not mean to bestow on these German states liberties, and laws too, after their mode; but those are not what have hitherto been understood as the laws and liberties of the Empire. These exist and have always existed under the principles of feodal tenure and succession, under imperial constitutions, grants and concessions of sovereigns, family compacts, and public treaties, made under the sanction, and some of them guaranteed by the sovereign powers of other nations, and particularly the old government of France, the author and natural support of the Treaty of Westphalia.

In short, the Germanic body is a vast mass of heterogeneous states, held together by that heterogeneous body of old principles which formed the public law positive and doctrinal. The modern laws and liberties, which the new power in France proposes to introduce into Germany, and to support with all its force of intrigue and of arms, is of a very different nature, utterly irreconcilable with the first, and indeed fundamentally the reverse of it: I mean the *rights and liberties of the man,* the *droit de l'homme.* . . .

France, the author of the Treaty of Westphalia, is the natural guardian of the independence and balance of Germany. Great Britain (to say nothing of the king's concern as one of that august body) has a serious interest in preserving it; but, except through the power of France, *acting upon the common old principles of state policy,* in the case we have supposed, she has no sort of means of supporting that interest. It is always the interest of Great Britain that the power of France should be kept within the bounds of moderation. It is not her interest that that power should be wholly annihilated in the system of Europe. Though at one time through France the independence of Europe was endangered, it is, and ever was, through her alone that the common liberty of Germany can be secured against the single or the combined ambition of any other power. In truth, within this century the aggrandizement of other sovereign houses has been such that there has been a great change in the whole state of Europe; and other nations as well as France may become objects of jealousy and apprehension.

In this state of things, a new principle of alliances and wars is opened. The Treaty of Westphalia is, with France, an antiquated fable. The rights and liberties she was bound to maintain are now a system of wrong and tyranny which she is bound to destroy. Her good and ill dispositions are shown by the same means. *To communicate peaceably* the rights of men is the true mode of her showing her *friendship;* to force sovereigns to *submit* to those rights is her mode of *hostility.* So that, either as friend or foe, her whole scheme has been, and is, to throw the Empire into confusion . . .

◇◇◇◇◇◇◇◇◇◇◇◇◇◇◇◇◇◇◇◇◇◇◇◇◇◇◇◇◇◇◇◇◇◇◇◇◇◇◇◇◇◇◇◇◇◇◇◇◇◇◇

# 40. The Depreciation of Forms

*During the course of the great debate over whether to adopt the new Federal Constitution for the newly independent states of America, one of the issues was precisely that of the effect of form of government on the relations of states. Alexander Hamilton, in his characteristically forthright and bold manner declared that the effect of such forms is historically negligible: states will find causes to enter into conflict because it is in the nature of political men to be engaged in competition. Hence, he rejects those arguments which would have it that republics, especially commercial ones, are necessarily "pacific."*

## ALEXANDER HAMILTON\*

. . . The genius of republics, [it is said] is pacific; the spirit of commerce has a tendency to soften the manners of men, and to extinguish those inflammable humors which have so often kindled into wars. Commercial republics, like ours, will never be disposed to waste themselves in ruinous contentions with each other. They will be governed by mutual interest, and will cultivate a spirit of mutual amity and concord.

We may ask these projectors in politics, whether it is not the true interest of all nations to cultivate the same benevolent and

---

\* From *The Federalist* (Hallowell: Masters, Smith and Co., 1857), No. 6. Footnotes renumbered.

philosophic spirit? If this be their true interest, have they in fact pursued it? Has it not, on the contrary, invariably been found that momentary passions, and immediate interests, have a more active and imperious control over human conduct than general or remote considerations of policy, utility or justice? Have republics in practice been less addicted to war than monarchies? Are not the former administered by men as well as the latter? Are there not aversions, predilections, rivalships and desires of unjust acquisition, that affect nations as well as kings? Are not popular assemblies frequently subject to the impulses of rage, resentment, jealousy, avarice, and of other irregular and violent propensities? Is it not well known, that their determinations are often governed by a few individuals in whom they place confidence, and that they are of course liable to be tinctured by the passions and views of these individuals? Has commerce hitherto done any thing more than changed the objects of war? Is not the love of wealth as domineering and enterprising a passion as that of power or glory? Have there not been as many wars founded upon commercial motives, since that has become the prevailing system of nations, as were before occasioned by the cupidity of territory or dominion? Has not the spirit of commerce, in many instances, administered new incentives to the appetite, both for the one and for the other? Let experience, the least fallible guide of human opinions, be appealed to for an answer to these inquiries.

Sparta, Athens, Rome and Carthage, were all republics; two of them, Athens and Carthage, of the commercial kind. Yet were they as often engaged in wars offensive and defensive, as the neighboring monarchies of the same times. Sparta was little better than a well regulated camp; and Rome was never sated of carnage and conquest.

Carthage, though a commercial republic, was the aggressor in the very war that ended in her destruction. Hannibal had carried her arms into the heart of Italy, and even to the gates of Rome, before Scipio, in turn, gave him an overthrow in the territories of Carthage, and made a conquest of the commonwealth.

Venice, in latter times, figured more than once in wars of ambition; till becoming an object of terror to the other Italian states, Pope Julius the second found means to accomplish that formidable league,[1] which gave a deadly blow to the power and pride of that haughty republic.

The provinces of Holland, till they were overwhelmed in debts and taxes, took a leading and conspicuous part in the wars of Europe. They had furious contests with England for the dominion of the sea; and were among the most persevering and most implacable of the opponents of Louis XIV.

In the government of Britain the representatives of the people compose one branch of the national legislature. Commerce has been for ages the predominant pursuit of that country. Yet few nations have been more frequently engaged in war; and the wars in which that kingdom has been engaged, have in numerous instances proceeded from the people. There have been, if I may so express it, almost as many popular as royal wars. The cries of the nation and the importunities of their representatives have, upon various occasions, dragged their monarchs into war, or continued them in it, contrary to their inclinations, and sometimes contrary to the real interests of the state. In that memorable struggle for superiority, between the rival houses of *Austria* and *Bourbon,* which so long kept Europe in a flame, it is well known that the antipathies of the English against the French, seconding the ambition, or rather the avarice of a favorite leader,[2] protracted the war beyond the limits marked out by sound policy, and for a considerable time in opposition to the views of the court.

The wars of these two last mentioned nations have in a great measure grown out of commercial considerations: the desire of supplanting, and the fear of being supplanted, either in particular branches of traffic, or in the general advantages of trade and navigation; and sometimes even the more culpable desire of sharing in the commerce of other nations, without their consent.

The last war but two between Britain and Spain, sprang from the attempts of the English merchants, to prosecute an illicit trade with the Spanish main. These unjustifiable practices, on

---

[1] The LEAGUE OF CAMBRAY, comprehending the emperor, the king of France, the king of Arragon, and most of the Italian princes and States.

[2] The duke of Marlborough.

their part, produced severities on the part of the Spaniards, towards the subjects of Great Britain, which were not more justifiable; because they exceeded the bounds of a just retaliation, and were chargeable with inhumanity and cruelty. Many of the English who were taken on the Spanish coasts, were sent to dig in the mines of Potosi; and by the usual progress of a spirit of resentment, the innocent were after a while confounded with the guilty in indiscriminate punishment. The complaints of the merchants kindled a violent flame throughout the nation, which soon after broke out in the house of commons, and was communicated from that body to the ministry. Letters of reprisal were granted and a war ensued, which, in its consequences, overthrew all the alliances that but twenty years before had been formed, with sanguine expectations of the most beneficial fruits.

From this summary of what has taken place in other countries, whose situations have borne the nearest resemblance to our own, what reason can we have to confide in those reveries, which would seduce us into the expectation of peace and cordiality between the members of the present confederacy, in a state of separation? Have we not already seen enough of the fallacy and extravagance of those idle theories which have amused us with promises of an exemption from the imperfections, the weaknesses, and the evils incident to society in every shape? Is it not time to awake from the deceitful dream of a golden age, and to adopt as a practical maxim for the direction of our political conduct, that we, as well as the other inhabitants of the globe, are yet remote from the happy empire of perfect wisdom and perfect virtue?

# 41. Democracy and Foreign Policy

*Alexis de Tocqueville's* Democracy in America, *first published well over a century ago, continues to be one of the most provocative works ever written on modern democracy, American*

*or any other. At the time when Tocqueville wrote, the United
States had only limited foreign interests, and certainly had never
been tested at any great length in the kind of international
politics characteristic of nineteenth-century Europe. All the
more compelling, therefore, are the remarks which follow on
the difficulty of democracy to conduct a prudent course in
foreign relations.*

## ALEXIS DE TOCQUEVILLE*

. . . As the Union takes no part in the affairs of Europe, it has,
properly speaking, no foreign interests to discuss, since it has at
present no powerful neighbours on the American continent. The
country is as much removed from the passions of the Old
World by its position as by the line of policy which it has
chosen, and it is neither called upon to repudiate nor to espouse
the conflicting interests of Europe; whilst the dissensions of the
New World are still concealed within the bosom of the future.

The Union is free from all pre-existing obligations, and it is
consequently enabled to profit by the experience of the old
nations of Europe, without being obliged, as they are, to make
the best of the past, and to adapt it to their present circumstances; or to accept that immense inheritance which they derive from their forefathers—an inheritance of glory mingled
with calamities, and of alliances conflicting with national antipathies. The foreign policy of the United States is reduced by
its very nature to await the chances of the future history of
the nation, and for the present it consists more in abstaining
from interference than in exerting its activity.

It is therefore very difficult to ascertain, at present, what
degree of sagacity the American democracy will display in the
conduct of the foreign policy of the country; and upon this
point its adversaries, as well as its advocates, must suspend
their judgment. As for myself, I have no hesitation in avowing
my conviction, that it is most especially in the conduct of foreign
relations that democratic governments appear to me to be de-

* From Alexis de Tocqueville, *Democracy in America*, trans. Henry
Reeve, Esq. (London: Longmans, Green, and Co., 1875), Vol. I, pp.
236–238.

cidedly inferior to governments carried on upon different principles. Experience, instruction, and habit may almost always succeed in creating a species of practical discretion in democracies, and that science of the daily occurrences of life which is called good sense. Good sense may suffice to direct the ordinary course of society; and amongst a people whose education has been provided for, the advantages of democratic liberty in the internal affairs of the country may more than compensate for the evils inherent in a democratic government. But such is not always the case in the mutual relations of foreign nations.

Foreign politics demand scarcely any of those qualities which a democracy possesses; and they require, on the contrary, the perfect use of almost all those faculties in which it is deficient. Democracy is favourable to the increase of the internal resources of the State; it tends to diffuse a moderate independence; it promotes the growth of public spirit, and fortifies the respect which is entertained for law in all classes of society; and these are advantages which only exercise an indirect influence over the relations which one people bears to another. But a democracy is unable to regulate the details of an important undertaking, to persevere in a design, and to work out its execution in the presence of serious obstacles. It cannot combine its measures with secrecy, and it will not await their consequences with patience. These are qualities which more especially belong to an individual or to an aristocracy; and they are precisely the means by which an individual people attains to a predominant position.

If, on the contrary, we observe the natural defects of aristocracy, we shall find that their influence is comparatively innoxious in the direction of the external affairs of a State. The capital fault of which aristocratic bodies may be accused is that they are more apt to contrive their own advantage than that of the mass of the people. In foreign politics it is rare for the interest of the aristocracy to be in any way distinct from that of the people.

The propensity which democracies have to obey the impulse of passion rather than the suggestions of prudence, and to abandon a mature design for the gratification of a momentary

caprice, was very clearly seen in America on the breaking out
of the French Revolution. It was then as evident to the simplest capacity as it is at the present time that the interest of
the Americans forbade them to take any part in the contest
which was about to deluge Europe with blood, but which could
by no means injure the welfare of their own country. Nevertheless the sympathies of the people declared themselves with
so much violence in behalf of France that nothing but the in-
flexible character of Washington, and the immense popularity
which he enjoyed, could have prevented the Americans from
declaring war against England. And even then, the exertions
which the austere reason of that great man made to repress
the generous but imprudent passions of his fellow-citizens,
very nearly deprived him of the sole recompense which he had
ever claimed—that of his country's love. . . . If the Constitution and the favour of the public had not entrusted the direction of the foreign affairs of the country to Washington, it is
certain that the American nation would at that time have taken
the very measures which it now condemns.

Almost all the nations which have ever exercised a powerful
influence upon the destinies of the world by conceiving, following up, and executing vast designs—from the Romans to the
English—have been governed by aristocratic institutions. Nor
will this be a subject of wonder when we recollect that nothing
in the world has so absolute a fixity of purpose as an aristocracy. The mass of the people may be led astray by ignorance
or passion; the mind of a king may be biassed, and his perse-
verance in his designs may be shaken—besides which a king is
not immortal—but an aristocratic body is too numerous to be
led astray by the blandishments of intrigue, and yet not numerous enough to yield readily to the intoxicating influence of un-
reflecting passion: it has the energy of a firm and enlightened
individual, added to the power which it derives from its per-
petuity.

5/16

# DATE DUE

| MAY 27 '65 | | | |
|---|---|---|---|
| | | | |
| | | | |
| | | | |
| | | | |
| | | | |
| | | | |
| | | | |
| | | | |
| | | | |
| | | | |
| | | | |
| | | | |
| | | | |
| | | | |
| | | | |
| | | | |
| | | | |
| GAYLORD | | | PRINTED IN U.S A. |